D1228322

Organized Crime

OTHER BOOKS OF RELATED INTEREST

OPPOSING VIEWPOINTS SERIES
America's Cities
America's Prisons
Civil Liberties
Crime and Criminals
Criminal Justice
The Death Penalty
Gangs
Gun Control
Juvenile Crime
The Legal System
Violence
The War on Drugs

CURRENT CONTROVERSIES SERIES
Crime
Drug Trafficking
Gun Control
Hate Crimes
Illegal Drugs
Urban Terrorism
Violence Against Women
Youth Violence

AT ISSUE SERIES
Does Capital Punishment Deter Crime?
The Jury System
The Militia Movement

Organized Crime

David L. Bender, *Publisher*
Bruno Leone, *Executive Editor*
Bonnie Szumski, *Editorial Director*
Brenda Stalcup, *Managing Editor*
Scott Barbour, *Senior Editor*
James D. Torr, *Book Editor*

Contemporary Issues
Companion

Greenhaven Press, Inc., San Diego, CA

Every effort has been made to trace the owners of copyrighted material. The articles in this volume may have been edited for content, length, and/or reading level. The titles have been changed to enhance the editorial purpose. Those interested in locating the original source will find the complete citation on the first page of each article.

Library of Congress Cataloging-in-Publication Data

Organized crime / James D. Torr, book editor.
    p.   cm. — (Contemporary issues companion)
  Includes bibliographical references and index.
  ISBN 1-56510-890-6 (pbk. : alk. paper). — ISBN 1-56510-891-4
(lib. : alk. paper)
  1. Organized crime. 2. Transnational crime. I. Torr, James D.,
1974– . II. Series.
HV6441.O739 1999
364.1'06—dc21   98-24228
                                                CIP

©1999 by Greenhaven Press, Inc.
P.O. Box 289009, San Diego, CA 92198-9009

Printed in the U.S.A.

CONTENTS

FOREWORD

In the news, on the streets, and in neighborhoods, individuals are confronted with a variety of social problems. Such problems may affect people directly: A young woman may struggle with depression, suspect a friend of having bulimia, or watch a loved one battle cancer. And even the issues that do not directly affect her private life—such as religious cults, domestic violence, or legalized gambling—still impact the larger society in which she lives. Discovering and analyzing the complexities of issues that encompass communal and societal realms as well as the world of personal experience is a valuable educational goal in the modern world.

Effectively addressing social problems requires familiarity with a constantly changing stream of data. Becoming well informed about today's controversies is an intricate process that often involves reading myriad primary and secondary sources, analyzing political debates, weighing various experts' opinions—even listening to firsthand accounts of those directly affected by the issue. For students and general observers, this can be a daunting task because of the sheer volume of information available in books, periodicals, on the evening news, and on the Internet. Researching the consequences of legalized gambling, for example, might entail sifting through congressional testimony on gambling's societal effects, examining private studies on Indian gaming, perusing numerous websites devoted to Internet betting, and reading essays written by lottery winners as well as interviews with recovering compulsive gamblers. Obtaining valuable information can be time-consuming—since it often requires researchers to pore over numerous documents and commentaries before discovering a source relevant to their particular investigation.

Greenhaven's Contemporary Issues Companion series seeks to assist this process of research by providing readers with useful and pertinent information about today's complex issues. Each volume in this anthology series focuses on a topic of current interest, presenting informative and thought-provoking selections written from a wide variety of viewpoints. The readings selected by the editors include such diverse sources as personal accounts and case studies, pertinent factual and statistical articles, and relevant commentaries and overviews. This diversity of sources and views, found in every Contemporary Issues Companion, offers readers a broad perspective in one convenient volume.

In addition, each title in the Contemporary Issues Companion series is designed especially for young adults. The selections included in every volume are chosen for their accessibility and are expertly edited in consideration of both the reading and comprehension levels of the audience. The structure of the anthologies also enhances accessibility. An introductory essay places each issue in context and provides helpful facts such as historical background or current statistics and legislation that pertain to the topic. The chapters that follow organize the material and focus on specific aspects of the book's topic. Every essay is introduced by a brief summary of its main points and biographical information about the author. These summaries aid in comprehension and can also serve to direct readers to material of immediate interest and need. Finally, a comprehensive index allows readers to efficiently scan and locate content.

The Contemporary Issues Companion series is an ideal launching point for research on a particular topic. Each anthology in the series is composed of readings taken from an extensive gamut of resources, including periodicals, newspapers, books, government documents, the publications of private and public organizations, and Internet websites. In these volumes, readers will find factual support suitable for use in reports, debates, speeches, and research papers. The anthologies also facilitate further research, featuring a book and periodical bibliography and a list of organizations to contact for additional information.

A perfect resource for both students and the general reader, Greenhaven's Contemporary Issues Companion series is sure to be a valued source of current, readable information on social problems that interest young adults. It is the editors' hope that readers will find the Contemporary Issues Companion series useful as a starting point to formulate their own opinions about and answers to the complex issues of the present day.

INTRODUCTION

Americans tend to think of organized crime as being synonymous with "the Mafia," a generic label that brings to mind images of bootlegging Prohibition-era gangsters, revered Sicilian godfathers, or flashy New York City wiseguys. These glamorized Hollywood images of American mobsters vary in their accuracy and are generally based more in legend than truth. The Sicilian Mafia and La Cosa Nostra, its American offshoot, are themselves more complex than their reputations suggest, and they are only two of the many organized crime groups worldwide. Organized crime groups in Russia, the so-called "Russian Mafia," enjoy far more power in their home country than La Cosa Nostra does in the United States. South American drug traffickers, also popular as movie villains, certainly rank among the world's most powerful criminal groups. Then there are the Chinese Triads, Japanese Yakuza, and many other smaller crime syndicates. Aside from their prominence as movie bad guys, what are the common characteristics of these different organized crime groups? What, exactly, is organized crime?

"The problem in defining organized crime lies not in the word 'crime,'" notes the Chicago Crime Commission in its 1997 report *The Changing Face of Organized Crime*, but rather "in what should be considered 'organized.'" After all, many types of criminals are organized to some extent. Economist Annelise Anderson offers the example of a group of bank robbers as criminals who are organized: "Someone drives the getaway car and someone else rides shotgun; positions in the structure may be vacant and need to be filled." But simply cooperating for one criminal act does not make the bank robbers an organized crime group. One feature of organized crime is longevity: Organized crime groups plan for and work toward long-term goals. Other characteristics include a sophisticated hierarchical structure, an ultimate goal of economic gain, the use of violence and bribery, and, among the major criminal organizations, the ability to exert significant influence over other criminal groups.

Many criminal groups possess only some of these characteristics and therefore are not considered part of organized crime. Street gangs that sell drugs, for example, may persist for years or decades and may be quite organized, but they usually do not meet all the criteria of an organized crime group. For instance, most gang activity lacks the more sophisticated command structure that is associated with organized crime. A law enforcement official quoted in a 1996 *Christian Science Monitor* report describes Chicago's Gangsta Disciples as "one of if not *the* largest and most successful gangs in the history of the United States," but he stops short of putting them in the same category as La Cosa Nostra.

Exactly what degree of organization is characteristic of organized crime? InterPol (the International Criminal Police Organization) defines organized crime as "having a corporate structure," while the Chicago Crime Commission states that organized crime groups "conduct their activities in a methodical, systematic or highly disciplined and secret fashion" and have "an intricate organizational structure." Complicating matters are new technologies that allow all types of criminals to become more organized. As Louise Shelley, an expert on Russian law and organized crime, explains:

> Advances in telecommunications and satellite technology, the development of fiber-optic cable and the miniaturization and complexity of computers have resulted in a communication explosion of international phone calls, fax transmissions and wire transfers. Crime groups benefiting from the "global village" and its instant and anonymous communications are able to operate without frontiers in unprecedented ways.

This interconnectedness has blurred the lines between various types of criminal activity, and criminals' increasing sophistication has resulted in more groups' being elevated to the status of organized crime.

Examining the major organized crime groups provides no single model of organized criminal structure or hierarchy. The Sicilian Mafia, for example, is sometimes called the "Honorable Society" because of the supposed code of honor that binds members together and governs their conduct. Many observers contend that the American Mafia has largely abandoned these rules of conduct, but it has retained the Sicilian system of organization based on families, with each family controlling a different U.S. city or region. Chinese Triads are structured so that most members know only their immediate superior, in order to maintain secrecy and protect top-level members. Their obsessive secrecy and respect for tradition give these criminal societies, as national security experts Roy Godson and William J. Olson put it, "a quasi-religious character." Yet in Triads, as in the American and Sicilian Mafias, membership is restricted either to family members or to individuals of a specific ethnicity. Restricted membership, which is necessary to ensure secrecy, and an ethnic base, which provides a cultural bond among members, are common—though not ubiquitous—features of organized crime groups.

The Medellin and Cali groups of Colombia operate differently. Less tied to tradition, these groups are, according to Godson and Olson, "vertically organized and fairly tightly controlled"; they are often referred to as drug "cartels" or "syndicates" precisely because they function much like sophisticated business conglomerates. The Colombian cartels epitomize the profit-oriented aspect of organized crime. This pursuit of profit is what differentiates gangsters from terrorists: Organized crime lacks ideology, whereas terrorism usually has a political or religious basis. Godson and Olson point out that while the Sicilian Mafia and the Chinese Triads both trace their origins to political movements, in the modern era their primary motivation is simple greed.

Phil Williams, director of the Ridgeway Center for International Security Studies at the University of Pittsburgh, adds that "although the Cali cartel may have devised the perfect blend of corporate and criminal cultures, even smaller [criminal] organizations display considerable business acumen." Organized crime groups can be described as businesses that operate outside the law, offering illegal goods and services such as drugs or gambling, and their management of these activities may sometimes seem merely entrepreneurial rather than criminal. However, one practice wholly separates organized crime from legitimate business: the use of violence to eliminate rivals, maintain monopolies, and intimidate innocent people. As the Chicago Crime Commission reports:

> Organized crime . . . contaminates the free market system and organized labor using fear, violence, intimidation and retribution. Organized crime–controlled businesses are not subject to the competitive pressures other businesses face. They undermine competition by controlling supplies, labor and transportation. They eliminate competition through extortion, violence and intimidation.

Violence may be used internally to discipline or silence organization members, but more often it is directed outward. In addition to waging outright warfare against rival criminal groups, organized crime groups often use violence, or the threat of violence, to extort money from legitimate businesses. Sometimes, however, such as when dealing with law enforcement, violence is not a feasible option: "Instead," write Godson and Olson, "they use bribery in order to corrupt the legal system and evade prosecution." While such corruption is a growing concern in Russia, the most notorious example is Colombia, where cartel influence has been a hallmark of government since the 1980s.

Although the Colombian cartels are some of the most dangerous and powerful organized crime groups, they are also one-dimensional, specializing almost exclusively in cocaine trafficking. Most of the other major criminal organizations are far more diverse. Moreover, the most powerful elements within the Sicilian and American Mafias—and possibly the Russian Mafia as well—do not themselves deal in illegal goods or services at all. Instead, as Annelise Anderson notes, they provide "governmental functions—such as law enforcement and criminal justice—in spheres where the legal system refuses to exercise power, or is unable to do so. . . . Their basic business is extortion from [other] criminal enterprises." Through such extortion and protection rackets, organized crime groups act as tax collectors and police for less powerful underworld elements.

In the American Mafia's heyday, this practice allowed its leaders to operate with relative impunity—top mobsters profited from the crimes of others, never dirtying their hands themselves. Once this aspect of organized crime was recognized by law enforcement, laws were changed so that all the group members that profit from a crime can receive harsh sentences, regardless of which individuals actually committed the criminal act. U.S. legislators and law enforcement officials have been able to fight organized crime much more effectively as they have begun to discover and understand how such criminals operate.

However, this ongoing effort to expose the nature of organized crime is especially difficult because organized crime is in a state of flux. Many experts believe La Cosa Nostra is losing its once-dominant position in the American underworld and that new crime groups are emerging to fill this power vacuum. The manner in which organized crime operates is becoming more sophisticated, and groups are becoming less territorial and more inclined to cooperate with each other in order to evade authorities and maximize profits. As their activities take on an increasingly international scope, some groups are obtaining unprecedented levels of power. Louise Shelley warns that in Russia, "organized crime provides many of the services that citizens expect from the state—protection of commercial businesses, employment for citizens, mediation in disputes. Private security, often run by organized crime, is replacing law enforcement." Some experts believe that criminal groups that gain this much power could threaten the security of nations.

Government leaders monitor the influence organized crime has on the stability and policies of nations, economists study the effects that black markets and mob-controlled unions have on economies, and, of course, politicians and law enforcement officials seek to curb the spread of crime and violence in society. The first step toward understanding organized crime is formulating an accurate definition of it that encompasses current trends. The selections in *Organized Crime: Contemporary Issues Companion* examine the significance of these trends and the nature of various organized crime groups.

CHAPTER 1

LA COSA NOSTRA: THE AMERICAN MAFIA

Contemporary Issues
Companion

AN OVERVIEW OF LA COSA NOSTRA

Federal Bureau of Investigation

> The Federal Bureau of Investigation has designated elimination
> of La Cosa Nostra as its number one priority in its fight against
> organized crime. (The FBI uses the term "La Cosa Nostra" to refer
> to the traditional American Mafia, in order to distinguish it from
> groups based in Italy.) In the following excerpt from its publica-
> tion, *An Introduction to Organized Crime in the United States*, the
> FBI describes the organizational structure of La Cosa Nostra and
> the code by which its members operate. The authors also provide
> a brief history of the origins of the American Mafia.

Various definitions have been used to distinguish an organized crime
group/enterprise from a group of individuals who band together to
commit a criminal act. The Federal Bureau of Investigation defines
organized crime group/enterprise as a continuing criminal conspiracy,
having an organized structure, fed by fear and corruption and motivated by greed.

Definitions

In the United States, "La Cosa Nostra" (LCN), is regarded as the primary organized crime group. The terms "La Cosa Nostra" (This Thing of
Ours), and "Mafia" are used in books, magazines, newspaper articles,
broadcast media, and by the general public when referring to organized crime groups or "families" based both in the United States and
Italy. To make things more confusing, both the American and Sicilian
organized crime groups call themselves "La Cosa Nostra" or Mafia.

There are various theories as to the origin of the word "Mafia.". . .

One version is that the word "mafia" means refuge in Arabic, and
the mafia organizations gave their members refuge from the outsiders
governing their land. Also from the Arabic comes the word "mahias,"
meaning bravery or boldness.

Another theory is that the word came from the Sicilian adjective
"mafiusu" which has been used by the Sicilians since the 18th century to describe objects as either beautiful or excellent. However, no
printed definition for the word mafia was found until around 1870,
when it first appeared in a Sicilian dictionary, defined as "any sign of

Reprinted from *An Introduction to Organized Crime in the United States*, a publication
of the Federal Bureau of Investigation, Organized Crime/Drug Branch, Criminal
Investigative Division, July 1993.

bravado." Whatever the true origin of the word, certain Mafia traditions can trace their beginning to the eleventh century the "omerta," or code of silence; the "vendetta," or blood feud; the "kiss of death"; the respect for the "Boss" or senior Mafia leader; and the "us against them" attitude, them being the government or ruling class, no matter if that was an Italian or even Sicilian one.

In order to clarify terminology, the FBI utilizes the term "La Cosa Nostra" or the abbreviation "LCN" to refer to the 25 ethnic Italian organized crime families based in the United States. Those organized crime groups/enterprises based in Italy or Sicily are labeled Italian Criminal Enterprises (ICE); more specifically ICE can be broken down into its components: the Sicilian Mafia, the Camorra, the 'Ndrangheta, and the Sacra Corona Unita (or Sacred Crown). . . .

Elimination of the LCN and its stranglehold on certain labor unions is the number one priority within the FBI's Organized Crime National Strategy. . . .

The LCN is the preeminent organized crime group in the United States. It represents a nationwide alliance linked not only to each other through familial and sinister conspiratorial ties, but also to non-LCN organizations by understandings and agreements. The FBI's intelligence base has conservatively identified over 2,000 LCN members belonging to 25 families across the country. For each LCN member there are ten or more associates whose illegal activities are directed by or dependent upon the LCN. . . .

The LCN has its own membership criteria, which was first divulged by Joseph Valachi in 1963. Membership in the LCN is not open. To qualify for membership in the days of Valachi, one had to be a male of Italian extraction on the father's side, and proposed for membership by a member in good standing. A prerequisite was for the prospective member to commit murder in the interest of his "family"; referred to as "making his bones." Currently, the prospective member must still be a male of Italian extraction, vouched for by a "Capo" and a good "earner." His candidacy is voted upon, and if accepted the individual must undergo an initiation ceremony during which he swears his allegiance to the family, and to live and die by the LCN code:

- To put the organization above wife, children, country or religion
- To follow orders of his captain without question, even to include murder
- To furnish no information or help to a law enforcement agency (omerta)
- To pay assessments imposed upon him by his captain, regardless of purpose
- To disclose nothing about the organization to outsiders
- To respect all members despite personal feelings, to pay debts owed other members, never to injure, steal from or make disparaging remarks about other members

- To refrain from associating with other members' wives, sisters or daughters except with honorable intentions

Membership in the LCN entitles the individual to share in the proceeds from illegal activity. The LCN amounts to a subculture complete with its own set of perverse human values and social rules, seeking to conceal itself by insulating its leaders from direct involvement in criminal acts.

The Structure of the LCN

The LCN has a pyramid-like structure composed of the following units:

Associate—Individuals who are not made members, but whose activities are directed by or dependent upon the LCN.

Soldier—Soldato, Wiseguy, Made Guy, Button Man, made member, one who has gone through initiation ceremony.

Crew—Group of "soldiers" under the direction and control of a "Capo."

Capo—Caporegima, Capodecina (Boss of ten), Captain, Skipper, Lieutenant, head of a "crew," reports to the "Boss."

Underboss—second in command to the Boss in a "family."

Consigliere—Advisor, generally an older member who advises the "Boss" and serves as a go-between soldiers and the Boss.

Boss—Head of an LCN "family," directives flow down from the Boss, profits flow up to the Boss.

Family—Individual unit of the LCN, comprising of a Boss, an Underboss, a Consigliere, several Capos and crews of soldiers and associates.

Commission—National organization comprised of the heads of the five New York Families, Philadelphia, Chicago and Detroit Families which plays a coordinating and mediating role between the families. Due to recent turmoil caused by incarceration of most commission members, the Chicago Family has assumed the responsibility for those functions west of Chicago, and the Genovese and Gambino New York Families in the East. . . .

Historical Roots

The origins of the LCN as well as the modern Italian Organized Crime groups known as the Sicilian Mafia, the Camorra, the 'Ndrangheta, and the Nuova Sacra Corona Unita can be traced to historical forces which shaped and developed a culture that is unique to southern Italy and the island of Sicily. Sicily, the largest and most populous island in the Mediterranean is and has been an autonomous region of Italy since 1949. It was first colonized by the Greeks and Phoenicians during the 8th century B.C. Other invaders include the Carthaginians, Romans (who made it their first province during the 3rd century B.C.), Vandals, Byzantines, Saracens, Normans, Angevins, Aragonese, Bourbons, fellow Italians, and the Allied army during World War II. Throughout its history, Sicily has always been ruled by what Sicilians consider foreigners or outsiders. The "Mafia" or "La Cosa Nostra" developed as an alternative to weak "outsider" governments and unfair laws that were viewed as tools of the ruling class.

The concept of a secret government or secret society strengthened over the centuries, and received its biggest boost during the rule of the Spanish Bourbon kings, whose barons and landowners controlled the land and ruled Sicily from 1735 until 1860. Landowners during this highly oppressive and corrupt regime lived primarily in the cities of Palermo or Naples and employed small armies of Sicilians referred to as caretakers or "compagnie di armi" to oversee and protect their property, as the government was too weak to maintain order. The "compagnie di armi" were recruited from the criminal element, so in fact they were "protecting" the estates from themselves. The various compagnie di armi developed into tightly knit organizations and began collecting tribute or "protection" from the peasants. The power of these caretakers grew, and based on their relationship with the landowners, which included the Catholic Church, they came to regard themselves as "Men of Honor."

Peasant revolts in 1820 and 1848 served to increase the power of the Mafia as "compagnie di armi" were used to suppress the peasants through violence and extortion. By the time of the unification of Italy in 1860, the Mafia had emerged as a major social and political force in Sicily.

A Brief History of the Mafia in America

Mass Italian immigration into the United States began in 1870. Prior to that year only about 100,000 Italians had immigrated to the United States, mostly from northern Italy. Of the approximately 5.3 million that have followed, approximately 80 percent were from Italy's rural south, and an estimated 25 percent from Sicily alone. This mass emigration was fueled by poverty, rampant inflation, social and economic immobility, a surging population growth rate, feuds and an anti-Mafia campaign conducted by the Italian Government during 1877–78. . . .

By the turn of the century, the Italian population of New York City had swelled to around 500,000. Nearly 80 percent of which had come from southern Italy and Sicily. Sicilian gangs known as "The Black Hand" formed and became involved in many of the traditional crimes that had existed in Italy for centuries, including kidnaping, gambling, and extortion. The Black Hand consisted of small, independent gangs of mostly Sicilian-born individuals that usually operated under the leadership of a single individual. Black Hand members preyed mainly on the Italian communities in the United States, taking advantage of their innate fear of the Mafia. There were no formal alliances nor is there any evidence of the existence of significant intercity connections among Black Hand gangs in America. . . .

In New York's Lower East Side there was the Five Points gang whose members came from Naples, Calabria, and Sicily, as well as from non-Italian backgrounds. Two Five Points veterans, Johnny Torrio and Al Capone, were largely responsible for solidifying the Chicago "Syndicate," and began to establish ties with Italian gangsters in other cities including New York, where they already had many contacts. They were significant contributors to the early development of organized crime. . . .

On January 16th, 1920, the 18th Amendment to the Constitution, also known as the Volstead Act, became effective, barring the sale or use of alcohol. Prior to Prohibition, Italian organized crime groups in America were fragmented by territorial disputes and were often subservient to Irish and Jewish gangs. Prohibition served as the catalyst for uniting opposing criminal factions within ethnic groups and led to the nationalization of organized crime. . . .

As each of the ethnic Italian organized crime groups in the United States became more influential, friction developed among them because of differing recruiting philosophies, turf disputes, and alliances with criminal groups of other ethnic backgrounds. The Italian groups (consisting mainly of Neapolitans and Calabrians) and Sicilian groups evolved into the most powerful forces in the underworld. Despite their many similarities, there were still some differences between these two factions. In 1929, these differences led to the bloody Castellamarese war, between the Italian (Neapolitans and Calabrians) families and the four Sicilian families. An estimated sixty persons lost their lives during its fourteen-month duration. This bloody war ended with the murder of Joseph Masseria, leader of the Italian faction, at Scarpato's Restaurant in Coney Island, New York, on April 14, 1931.

Following the murder of Masseria, Salvatore Maranzano, head of the Sicilian faction, proclaimed himself "boss of bosses." Within two weeks, he convened a meeting in the Bronx, New York, of all Mafia members. At that meeting, he established the official codes by which these criminal groups of Italian origin would be governed and collectively gave them the name of La Cosa Nostra. Maranzano divided the new American Mafia into families, described the structure of each family, and forbade the Sicilians, Neapolitans, and Calabrians to wage war against each other.

The Commission

Maranzano was himself murdered on September 11, 1931, and Salvatore Lucania more commonly known as Charles "Lucky" Luciano was then acclaimed as the undisputed if unofficial leader of the newly formed LCN. One of the first actions Luciano took was to "close the books" on the admission of immigrant Italian organized crime members. The "books" remained closed from 1931 until 1954. During this time, membership in the Sicilian Mafia was no longer sufficient qualification for membership in the American LCN. Luciano also abolished the old title of "boss of all bosses" and created a "Commission" system to assign territories, adjudicate disputes, and exercise internal discipline. The "Commission" was originally composed of the five New York families and Al Capone from Chicago. It was later expanded to include bosses from other families across the country.

The new LCN abandoned many of the traditional Sicilian customs and placed more emphasis on monopolizing the criminal rackets. While "omerta" was still practiced, many of the "man of honor" ideals were lost in the American culture. Also, whereas Italian gangs had cooperated with other groups such as Irish and Jewish ethnic gangs, the LCN refused to ally itself with other criminal groups. During the remainder of the 1930s, until the outbreak of World War II, the new LCN bosses consolidated their power bases and succeeded the Irish, Jewish and other ethnic groups as the most influential and most powerful criminal organizations in America. By establishing itself as an independent entity, the LCN soon became the undisputed ruler of organized crime in the United States.

The first glimpse American law enforcement had at this national crime organization came during a murder investigation conducted by the district attorney's office in Brooklyn, New York. Abe (Kid Twist) Reles, facing murder charges, decided to "tell all" and uncovered the existence of "Murder Inc." Reles told details of 50 separate murders all over the country, which he'd been in on as a member of Albert Anastasia's "Murder Inc." Reles' testimony sent seven men to the electric chair and got another sentenced to 80 years. During one of the trials, the Brooklyn district attorney's office had been keeping him and three other witnesses in the sixth floor of the Half Moon Hotel in Coney Island, New York, and the entire floor was guarded at all times by five armed policemen, to ensure their safety. Yet, on November 12, 1941, Reles himself had the misfortune of falling six floors to his death.

In 1950, the Senate Special Committee to Investigate Organized Crime in Interstate Commerce, or Kefauver Committee (Senator Estes Kefauver was its chairman) was formed. The committee went from city to city, holding hearings, some behind closed doors, others televised and seen by over 20 million people. The committee concluded that a "nationwide crime syndicate did exist in the United States," and that "behind local mobs there was a shadowy international criminal organization known as the Mafia."

The next evidence of the LCN's national scope came to light in November, 1957, in what has come to be known only as "Apalachin." On October 10–14, of that year, LCN delegates met with Sicilian Mafia representatives at the Hotel des Palmes in Palermo, Sicily. The purpose of the meeting was to reestablish ties and to formulate a strategy for international cooperation in drug trafficking. It resulted in an accord that authorized the Sicilian Mafia to import and distribute heroin in the United States, while the LCN provided marketing territory and collected a percentage of the profits. A follow-up meeting was scheduled in the United States to deal with the American questions of the new LCN–Sicilian Mafia relationship.

That meeting took place on November 14, 1957, in Apalachin, New York, at the estate of Joseph Barbera, a senior member of the Buffalo Family. For a day or so preceding the meeting big cars, some of them rented and occupied by men wearing flashy silk suits, arrived in the small town of Apalachin near the Pennsylvania State line and filled almost every motel in the area. New York State Police (NYSP) Sergeant Edgar D. Crosswell was one of the many who took notice of the invasion of the silk suits. Out of curiosity, he followed one of the cars to the home of Barbera, an Apalachin resident who had been under suspicion and intermittent surveillance for quite some time. Crosswell was aware that Barbera carried a gun and had twice been arrested in connection with two Pennsylvania murder cases. Crosswell, another NYSP trooper and two Treasury agents paid the Barbera estate a visit. They discovered the driveway jammed with limousines, and as they entered the driveway, one of the drivers gave the alarm. Within seconds dozens of the silk-suited men swarmed from the house, running across the fields in all directions. Utilizing roadblocks, Crosswell with reinforcements arrested and identified 61 of the men that had been at Barbera estate. All of the LCN families around the country were represented.

Twenty-seven of the men were tried and convicted for conspiracy to obstruct justice by refusing to state the purpose of their meeting. Their conviction was later overturned on appeal. The publicity brought on by the Apalachin fiasco served not only to embarrass the LCN, but also to prove the existence of a nationwide criminal organization.

In 1963, Joseph Valachi, a 30-year LCN member and a soldier in the Genovese Family, gave the world the first inside look at the LCN. Valachi had been serving a 15-year and a 20-year sentence in Atlanta since 1960 for heroin smuggling. Vito Genovese, then boss of the Genovese Family suspected Valachi of conspiring against him, and according to Valachi, ordered him killed. Valachi was placed in solitary confinement at his own request, but on June 22, 1962, he was forcefully released into the general prison population. Within an hour of his release, Valachi beat a fellow inmate to death with a pipe, mistaking him for an LCN assassin. Valachi then decided to tell all.

Valachi cooperated fully with the FBI and on September 27, 1963, he testified before the U.S. Senate Permanent Subcommittee on Investigations of the Subcommittee on Government Operations, also known as the McClellan Committee. After Valachi's testimony, the LCN became recognized as a national conspiracy. He exposed to the committee, and to all America, the structure, codes, identities and the extent of the criminal web of the LCN. Labor racketeering, narcotics, murder, gambling, loansharking, public corruption, pornography, and extortion were and continue to be the LCN's stock and trade.

Commerce

THE FIGHT AGAINST ORGANIZED CRIME

James B. Jacobs

In the following excerpt from his book *Busting the Mob: United States v. Cosa Nostra*, James B. Jacobs describes the tools and methods that the FBI and federal prosecutors use to investigate and prosecute organized crime. He explores the factors behind the U.S. government's apparent success in weakening La Cosa Nostra, discusses the organization's current status, and offers predictions for the future of organized crime in America. Jacobs is a law professor and the director of the Center for Research in Crime and Corruption at New York University in New York City.

For most of the twentieth century, what has been called the "Mafia," "Cosa Nostra," or simply "organized crime" seemed as inevitable as increased taxes. Some Mafia chieftains even attained widespread public notoriety and were treated like folk heroes in their neighborhoods, cities, and beyond. People who understood power and "the way things worked" in New York and other large cities recognized organized crime as a key player in politics, vice, and legitimate industry ranging from shipping and trucking to garbage disposal and the garment trade.

Despite, or perhaps because of, its power and pervasiveness, with a few notable exceptions Cosa Nostra faced relatively little opposition from law enforcement. Local police forces did not have the resources, strategies, or tools to engage in long-term investigations of secret societies that carefully covered their tracks and insulated their leaders from scrutiny through hierarchical organization and a code of silence. Sometimes local law enforcement personnel, as well as prosecutors and judges, were dissuaded from organized-crime control initiatives by potentially adverse political or even professional consequences; sometimes they were just bribed. Remarkably, until well into the 1960s the FBI, under the leadership of J. Edgar Hoover, disputed the very existence of an American Mafia.

Congressional attention to organized crime dates back to the Kefauver Committee hearings in 1951 and the McClellan Committee hearings in 1957. The Department of Justice began to focus on organized crime during Robert Kennedy's tenure as attorney general in the early 1960s. He sponsored antiracketeering legislation in the early 1960s. By the end of the decade Congress had passed the Organized Crime Control Act; Title III provided a comprehensive regimen for electronic surveillance by federal, state, and local police. After Hoover's departure from the FBI in 1972, that agency began to devote significant resources to organized-crime control. Various successes can be identified throughout the 1960s and 1970s, but there can be no mistaking the proliferation of achievements beginning in the late 1970s.

The United States Versus Cosa Nostra

From approximately 1978, the federal government mounted an extraordinary effort to eradicate Cosa Nostra. Utilizing extensive electronic surveillance, undercover government agents, and mob turncoats, the FBI, the federal Organized Crime Strike Forces, and the United States attorneys' offices initiated a steady stream of intensive investigations and produced a regular flow of Cosa Nostra prosecutions throughout the country. The federal effort was supplemented by more limited, but not inconsequential, efforts by state and local investigative and prosecutorial agencies. Joint task forces involving federal, state, and local agencies became routine. No other period in American history comes close in terms of the number of investigations and prosecutions. Ultimately, whether this effort will prove sufficient to destroy Cosa Nostra or whether, phoenixlike, organized crime will rise from the ashes, remains to be seen. . . .

There is no exact figure on how many criminal and civil cases were brought by the federal government (much less state and local prosecutors) against organized crime in the 1980s. However, in 1988, FBI Director William Sessions reported to the Senate Subcommittee on Investigations that since 1981 nineteen bosses, thirteen underbosses, and forty-three capos (crew chiefs) had been convicted. Another witness, David Williams, director of the General Accounting Office's (GAO's) Office of Special Investigations, stated that between 1983 and 1986, there had been twenty-five hundred indictments of Cosa Nostra members and associates.

The magnitude of the government's attack on Cosa Nostra is nothing short of incredible. There were major prosecutions in every city where organized-crime families have been identified. . . .

These federal cases, supplemented by some state and local prosecutions, systematically decimated whole organized-crime families. In New York City, the leadership and many soldiers of each of the five Cosa Nostra crime families (Bonanno, Colombo, Gambino, Genovese, Lucchese) were prosecuted in separate Racketeer Influenced and Corrupt Organizations (RICO) suits on the theory that the defendants conducted the affairs of an "enterprise" (their respective crime families) through a pattern of racketeering activity (their many rackets, extortions, and crimes of violence). In *United States v. Salerno,* the heads of four of the five families, and several other key figures, were prosecuted together for constituting and operating a "commission," in effect a regional and perhaps national board of directors for the mob. . . .

By the early 1990s, the accumulated prosecutions had been so extensive and the internal deterioration of the families so severe that some law enforcement experts began to predict the end of Cosa Nostra. . . .

The most important legal weapons deployed in the government's attack on organized crime have been electronic surveillance authority, the Racketeer Influenced and Corrupt Organizations (RICO) Act, and the Witness Security Program.

Electronic Surveillance

Title III of the Omnibus Crime Control and Safe Streets Act of 1968 provided comprehensive authority for electronic surveillance by federal, state, and local law enforcement agencies. The two main justifications for the act, according to its proponents, were the necessity for electronic surveillance in national security and in organized-crime investigations. Title III brought federal, state, and local wire tapping within the framework of a comprehensive statute. It permits electronic eavesdropping only with a judicial warrant issued upon a showing of probable cause and of necessity due to the absence of alternative means. The interception is limited to thirty days, although extensions can be obtained. The law requires "minimization"; the eavesdropping device must be turned off if, after a brief period of listening, it is apparent that the intercepted conversation is not relevant to the subject of the warrant. Amendments in 1986 strengthened the law and, for the first time, authorized "roving surveillance" to cover sophisticated criminals who use a number of different phones or sites to conduct business. . . .

Electronic eavesdropping figured prominently in almost every organized-crime prosecution of the modern period; some prosecutions were based almost entirely on intercepted conversations. The FBI and state and local agencies utilized both telephone intercepts and hidden microphones in cars, homes, restaurants, and social clubs. In some cases, the FBI was able to pick up conversations on the streets with high-power surveillance microphones. By the end of the decade, there was no place where Cosa Nostra members could converse without concern for government eavesdroppers. . . .

RICO

The Racketeer Influenced and Corrupt Organizations (RICO) Act, part of the 1970 Organized Crime Control Act, created the most important substantive and procedural law tool in the history of organized-crime control. A brainchild of Professor G. Robert Blakey (who worked on Senator McClellan's organized-crime hearings in the late 1950s and later with the Organized Crime and Racketeering Section of the Department of Justice when Robert F. Kennedy was attorney general) brought into existence a new kind of law punishing "enterprise criminality." RICO was explicitly aimed at organized crime, especially its infiltration of legitimate business. It took investigators and prosecutors some years to become fully familiar and comfortable with the new law; after 1980, almost every major organized-crime case was brought as a RICO prosecution. Moreover, the concept of enterprise racketeering changed the way organized-crime investigations were conceived and executed. The FBI began to think in terms of gathering evidence and obtaining indictments against entire "enterprises" like each organized crime family and the Cosa Nostra commission.

RICO makes it a crime to infiltrate, participate in, or conduct the affairs of an enterprise through a pattern of racketeering activity. An enterprise is defined as any "association in fact" comprised of two or more people. In *United States v. Turkette,* the United States Supreme Court held that an enterprise could be a wholly illegitimate group. This provided a green light for prosecuting individuals for participating in criminal syndicates like Cosa Nostra crews, families, and the commission.

Having to prove an "association in fact" in an organized-crime case provides prosecutors with an excellent opportunity to introduce extensive evidence, complete with charts and tables of organization, depicting the structure of an organized-crime family. In the Commission case and other organized-crime prosecutions, the government has been able to introduce testimony about the history of organized crime in order to establish the enterprise's existence over time. Angelo Lonardo's (former underboss of the Cleveland crime family) lengthy account of the history of the Cosa Nostra commission provided some of the most valuable evidence in the Commission case. In the Pizza Connection case, the prosecution used Tomasso Buscetta, a former leader of the Sicilian Mafia, to lay out the history and structure of both the Sicilian Mafia and the American Cosa Nostra.

The Advantages of RICO

RICO requires the government to prove that a defendant conducted or participated in the affairs of an enterprise through "a pattern of racketeering activity," defined as at least two racketeering acts committed within ten years of one another. A racketeering act (also called a "RICO predicate") is defined as virtually any serious federal felony and most state felonies. Thus, in a RICO trial, the defendant may find himself charged with all sorts of different crimes, allegedly committed at different times and places. The prosecution need only prove that the defendant committed all these crimes in furtherance of the defendant's participation in conducting the affairs of the same enterprise. Critics complain that this puts a defendant at an enormous disadvantage because the judge or jury can hardly help concluding that he must be guilty of at least some of the diverse offenses being alleged, especially given his connection to a racketeering enterprise like Cosa Nostra. Proponents of RICO argue that it simply allows the government to present a complete picture of what the defendant was doing and why—instead of the artificially fragmented picture that traditional criminal law demands.

From the prosecutor's standpoint, another of RICO's advantageous procedural features is its ability to join all the members of a criminal enterprise in a single trial, even though they are not all charged with the same predicate offenses. For example, in a single trial some defendants may be charged with participating in the affairs of the enterprise (e.g., a Cosa Nostra crime family) through murders and loansharking, while others are charged with participating in the affairs of the same enterprise through drug trafficking. Moreover, where two or more defendants are charged with racketeering related to the same enterprise, a RICO conspiracy count can also be brought. The consequence is the potential for "megatrials" (like the Pizza Connection case) in which all the members and associates of a crime syndicate are tried together because two predicate offenses are alleged against each one of them. The advantages to the government are obvious; it can pour into the trial masses of evidence about murders, drug deals, extortions, labor racketeering, and so forth, allegedly committed by each defendant. The prosecution can present a complete picture of a large-scale, ongoing, organized-crime group engaged in diverse rackets and episodic explosions of violence. At the end of the trial, the jurors will be admonished not to allow evidence against one defendant to affect their judgment about the guilt of the others, but it is hard to believe that "guilt by association" is not a danger in such megatrials. . . .

The Witness Security Program

Historically, the unwillingness of victims and other witnesses to testify posed a major impediment to successful organized-crime prosecutions. Fear of retribution was well founded since there were many examples of potential witnesses having been murdered or beaten. The Witness Security Program, authorized in the Organized Crime Control Act of 1970, sought to guarantee the safety of witnesses who agreed to testify for the government in organized-crime cases.

Run by the United States Marshalls Service, the Witness Security Program applies to witnesses before, during, and after trial. It protects them during their prison terms and, if they are released provides them with new identities, jobs, and homes in new locations. This protection makes it feasible to testify against Cosa Nostra and survive.

The Witness Security Program has encouraged, or at least facilitated, a number of major defections from organized crime. Up until the trials of the 1980s, no member of organized crime, with the single exception of Joseph Valachi in 1963, had ever broken the code of *"omerta"* [silence] and gone public, much less testified at a criminal trial against fellow Cosa Nostra members. In the 1980s, facing the prospect of long prison terms, a number of mob figures "flipped," agreeing to testify for the government in exchange for concessions in the charges against them and admission into the Witness Security Program. . . .

Developments in the FBI

One reason for the success of the FBI's organized-crime program was its ability to develop an intelligence base on the structure, makeup, and activities of Cosa Nostra over many years and to disseminate intelligence from one field division to another. This was facilitated by the development and implementation of the Organized Crime Information System (OCIS), a computer network (initiated in 1980) designed to collect, evaluate, store, and disseminate organized-crime intelligence information.

Given the concentration of Cosa Nostra families and members in New York City, the New York City FBI office was, not surprisingly, the Bureau office most involved in organized-crime investigations throughout the 1980s. In 1979, that office's coordinator of organized-crime investigations, James Kossler, attended G. Robert Blakey's summer institute on organized crime at Cornell University. Blakey explained how RICO could be used to attack Cosa Nostra and argued for the targeting of organized criminal *enterprises*. Kossler, maintaining close touch with Blakey, redeployed resources on New York City's five Cosa Nostra crime families. Under operation GENUS teams of FBI agents were assigned to develop intelligence on each family. Each team's job was to develop a table of organization for each family, identify all the members and their status in the organization, and then determine which rackets and industries the family was involved in. After that, the prosecutions would fall into place. By the mid-1980s, the New York FBI office had 165 agents assigned to the organized-crime division.

FBI agent Joseph Pistone's penetration of the Bonanno family in New York City from 1976 to 1982 constitutes one of the most extraordinary chapters in the modern history of law enforcement's attack on Cosa Nostra. No law enforcement agent had ever before been able, through disguise and guile, to get so deeply inside a Cosa Nostra family. Indeed, that the FBI would even attempt to place a secret agent in the ranks of organized crime reveals how committed, confident, and creative the agency had become. Pistone hung out at the bars and restaurants frequented by organized-crime members and associates. Eventually, he was noticed by organized-crime figures, whom he cut in on a number of phony schemes. In the course of some of these "crimes," he was able to bring other agents into contact with members of Cosa Nostra. Pistone's undercover operation lasted six years; just before he had to surface and break his cover, he was promised

FBI = CIA

induction into the Bonanno family. Pistone provided a mountain of intelligence material and served as a witness at a number of key Cosa Nostra trials, especially the Commission case. No doubt, this infiltration was a blow to Cosa Nostra morale, raising doubts about how many of its secrets had been revealed. . . .

Why the 1980s?

Why did the government's attack on Cosa Nostra reach its zenith in the 1980s? Perhaps the 1980s' successes were simply the culmination of an organized-crime control process that began in the 1950s and steadily gained strength and momentum thereafter. Perhaps the 1951 Senate hearings organized by Senator Estes Kefauver, the 1957 revelation of a secret meeting of organized-crime bosses from all over the country at Apalachin, New York, Kennedy's tenure as attorney general, the Valachi revelations, and the passage of organized-crime control legislation provided the foundation for a gradual, sometimes halting, process that led to the investigations and prosecutions of the 1980s. This "explanation," however, does not focus on key decisions or decisionmakers or major shifts in formal policy. It interprets organized-crime control initiatives as having "evolved" or "matured," perhaps following their own internal logic or time clock. Those who favor such an interpretation tend to speak in terms like the following: "It took ten years for federal prosecutors to learn to use RICO."

We believe that the evidence will ultimately support a different hypothesis, albeit one that could be reconciled with the evolutionary hypothesis. While maturation, evolution, and internal logic are certainly part of the story, there were also key decisions and decisionmakers who consciously chose to make organized-crime control an important priority despite relentless pressure to accord preference to other crime problems.

The attitude, politics, priorities, and policies of presidents and the attorneys general have surely had an impact on federal organized crime-control initiatives. The president can have a positive impact via his choice of attorney general and FBI director, his support for enhanced crime-control budgets, and his "jawboning" on organized-crime themes. On the other hand, a president can have a negative impact if, for political or other reasons, he chooses an attorney general disinclined to pursue organized crime or makes it clear to the attorney general and other subordinates either that attacking organized crime is not a priority or that some other goals are higher priorities.

Likewise, the attorney general can have great impact on organized-crime control by lobbying or not lobbying for legislation (e.g., RICO, electronic eavesdropping, Witness Security Program) and by allocating or not allocating substantial resources to the Organized Crime and Racketeering Section. While the United States attorneys have some independence from the central Justice Department, there is little doubt that the attorney general has the power to establish priorities through persuasion and manipulation of resources. . . .

Internal Weakening of Cosa Nostra

Ronald Goldstock, long-time director of the New York State Organized Crime Task Force, echoing the thesis of mob-boss-turned-author Joe Bonanno, has argued that Cosa Nostra has been weakened as much by internal forces as by external forces. In Goldstock's opinion, the modern generation of Cosa Nostra leaders has different values from its predecessors. Honor, respect, and family have given way to greed and the fast buck. Moreover, Goldstock argues that with the demise of "Little Italies" around the United States, the mob lost its recruitment base and did not, perhaps could not, adequately replenish itself with young members. He concludes that Cosa Nostra became less competent at the very time when law enforcement was becoming more competent.

Goldstock's thesis deserves serious consideration because of its plausibility and the author's expertise. All organizations experience change resulting from leadership transitions, alterations in environment, and oscillations in the economy. Some changes are merely deviations from long-term patterns and others permanent changes in goals, priorities, strategies, and culture. Goldstock believes cultural change has diminished organized crime's capacity to carry out its goals and strategies effectively. The strongest evidence in favor of Goldstock's thesis is the apparent breakdown of *omerta*, the code of silence, and the willingness of scores of mobsters to cooperate with the government. This certainly reflects some sort of change, either much more powerful and effective law enforcement than ever before (including especially the draconian RICO sentences) and the possibility of defecting without being killed (thanks to the Witness Security Program) or a different attitude among Cosa Nostra members about the importance of loyalty to their organization.

While plausible, Goldstock's thesis is difficult to evaluate because it is hard to compare the "values" of yesterday's organized-crime leaders, middle managers, and soldiers with today's. There is a tendency in many contexts to romanticize the values and accomplishments of past generations. Just as many of us do not believe that this generation's political leaders or college presidents measure up to their counterparts of the past, so it is not surprising that Joe Bonanno believes that today's mob leaders are less capable and worthy than he.

This romanticizing tendency is compounded by the methodological error of comparing all (or the average) of today's leaders with only the best of yesterday's leaders. Not all of yesterday's mob members and bosses were like Marlon Brando's depiction of a man of honor in *The Godfather*. The Goldstock thesis is intriguing, but it needs to be carefully and critically examined.

Organized-Crime Control and Civil Liberties

[The U.S. government's fight against organized crime] is not a case of law enforcement agencies' ignoring or taking the law into their own hands; rather it is an example of how substantive and procedural criminal laws have been expansively amended and recast in order to provide law enforcement agencies powerful means for defeating Cosa Nostra and other organized-crime groups. While some observers may applaud the government's attack on Cosa Nostra as an impressive example of how a democratic government can defeat an immensely powerful crime syndicate while respecting the rule of law and due process of law, other observers may conclude that the rule of law and important principles of fairness, due process, and substantive justice have been stretched too far in the relentless effort to put the leaders of Cosa Nostra behind bars. Such critics would point to the expansion of accessorial and conspiratorial liability under RICO, electronic eaves-dropping, grand jury subpoenas, making deals with dangerous and reprehensible criminals, mass trials, and draconian punishments as too great a price to pay, even for the dismantling of Cosa Nostra.

Politicians have shown no concern for the privacy of or justice for organized-crime figures. Senators and representatives have competed with one another to be toughest on organized crime. The only doubts raised in congressional debates over organized-crime legislation have involved the possibility that organized-crime-control tactics would be used against people other than organized-crime members, especially unpopular political groups.

Cosa Nostra members have been demonized in Congress and defined as social pariahs against whom extraordinary rules ought to apply. Thus, a system of substantive and procedural law has evolved so that once a person is identified as head of an organized-crime fam-ily, there is usually probable cause to bug his home and car and tap his phones. Under RICO the crime boss can practically be automati-cally charged with participating in an enterprise (his crime family) through racketeering activity (the crimes committed by his under-lings). No matter what the underlying crimes proved against him, the sentencing law is structured so that the boss can be imprisoned for a very long time, probably for life.

For the most part, the appellate courts have not rejected the gov-ernment's aggressive use of RICO and other anti-organized-crime tac-tics. The appellate courts are loathe to reverse a conviction resulting from many months of trial against a defendant whom "everybody knows" is a major organized-crime figure. Even when they are obvi-ously troubled by such things as megatrials and status crimes, the appellate judges have upheld organized-crime convictions, while expressing their "doubts" and "concerns."

Civil libertarians have rarely chosen organized-crime cases to chal-lenge government over-reaching and abuse of authority. Indeed, from a civil liberties standpoint, major organized-crime cases provide the worst set of facts on which to test the propriety and constitutionality of new law enforcement and crime control tactics. Perhaps there is an implicit assumption that the rules are different in organized-crime cases. Perhaps it is generally accepted that Cosa Nostra bosses and members assume the risk of (and have no justifiable complaint about) whatever law enforcement tactics the legislative and the executive branches come up with.

Rather than defend the rights of organized-crime figures, civil liberties groups have often warned against and opposed the tactics designed for the "war on organized crime" on the ground that they would inevitably be used in other contexts, especially to chill bona fide political expression. In fact, organized-crime-control devices, from conspiracy law to RICO, and from electronic eavesdropping to criminal and civil forfeitures, have inexorably seeped into other contexts. One reason for this is the plasticity of the term "organized crime." Many kinds of criminality can plausibly be labeled organized crime. The RICO statute, for example, has frequently been used against non–Cosa Nostra defendants who, under even the broadest definition, could not be linked to an organized-crime group. Furthermore, the use of civil RICO provisions in disputes among corporations has triggered repeated, albeit unsuccessful, efforts to reign in the reach of the statute. If anything, however, the tactics that have proven so successful against Cosa Nostra are being transplanted to the war against drugs, and even to "wars" against official corruption, violent crime, and pornography.

The Future of Cosa Nostra

After each of the major organized-crime cases, some law enforcement officials and academic observers predicted that America was on the threshold of defeating Cosa Nostra. While one cannot help being impressed by the government's overwhelming successes in organized-crime prosecutions across the United States since 1980, one must also be impressed by Cosa Nostra's power and expansive reach as evidenced in the testimony, wiretaps, and physical evidence that have been adduced in these same trials. It is sobering to consider that, at least until recently, Cosa Nostra exerted powerful influence over the nation's largest union (the Teamsters), several other important national unions (Longshoreman's Association, Hotel Employees and Restaurant Employees International Union, and the Laborers International Union of North America), the New York City/New Jersey waterfront, the Fulton Fish Market, the New York City construction industry, garment industry, and trash-hauling industry, and numerous other businesses throughout the country. Over the last several decades, Cosa Nostra leaders have stood at the side of mayors, governors, and even presidents. The sum total of this much influence and power makes organized crime a significant part of the political economy of the United States.

Unfortunately, there is no systematic way to determine how successful the government's organized-crime-control campaign has been, much less *will be*, in weakening or eliminating Cosa Nostra or in reducing the amount of racketeering and harm associated with Cosa Nostra. There are no systematic and reliable data on the health, wealth, and power of Cosa Nostra as a whole or of its individual crime families. Hundreds of Cosa Nostra members have been sentenced to long prison terms, but we do not know whether replacements have or will move into their vacated roles. Many law enforcement professionals see the Cosa Nostra families as being in disarray and in permanent decline. But these observations are generally ad hoc and not part of systematic nationwide intelligence gathering and analysis effort. Electronic monitoring, computer systems, and the emergence of well-trained organized-crime-control units and specialists make conceivable the implementation of an extensive intelligence operation. But resources and technology have to be supported by political will and organizational commitment. The danger is that attention will be drawn away from organized-crime control to other pressing law enforcement priorities and that, while the law enforcement machinery sleeps, Cosa Nostra will reconstitute itself. Finally, even if Cosa Nostra as an organization has been substantially weakened, we obviously cannot be sure that Cosa Nostra's racketeering activities have not been (or will not be) taken over by newly emerging crime groups, thereby negating any reduction in racketeering or societal harm.

Many of the economic and social forces that allowed organized crime to achieve such immense power are still operative. The citizenry's demand for illicit goods and services remains strong. Many unions remain vulnerable to labor racketeering, and those that have been "liberated" from organized crime have been very slow to repudiate their mob ties, if they have done so at all. Thus, it may be premature to predict that the investigations and trials of the 1980s constitute the beginning of the last chapter in the history of Cosa Nostra. Whatever the future may hold, the period from the late 1970s to the early 1990s has been marked by the most concerted and sophisticated attack on organized crime in the history of the United States.

RACKETS AND SHAKEDOWNS: THE GAMBINO FAMILY

John H. Davis

New York City has traditionally been a major center of organized crime activity, and New York's five families are some of La Cosa Nostra's most notorious. Not only are these families involved in criminal endeavors such as drug trafficking, auto theft, and fraud, but they also have a long history of racketeering that includes the corruption of otherwise legitimate industries through control of labor unions and other means. In the following excerpt from *Mafia Dynasty: The Rise and Fall of the Gambino Crime Family*, John H. Davis details the varied and often complex criminal operations that the Gambino crime family was pursuing when John Gotti became leader of the organization in 1985. An expert on the Mafia, Davis is the author of several books on organized crime, including *The Kennedy Contract* and *Mafia Kingfish*.

The criminal enterprise John Gotti inherited upon the assassination of Paul Castellano in 1985 had been growing steadily for the past fifty-four years. By the time it fell under Gotti's control, it had achieved a stranglehold on many New York industries—from meat distribution and building construction to waste disposal and garment trucking—and was grossing at least $500 million a year, probably much more. As one former Gambino associate told me: "You have no idea how much money keeps pouring in. It's unbelievable. It's like twenty-three mighty rivers all emptying into one lake."

How was this conglomerate organized, how did it operate, what were its major activities? . .

Organizational Structure

According to the New York State Organized Crime Task Force and tapes of Gambino wiseguys' conversations recorded by FBI bugs, the Gambino family in 1986 consisted of twenty-three *regimes,* or crews of soldiers, each headed by a *caporegime,* or captain, who reported to the family underboss, who in turn reported to the boss. The family's *consigliere,* or counselor, dispensed advice to the boss and underboss and

Edited excerpt from Chapter 31, "The Gambino Legacy," in *Mafia Dynasty: The Rise and Fall of the Gambino Crime Family* by John H. Davis. Copyright ©1993 by John H. Davis. Reprinted by permission of HarperCollins Publishers, Inc.

also to the captains and soldiers. The money earned by a given crew would travel upward, with each level in the hierarchy collecting its share of the spoils. Thus the boss, the underboss, and the *consiglière* would each receive cuts from the profits of all twenty-three crews after the crew captains and soldiers were paid off. Twice a year, on his birthday and at Christmas, the boss would receive a tribute from each of his crews that totaled around $100,000. With an average of twenty to twenty-five soldiers in each crew, the Gambino family numbered almost five hundred men. Affiliated with them were several thousand "associates," mostly from the labor unions, political machines, and industries the family controlled or did business with.

Some of the crews were highly specialized. Thomas Gambino's crew was wholly concerned with racketeering in the garment trucking industry. The crew once headed by Tony Scotto was wholly concerned with labor racketeering on the New York and New Jersey waterfront. Robert "Di B" DiBernardo's crew specialized in pornography. Carmine "The Doctor" Lombardozzi's crew specialized in securities theft and stock market swindles. James "Jimmy Brown" Failla and his crew monopolized private waste carting in New York and were masters at illegal waste disposal. Pasquale Conte, a member of the board of directors of the Key Food supermarket chain, was also a Gambino capo. The crew run by Nino Gaggi and Roy DeMeo specialized in car theft and the selling of stolen cars in the Middle East. For most of the crews the standard staples were loan-sharking, gambling, hijacking, and shakedowns, with the specialty being carried on by only a few members of a given crew.

Controlling the Unions

Paul Castellano had been recorded by an FBI bug telling one of his captains, "Our job is to run the unions." The reasoning behind the dictum was that if you controlled the labor supply of a given industry, you controlled that industry. Thus the Gambinos had for many years been heavily involved in labor racketeering, notably in the waterfront, hotel and restaurant, construction, garment, meat, and waste disposal industries. Through control of key locals and district councils of the International Longshoremen's Association they were able to dominate most of the Manhattan and Brooklyn waterfront. Likewise their control of key locals of the Hotel and Restaurant Employees International enabled the Gambinos to shake down restaurants, bars, nightclubs, and hotels in return for guaranteeing labor peace. By occupying key positions within the unions serving New York's construction industry the Gambinos, in conjunction with the other New York families, were able to charge contractors a two percent fee on their overall construction projects' budgets again in return for guaranteeing labor peace, but also for guaranteeing the safe and prompt arrival of essential building materials, such as concrete, to construction sites. The division of the fees among the five families would be decided at meetings of the Commission. Some of the construction unions in which the Gambinos exercised considerable influence were, according to the State Organized Crime Task Force, the International Brotherhood of Teamsters, Local 282; the Cement and Concrete Workers Union, Local 20; the Mason Tenders Union, Local 23; and the Steam Fitters Union, Local 638. Mob control of the construction industry was directly responsible for construction costs in New York being the highest in the nation.

The Construction Industry

But the Gambinos' influence in the construction industry was not confined to the unions serving the industry. Various Gambino men owned, controlled, or held employment with important construction companies. Paul Castellano and his sons owned the Scara-Mix Concrete Company on Staten Island. John Gotti's former *consiglière*, Salvatore "Sammy the Bull" Gravano, was president of the JJS Construction Company of Brooklyn and the owner of half a dozen companies serving the construction industry. John Gotti, Jr., is president of the Sampson Trucking Company. Alphonse Mosca, a Gambino family capo, was the owner of Glenwood Concrete Flooring, Inc. John Gotti held the position of salesman with the ARC Plumbing Company of Queens, a firm holding contracts with the city of New York worth $20 million. According to public testimony given before the New York State Investigation Commission in 1985, Frank DiCicco, Gotti's underboss, was on the payroll of the Leon DeMatteis Construction Corporation, a major New York State builder.

The Gambinos were also active in industries allied to the construction industry. In 1990 John Gotti's older brother, Peter, was indicted for allegedly splitting, with the Lucchese family, a $2 fee from Local 580 of the Architectural and Ornamental Ironworkers Union on each of over a million replacement windows union workers put up in New York public housing projects. Peter Gotti was later acquitted of these charges.

Other Industries

Another legitimate business in which the Gambino family wielded considerable clout was the meat business. Twenty percent of all the meat sold in the United States changed hands on the New York meat market, which was controlled by three organized crime families: Genovese, Lucchese, and Gambino.

Since the 1930s Paul Castellano and various members of his family had been involved in both the wholesale and retail meat business. Big Paul had owned two large retail meat markets in Brooklyn and controlled the Ranbar Meat Packing Company; the Dial Poultry and Meat Company, which distributed chicken and meat to three hundred retail butchers and several supermarket chains; and Quarex Industries, a major meat distributor. He also had influence with two big supermarket chains, Key Food and Waldbaum's, that bought large quantities of meat. And, as might be expected, he had representatives within the Amalgamated Meat Cutters Union, the Butcher Workmen of North America, and the United Food and Commercial Workers Union, which bargained on behalf of 525,000 meat industry workers.

According to author Jonathan Kwitny, in his book *Vicious Circles,* the Castellano meat businesses had a long record of "suffering suspicious hijackings, which can lead to insurance claims; and of selling meat products that were later found to have been stolen off docks and trucks."

In 1977 Castellano's Ranbar Packing, Inc., was indicted by a federal grand jury in Brooklyn on charges of defrauding the government with counterfeit or stolen food stamps. According to Jonathan Kwitny's book the company apparently made $660,000 worth of fraudulent claims to the government.

Waste disposal was another business in which the Gambinos were active. As has been noted, this was Jimmy Failla's specialty. Failla, an officer in the Manhattan Trade Waste Association, controlled Rosedale Carting and the National-Stage Carting Company. Rosedale disposed of most of the waste it collected at a Staten Island landfill near the Arlington Railroad yard. In 1989 it was discovered that among the waste deposited in the landfill were hypodermic needles, catheters, and surgical gloves. In 1991 federal investigators found out that Failla's trucks were dumping toxic waste from the New York metropolitan area as far away as the mountains of West Virginia.

Pornography was a major earner for the Gambino family. It was the specialty of the crew headed by Robert "Di B" DiBernardo, who controlled a huge network of Times Square area "adult" peep shows and bookstores that sold pornographic books, videos, and photographs at considerable markup. An FBI investigation of DiBernardo revealed he was the biggest pornographer in the United States. His company, Star Distributors, the nation's largest pornography distributor, was located in a building in downtown Manhattan owned by former vice-presidential candidate Geraldine Ferraro's husband, John Zaccaro. According to reliable sources, Ms. Ferraro collected $350,000 in rent from DiBernardo which she used to finance her political campaigns.

Eventually the FBI ensnared Di B in a sting operation and he was indicted and convicted. Not long after he appealed his conviction, Di B DiBernardo disappeared. Police detectives now suspect he was murdered and that John Gotti and his underboss, Salvatore Gravano, were involved in the crime. Apparently Gotti had heard that Di B was talking against him behind his back.

Drug Trafficking and Other Scams

Then there was the narcotics trade, specifically the heroin business. Both Big Paul Castellano and his underboss, Aniello Dellacroce, profited off the Sicilian heroin pipeline through their association with the Sicilian Zips [Italian-born mafiosi]. And we know that three members of John Gotti's crew, his brother Gene, *gumbah* Angelo Ruggiero, and John Carneglia, were deeply involved in heroin trafficking. Dealing heroin was the most dangerous and lucrative of all the family's operations.

But these criminal activities in and around New York did not define the limits of Gambino operations. The Gambinos were also active throughout Long Island, Connecticut, Pennsylvania, and New Jersey, especially in Atlantic City, and in Fort Lauderdale and New Orleans.

Loan-sharking, running illegal gambling casinos, stealing cars, stealing securities, hijacking trucks, selling heroin, distributing pornographic materials, labor racketeering, construction job shakedowns, waterfront shakedowns, garment trucking rackets. . . . As Big Paul Castellano had once told Joe "Piney" Armone: "This life of ours, this is a wonderful life."

THE FIVE FAMILIES IN TURMOIL

Jeffrey Goldberg

Genovese, Gambino, Lucchese, Colombo, Bonanno—the names of these five families of New York have long been synonymous with organized crime, but they have also been associated with a certain prestige, a legacy that dates back to Prohibition and that has been glorified in movies like *The Godfather*. In the 1980s and 1990s, however, the five families have experienced many setbacks. Some blame the families' troubles on the younger mobsters' lack of discipline and respect for tradition. Jeffrey Goldberg, a contributing editor for *New York* magazine, profiles some of the personalities of this younger generation and offers insight into the increasing dysfunctionality of the five families.

Dominick Montiglio looks around skeptically. "What's this ride called?" he asks. " 'Little Fucks'?"

"It's called 'It's a Small World,'" he is told. We're in Disney World.

"What's this ride *about*?" he asks.

"Togetherness and harmony," I say.

"Fuck," he says.

We push off into Disney's treacly celebration of multicultural awareness. "It's a world of laughter, a world of tears," hundreds of smiling dolls sing at us. "It's a world of hopes and a world of fears."

"This place is like hell," Montiglio says. "Hell would be having to stay in this place forever."

Suddenly, he sees something he likes. "Look down in the water," he barks. "Money! There's tons of money down there."

The good people of the world have cast hundreds of dollars in coins into the water, and Montiglio's got a plan. "We can get some vacuums and just suck all the money up. We could just suck it all up." In another boat, little towheaded children stare at us.

Montiglio's getup is antithetical to the saccharine surroundings: He's dressed in black jeans, shiny black shirt, dark boots, a Yankees cap, and mirrored sunglasses. There's little chance the people who want Montiglio dead would have trouble picking him out of this crowd.

He was once an enforcer for the Gambino crime family; after years of drug dealing and mayhem-making, he flipped, testified, and disap-

Abridged and edited from "The Mafia's Morality Crisis," by Jeffrey Goldberg, *New York*, January 9, 1995, with permission of the author.

peared. Now in hiding, the 47-year-old Montiglio is one of dozens of ex-mobsters trapped in Middle American purgatory.

We meet in Orlando to discuss the decline of the Mafia, something he's watched close-up. He grew up a minor prince in a royal mob family; his uncle, Nino Gaggi, was a powerful Bensonhurst, New York, capo related by blood to Carlo Gambino and Paul Castellano [former heads of New York's Gambino crime family].

Montiglio watched as the family leadership grew more pigheaded, soiling Gambino's vision of an elegant and discreet crime syndicate. It was the drugs more than anything else, Montiglio says, that led to the collapse of the old ways.

"Carlo, the real men of honor, they would never touch the stuff," Montiglio says. As time went on, though, "you had people putting the product up their nose. That weakens your moral fiber. It makes you not trust your own friends. . . . There's no loyalty anymore. They don't fear the boss enough."

Montiglio wasn't always a criminal. He joined the army after high school, and fought in Vietnam—"I whacked a lot of people over there." He came back to America and put a continent between himself and Bensonhurst, settling in San Francisco. But then he went to the movies, he says, and he knew it was time to go home—the movie, of course, was *The Godfather*.

He started out doing jobs for his uncle, who dispatched him to work with a lunatic Gambino crew run by a gangster named Roy DeMeo. It was the DeMeo crew's job to kill people and butcher their bodies.

"I remember one time, Joey Dracula had these two bodies hanging upside down in the shower, and I said, 'Joey, what are you doing?' and he said, 'I'm bleeding them by the neck'—he would do this so when they chopped them up there wouldn't be blood," he says as we float down Disney's river of costumed dolls. "Another time he was chopping up bodies and eating pizza at the same time."

The air is filled with music: "There's so much that we share/ That it's time we're aware/ It's a small world after all."

"I need a beer," Montiglio says.

We leave the ride, and I ask an ice-cream lady where the beer is. "There's no alcohol sold in the Magic Kingdom," she says officiously. "This is a family park."

Montiglio stares her down. "What about heroin?" he asks. "You got any heroin?"

The Mafia Code of Silence

Pasquale "Patsy" Conte, a lumpy and sour Gambino captain, heaved his bulk to the defense table in a Brooklyn courtroom in 1994. And another Mafia myth was about to die. Life until then had been sweet to Patsy—he sold groceries, and, reputedly, heroin, for a living; at one point, he owned several Key Food supermarkets. Life was not so kind to his younger brother, Anthony. Prosecutors call Patsy a gifted drug pusher; as for Anthony, well, Anthony couldn't fight his way out of a glassine envelope. Patsy ran supermarkets; Anthony boosted from them—he's a convicted shoplifter. Patsy even had to put Anthony through college.

By way of thanks, Anthony Conte strolled into a federal prosecutor's office in 1994, and—one, two, three—Patsy Conte was pleading guilty to murder-conspiracy charges. He was charged with plotting to kill a man who failed to show proper respect to his boss, John Gotti.

Anthony's sellout of his brother may be the worst act of fraternal betrayal this side of Michael and Fredo Corleone. Sources say Anthony Conte told prosecutors about his brother's search for the man Gotti wanted dead, Louis DiBono. In 1991, DiBono's corpse was found stuffed in a car trunk in the World Trade Center garage.

Anthony Conte turned in his brother for seemingly self-evident reasons: Anthony had recently been convicted in a mob-involved money-laundering case and wanted the judge to go light on the sentence. But there was more to the betrayal than that.

Omertà, the Mafia "code of silence," is said to be the social glue that keeps Italian-American mobsters—and their associates and families—together. Literally, *omertà* means the "ability to act like a man."

But even that code has fallen in the face of contemporary doubt. According to a psychiatrist's report prepared for his sentencing, Anthony Conte's problem was an "unacceptable sense of self as a masculine figure."

It is a strange turn of events when a twelve-stepping shoplifter rats out his capo brother, but these are strange and confusing days for the American mob.

Hard Times for the Five Families

The mob isn't dead yet—not quite. Ignore the periodic obituaries issued by wishful or self-promoting prosecutors; the Mafia may never die. But Italian-American organized crime is in a state of flux unique in its history. In most parts of the country, the Mafia is in free fall; the mob's misfit collection of espresso-sipping geriatrics and 20-year-old thugs with disabled mental equipment is no match for RICO-wielding U.S. Attorneys. The mob in New York is bigger and more resilient than its counterparts elsewhere, but here too it is taking its hits. The bosses of three of New York's five families are in jail for life, though law enforcement is finding that the removal of the godfather doesn't mean the end of a family. Still, the business of three of the five families has been disrupted enough for some law-enforcement types to predict that within ten or twenty years, these families—the Colombo, Lucchese, and Bonanno—might not even exist. They may devolve into street gangs or be absorbed into cannier families.

Or family. Of the five families born in the Castellammarese War—the legendary 1930–31 conflict that gave rise to Lucky Luciano's modernized Cosa Nostra—only the Genovese seems savvy enough to flourish in the coming age. Law-enforcement sources tell *New York* that the Genovese family has even "opened the books," initiating 30 new members in 1993 and 1994. It is an extraordinarily confident move at a time when other families are in full-bunker mode.

But the survival of the Genovese has come at a cost. Law-enforcement experts tell *New York* that the Genovese family has survived only by enforcing an ethic of severe self-abnegation—no Armani suits, no Robin Hood-ish festivals, no social-club sitdowns, no preening bravos circling a cheese-ball, made-for-TV boss. The family now resembles the operations branch of an intelligence agency—which means that if the mob survives, it will do so in a form unrecognizable to fans of Mafia mythology.

Mob Family Values

The changes in the Genovese family are a response to the numbing success of prosecutors, the New York Police Department (NYPD), the FBI, and the state's Organized Crime Task Force. Aided by RICO statutes and digital-age eavesdropping equipment, these agencies can take credit for nailing the recent decline of the New York mob. But law enforcement has been helped by more than just new laws and new technology. The biggest ally the government has is the mob itself: Over the past twenty years, the Mafia has abandoned the strict "values" system that kept it immune from attack for so long. Dan Quayle was right: There *has* been a decline in family values.

"I think what has happened is that the younger mobsters are growing up with the values of their contemporaries," says Ronald Goldstock, the former director of the Organized Crime Task Force. "Honor is seen as a quaint throwback, both inside and outside the mob."

Law-enforcement officials—and mafiosi themselves—say the rise of the yuppie mobsters has led to the death of all the things the old-timers stood for: circumspection, respect, moderation. Not only do the "yuppies" sell drugs—a racket ostensibly banned by the mob's ruling commission—but they use drugs themselves. Look at the sad-sack case of Daniel "Danny Squires" Latella, a Lucchese soldier in the Bronx. In October 1994, Latella was arrested during a Bronx "john sweep" after cops discovered a trifecta of vice in his car: crack, a gun, and a prostitute.

"Things change," onetime Gambino underboss Aniello Dellacroce unknowingly told an FBI bug several years back. "Things change now because there's too much conflict. People do whatever they feel like. . . . They don't train their people no more. There's no more—there's no more respect."

Behavior that 30 years ago would get a man killed is written off today as the excess of a slack, hopelessly Americanized generation. Take the antics of Carmine Agnello, a Gambino associate and John Gotti's son-in-law. Agnello runs an auto-parts shop in Jamaica, Queens, on a street clogged with double-parked cars. In the mob, the rule was, don't mess with the police—it only attracts attention. So what did Carmine Agnello do in February 1994 when a cop began writing traffic tickets? He rammed the cop's scooter with a tow truck. Said one high-ranking law-enforcement official: "Even his father-in-law wouldn't do something this stupid.". . .

And then, of course, there's "ratting," which used to get you killed but now seems to be as common as becoming a lobbyist after a stint in the government (until the eighties, only a handful of made men ever divulged mob secrets). Most Mafia chieftains have been hurt by it—John Gotti certainly was—but none were wounded like the leaders of the Lucchese family. It was the testimony of Lucchese turncoats that put boss Vittorio "Little Vic" Amuso away for life; the only reason more Lucchese bigwigs haven't gone away is that many have become witnesses themselves, latecomers to the free-for-all snitcha-thon. The Lucchese family is a particularly apt case study in what happens when a long-held "values system" begins to fall apart.

Lucchese Paranoia

If Peter Chiodo weren't so fat, the twelve bullets fired into his body by a Lucchese hit squad at a Staten Island gas station in 1991 would have met with a sufficient number of vital organs to induce death. But Chiodo's weight hovered around 500 pounds, and his avoirdupois kept death at bay.

Naturally, Chiodo, a Lucchese captain, took offense at this attempt to end his life. But little did he know that by surviving, he was bringing the government not one but two high-level informants—the second was the man who actually engineered the botched hit.

That man, Alphonse D'Arco, is proving to be the most important Mafia turncoat in history, more important than Joseph Valachi in the sixties, more important even than Gotti's man Sammy "The Bull" Gravano. "In thousands of hours of conversation, we have never caught him in a contradiction," says Donald North, the FBI's chief organized-crime investigator in New York.

D'Arco, who at the time of the 1991 hit was the acting Lucchese boss, trusted the competence of the squad he assembled to kill Chiodo. After all, the team included his own son, Joseph. So he was surprised, and displeased, when Chiodo didn't die. But D'Arco's displeasure was more than matched by that of the two men who had ordered him to kill Chiodo—Vittorio Amuso and Anthony "Gaspipe" Casso, the most powerful members of the family.

Amuso and Casso apparently wanted Chiodo dead because they believed he was informing on them. Here, they may have been right.

New York has learned that on the day Chiodo was shot, his address book contained several FBI phone numbers. Sources say Chiodo had been warned by the government that his life was in danger, and he may have been preparing to flip.

But Amuso and Casso did not know this—they tended to believe, facts notwithstanding, that *everybody* was ratting them out. And if they didn't suspect their compatriots of snitching, they suspected them of stealing—at one point, the two ordered the murders of most members of the New Jersey Lucchese faction.

If the Gambinos of the early nineties were heavily into trucking and loan-sharking, the Luccheses of the early nineties were deep into paranoia and violence—eventually, they would target even Chiodo's innocent relatives for death, a gross violation of unwritten mob rules. But this is how mob families operate as they move into their third and fourth generation in America. "This third generation has no work ethic, no loyalty," the FBI's North says disapprovingly. . . .

Infighting and Defection

When Lucchese family head Tony Corallo was convicted of racketeering in 1987 and sentenced to life in prison, the family was left in the hands of Amuso and his aide-de-camp Casso. They were not Corallo's first choices; one of his preferences, Anthony "Buddy" Luongo, disappeared around the time succession became an issue. Both Casso and Amuso were drug dealers and inexperienced managers, law-enforcement sources say, and they were temperamentally unsuited to be dons. They are paranoid, rash, unskilled in diplomacy, and needlessly violent— especially Casso. . . .

Casso, law-enforcement officials say, has had a hand in at least 36 murders, including that of Anthony Fava, the unluckiest architect in New York history. Fava, building a million-dollar home for the Casso family in Mill Basin, Brooklyn, once complained to Casso about late payment. He didn't have time to complain twice. He was tortured— burned, gouged, shot in the knees—and murdered.

The old-line Lucchese leaders knew Amuso and Casso were trouble. Corallo's underboss Salvatore Santoro once told a person who visited him in jail that "these guys are nuts."

Throughout the late eighties and early nineties, the Luccheses con- tinued to make money in the traditional manner—extortion, loan- sharking, sports betting, garbage carting, garment trucking. The mon- ey flowed in, but Amuso and Casso killed anyway—not only the family's "cripples," soldiers who didn't make money, but its earners too. It was plain paranoia.

Many died; Chiodo didn't. Upset that D'Arco couldn't pull off the hit, Casso and Amuso apparently plotted to kill *him*. . . .

D'Arco collected his family and fled to the welcoming arms of the government. He's been testifying ever since. Casso may soon be doing the same. Captured by the FBI in 1993 while taking a shower in a New Jersey safe house, Casso offered his services to the government. In 1995, sources said he was in the Justice Department equivalent of charm school, learning how to talk to juries without scaring them.

Now that D'Arco, Casso, Chiodo, and former New Jersey Lucchese boss Anthony Acceturo are all employed by the government, whole Lucchese crews have applied for membership in other families, the FBI's North says. The other families have so far said no, fearing the Lucchese men as potential turncoats.

"The Lucchese family has lost its leadership," says Gregory O'Connell, a former assistant U.S. Attorney who prosecuted Amuso and other big-time bosses. "They've lost a treasure trove of knowledge about arrangements with other families and industries, and as a result, they've lost much of their ability to run sophisticated racketeering operations."

Other families are also burdened by succession disputes. The Colombos have been murdering one another over the right to run their family. In the Gambino family, John Gotti [who is serving a life sentence for racketeering and murder] has not relinquished power— he runs the family through his roughneck son, John Jr. But it's unclear whether "Junior" has either the brainpower or the backing of enough Gambino captains to assert definitive control. Like his father, Junior is said to be too thick to understand the Gambinos' complex holdings in legitimate business. And for the Gambinos, like the rest of the families, this is where the real money is. . . .

The Mob Perseveres

The secret of the mob's continued survival is that it involves itself in anything that makes money. Even today, the mob is the secret force behind dozens of industries and unions in the New York region. Food, clothing, and shelter: The mob supplies all three.

It is the essential contradiction in the government's war on the mob: Why, despite so many gang-busting successes, is the Mafia still a power in legitimate industry? And why is it still more successful than fresher, less strife-ridden, non-Italian ethnic syndicates? So far, the Russian Organizatsiya has made only modest inroads into aboveboard commerce, and no one expects the Chinese to take over the roofers union anytime soon.

The mob benefited by its special dispensation from J. Edgar Hoover, who gave the Mafia a 40-year head start, something none of the other groups will get. That's a key reason that pushing the Mafia out of legitimate industry is a bit like squeezing yeast from bread.

Take the fish business. Fish has been very good to the Genovese family. The family is heavily involved in the Fulton Fish Market, despite repeated government efforts to push it out, and Genovese associates are said to be behind regular attempts to hijack truckloads of shrimp around the region. Besides running fish, the Genovese are in unions, in construction, in the recording industry, in carting, and in fireworks, as well as in loan-sharking, drug pushing, and numbers running. Even dysfunctional families like the Luccheses still earn. The FBI's North says the Luccheses, shell-shocked as they are, are hoping to strengthen their position in the garment industry now that Thomas Gambino, the longtime garment-trucking boss, is in legal trouble. In truth, North says, it doesn't matter whether Gambino goes to jail or not. "The system is what's important," he says. "Any mob guy can be put in to take another's place."

The garment center resists change, but no industry has been as impervious to government assault as garbage carting. Nowhere has this been more true than on Long Island, the laboratory in a government experiment to cleanse the industry of mob ties. The first step has already been taken—the Lucchese captain who ran Long Island, Sal Avellino Jr., is in prison, serving a ten-year sentence for organizing the murders of two rebel carters. But investigators—and those garbagemen yearning to breathe free—find mob influence so ingrained that the removal of the gangster-in-chief has not meant the death of a system. . . .

The Genovese Family

It's one of the greatest shows running in New York City, and it's free. The star is a burly, disheveled man in a bathrobe and slippers, and the stage is Sullivan Street in the West Village. The show runs throughout the year, but since it's outdoor theater, it often shuts down on cold nights. The star isn't crazy, after all.

Or is he?

"Vincent Gigante has been found incompetent by four psychiatrists, including two psychiatrists recommended by the prosecution," says Barry Slotnick, who represents the West Village wanderer, the reputed boss of the Genovese crime family. "I've known Gigante for a long time. There is no question in my mind that he is incompetent."

Certainly, if Vincent "Chin" Gigante is competent, he's doing a good job hiding it. He may soon be involuntarily committed for yet another check to see whether he's fit to stand trial on murder and racketeering charges. So far, his life proves the old Mafia adage that it's better to have a good doctor than a good lawyer.

On a balmy evening this fall, Gigante was out wandering the neighborhood, a cap pulled down over his head. No one on the street seemed to notice the man the government calls the most powerful mobster in America. He was mumbling to himself, hands in the pockets of his bathrobe; there's a laminated card in one pocket, law-enforcement sources say, that contains his mother's telephone number, as well as the number to the Ghent, New York, estate of the late, felonious record mogul Morris Levy, a Genovese crony. Sources say Gigante's brother, Louis Gigante—the Catholic priest and controversial Bronx low-income-housing activist—lives at the estate.

On some nights, Vincent Gigante stops to chat with parking meters and fire hydrants, but on this particular night he soon disappears into the West Village shadows.

Slotnick says he's sure his client is mentally ill; law-enforcement officials are equally adamant that he's not, and sources say the government is about to produce several Mafia turncoats who will testify that they've seen Gigante talk business cogently.

Gigante is said to be not only cogent but intimidating. He is by far the most feared mafioso on the streets today, law-enforcement sources say. At the 1986 wake for a Genovese soldier, Gigante pulled "Little Vic" Amuso aside to discuss the Lucchese family's encroachment on the Genovese family's then-lucrative window-replacement business. According to sources, Gigante told Amuso he would be "lucky to leave this wake alive." Amuso, a stone killer in his own right, left trembling. "The Luccheses backed off after that," a source says.

Obsessive Secrecy

By all accounts, Gigante has radically cut back his exposure to other bosses; he certainly doesn't see his underlings very much. In so doing, he seems to be perfecting a new model for the running of an organized-crime family.

No one in the family is allowed to mention Gigante by name—when someone wants to refer to the boss, he is supposed to pull on his chin. The punishment for breaking this rule, sources say, can be death—it's the Genovese version of Total Quality Management. Outside the family, mobsters call Gigante the Robe.

According to law-enforcement sources, Gigante speaks most often with Vito "Bruce" Palmeri, a childhood friend and a soldier in the family. Palmeri passes cryptic messages on to Dominick "Quiet Dom" Cirillo, a Gigante deputy, who then relays encoded messages to other important leaders. Word then gets passed down the chain of command. Of course, Gigante could communicate quite easily with Cirillo if he chose to, since Cirillo is seen regularly at Il Mulino, the Italian restaurant on 3rd Street ("Superb people-watching," a recent Zagat's says). Gigante often passes by Il Mulino on his strolls through the neighborhood.

Genovese-family members mask their activities in other ways—they know that most law-enforcement agencies don't have surveillance running overnight, so they hold many of their meetings at 3 and 4 A.M.; they have traveled to meetings curled up underneath blankets on the backseats of cars. They dress like bums—reputed street boss Liborio "Big Barney" Bellomo showed up to a family wedding in a T-shirt. The family is also broken down into cells—no inter-crew dinners for the Genoveses. Soldiers are isolated from one another as a protective measure against informers. The 30 newly made members of the family are being kept under wraps for at least two years in order to give the bosses time to assess their loyalty.

All of these countermeasures make law enforcement surpassingly difficult. There have been few significant prosecutions and virtually no defections. The Genovese family is the "Ivy League of the underworld," says Joseph Coffey, the chief of intelligence for the state's Organized Crime Task Force.

A Less Glamorous Image

By changing the way mobsters conduct themselves, the Genovese family will also change the way outsiders see the Mafia. The cost of succeeding in a world crowded with snooping detectives and disloyal confederates is to give up everything that made Mafia life fun in the first place. Gigante is feared by young mob wannabes, but his world is empty of the brand of high-stepping outlaw romance John Gotti personified. There are still young Italian-Americans who are attracted to the life, mob experts say, but assimilation and suburbanization are helping to thin their ranks to the point that the Italian street gangs are no longer an effective Mafia minor league.

But there are still farm teams out there. They're in the necklace of New York City neighborhoods that stretches from Bay Ridge and Bensonhurst to Ozone Park and Howard Beach. There's a young Bonanno-family crew in Maspeth; in Canarsie, there's a Lucchese crew led by soldier Angelo DeFendis that consists almost entirely of twentysomethings. In September 1994, a group of young would-be mobsters in Dyker Beach Park beat to death an Ecuadorean immigrant in a turf dispute. The daily press reported the killing as an example of teenagers gone haywire. "Just 4 'Ordinary' Kids," *Newsday* headlined one of its stories. But law-enforcement sources say that two of the teenagers charged in the killing are nephews of Robert Scarpaci, a Gambino soldier. One of the nephews, Steven Ruiz, even worked part-time in the Scarpaci family's funeral home, the Scarpacis being the undertakers to the underworld.

"These kids were trying to make their bones by protecting turf," says one law-enforcement source. "They wanted to be seen as connected. There are still people like that out there."

The Gambino Family Without John Gotti

There is nothing particularly clubby, and there's certainly nothing sociable, about Caffè 2000, an espresso bar-cum-social club on 101st Avenue in Ozone Park, the Via Dolorosa of the Gambino family. The wiring is exposed; the chairs are orange plastic. In the pastry case sits a handful of damp cannoli. Across the street, at the St. Mary Gate of Heaven church, the people of Ozone Park are celebrating Saturday-night mass. In Caffè 2000, there's a card game on.

The proprietor is irascible. I order an espresso. "That's to go," he announces.

But he lets me sit by the pay phone, and I watch the regulars, who are reputed members of an autonomous Sicilian crew that nevertheless pays allegiance to the Gottis. There are a few English-speaking men in the club, one of whom looks like a stereotypical Gambino— see-through socks, thin gold watch, swept-up, bouffy hair. The rest look like peasants. It's a decrepit-looking scene, and it's improbable that the people of Ozone Park come here looking for "justice," the way the undertaker Bonasera sought justice from Vito Corleone. In fact, the people of Ozone Park probably don't even come here looking for cannoli.

Down 101st Avenue, at Aldo's Pizzeria, a framed photograph hangs behind the counter. It's a picture of Robert De Niro and Joe Pesci eating Aldo's pizza. Life imitating art imitating life. Some of the Gotti brothers, the obscure Gotti brothers, are said to eat at Aldo's on occasion.

There are people in Ozone Park who say the neighborhood's gone to seed since John Gotti went away. "The colored are moving in," one man outside Aldo's says, nodding toward East New York. "It wouldn't have happened before."

But there are people who will talk to a reporter, anonymously, about the real John Gotti. "It's all bullshit. He didn't do shit for us," a man in his twenties says. "At this point, it's the losers who go with these guys. Anybody who can get a real job gets a real job." Still, there are some in Ozone Park who respect Gotti and would like to imitate his style. "The guy was treated like a king," the man says. "Everybody wants that respect."

But John Gotti is now paying for his way of life; he believed the myth, as William Bastone of *The Village Voice* has written, and the myth is what beat him. The smart mafiosi know it.

The mob may be far from dead, but the romance is almost certainly gone. *The Godfather* created the myth; *GoodFellas* deconstructed it; a movie featuring the shlimazls of the Lucchese family would destroy it. John Gotti is the end of the line that reaches back to Lucky Luciano and Al Capone, and even further, to Billy the Kid and Jesse James.

Nostalgia

Dominick Montiglio and I are drinking Cokes in Frontierland, Disney's G-rated paean to the Wild West. Shots ring out; time for the show. On the rooftops, pink-faced outlaws fire caps at each other. The tourists love it. "Shoot 'em, shoot 'em!" a 12-year-old near us screams.

"It's a Small World" is the exception at Disney World. Many of the attractions feature violence, even glorify it. One of Montiglio's favorites turns out to be "Pirates of the Caribbean," which celebrates sacking, pillaging, and prostitution.

"I would have liked to live back then," he says, as Animatronic whores kick their plastic legs in our direction. "Looting and shit."

At the Frontierland show, an actor dressed all in black—the only person in Disney World who looks like Montiglio—pushes his way through the crowd. "Uh-oh—Black Bart," Montiglio whispers.

"Get outta here before I blow your brains out," the actor yells, pushing Montiglio aside. Not a good move, I want to tell Black Bart.

Montiglio grunts. "He's probably gay anyway."

The show ends, the people applaud, and the dead actors scrape themselves off the plaza and go for ice cream. As we walk through Frontierland, Montiglio is telling me about an idea he has for a board game. It's called Boss of Bosses.

"The goal is to reach the top of the family," he says. Players compete for "whack" cards, which allow you to kill off the competition.

"Maybe Disney will buy it," he says hopefully.

Why not? The Mafia, in some respects, seems just as self-consciously stylized as Black Bart, as immutably part of a bygone era as Porfirio Rubirosa or the Rat Pack. The mob's new generation has abandoned family values because they seem more like a campy relic to put under glass than a code to live by.

Montiglio and I head out of the Magic Kingdom—he really needs that drink. "They got whores and guns and shit, but you can't get a beer," he says. "Fuckin' hypocrisy."

Disney World has left him philosophical. "Americans love their violence. They don't want to admit it, but they love it."

I ask him whether that's why they love mobsters. Montiglio's answer is telling. "What people like is the whole thing of *respect*," he says. But what he's talking about has nothing to do with loyalty and virtue. "You know, when I was in the life, it was great. I mean, we got respect. I got in once at Studio 54 ahead of Burt Reynolds. That's what we were attracted to, the glitz. It doesn't exist anymore. . . . The new generation ruined it."

THE DECLINE OF THE AMERICAN MAFIA

Peter Reuter

Peter Reuter, an economist and author, is noted for his research on drug trafficking and criminal justice and his work with the federal government in these areas. The American Mafia is on its way out, Reuter maintains. He contends that the Mafia is under increased pressure from law enforcement and from growing competition from other organized crime groups. Due to these and other factors, he asserts, the Mafia has become less threatening, powerful, and competent than it was in the past.

The American Mafia emerged during Prohibition as the wealthier and more violent successor to local city gangs involved in prostitution and gambling. It is thus a contemporary of the Soviet Union, another long-standing problem for the United States government. Coincidentally, the Mafia and Soviet Union have ceased to be significant strategic adversaries at almost the same time. The Mafia is almost extinguished now as a major actor in the United States' criminal world. And, to extend the comparison with the Soviet Union perhaps beyond its fair limits, the Mafia's decline is the result of both its conservatism and of federal government actions.

The Mafia's Heyday

Initially, the American Mafia was a prominent supplier of bootlegged liquor. That required good connections with the local police department and political machines. Paying off the local beat cop provided a speakeasy, with its conspicuous and regular flow of traffic, little effective protection. Instead, it was necessary to guard against any cop who might be on that beat; the efficient solution was buying the whole department, if it was for sale. In many cities it was. Frequently, that also meant connections with urban political machines. While Al Capone's control of Chicago (though some scholars question Capone's Mafia membership) in the 1920s is the most notorious instance, almost 50 years later the Mayor of Newark, New Jersey, Hugh Addonizio, retained strong connections to the local Mafia family. Elliot Ness

Reprinted with permission of the author from "The Decline of the American Mafia," by Peter Reuter, *The Public Interest*, No. 120 (Summer 1995), pp. 89–99; ©1995 by National Affairs, Inc.

and the federal revenuers, frequently less honest than legend, were a nuisance but not a major one.

At the same time, the Mafia acquired control of many unions, largely through direct intimidation of members. By 1929, when John Landesco did his classic study of organized crime in Chicago, he could already list a dozen local industries that the Mafia dominated through the unions. Prices were fixed and/or territories were allocated, with the threat of union strikes or picketing of customers as the enforcement mechanism. The Depression, which created a demand for cartel-organizing services later met by various New Deal agencies, such as the Reconstruction Financing Administration, added a few more industries (e.g., fur manufacturing) to the Mafia list, particularly in New York.

By the 1960s, the Mafia had mostly shifted from direct provision of illegal services, like bookmaking and loansharking, to selling services to bookmakers, loansharks, and other criminal entrepreneurs. The organization's reputation for being able to deliver on threats was good enough that it could, in effect, sell these entrepreneurs contract insurance and dispute-settlement services. A bookmaker could insure himself against extortion by other gangsters or customer welching by making regular payments to some Mafioso. The organizational reputation, painstakingly and bloodily acquired earlier, was now the principal asset.

Signs of Weakness

The evidence of the Mafia's decline is partly of the "dog didn't bark" variety. A Senate committee has a hearing on international fraud and organized crime, and the American Mafia goes unmentioned. The Department of Justice lists its principal targets for drug enforcement, and Mafia leaders don't make the cut. The New York City Police Department has yet another major corruption scandal, and none of the events involve the Mafia. A major numbers banker in New York, "Spanish Raymond" Marquez, who paid 5 percent of his profits to the Mafia in the 1960s, now pays only $300 per week.

There are a few more direct indicia as well. At least one family, based in Cleveland, has effectively disbanded. The *New York Times*, long the newspaper of record for Mafia events, now lists the membership of the five major New York families as only 1,200, down from 3,000 in the early 1970s. The DeCavalcante family of New Jersey, admittedly a weaker family even then, now has only 10 members, scarcely enough to fill a good-sized dining table, let alone an organization chart of the type so dramatically displayed by the FBI at numerous Senate hearings.

The Mafia has failed to maintain control of the New York heroin market and has been a marginal player in the cocaine business everywhere. Mexican-source heroin became available when the heroin market first expanded in the early 1970s, and the Mafia was never able to prevent its distribution in New York City, the home of perhaps one-third of the nation's heroin addicts. Its earlier control of the market had apparently rested on its domination of the New York docks, through the longshoremen's union as well as its connections with southern European processors. Mexican imports evaded that bottleneck. By the late 1980s, the traditional circuitous route for Southeast Asian heroin, through Sicily, southern Italy, or France, had primarily been replaced by direct importation, via the West coast, by Chinese and Vietnamese entrepreneurs. The Mafia proved helpless to deal with any of these incursions on its traditional territories.

Asian drug distributors have major advantages as heroin importers and domestic wholesalers. In the source countries for heroin, they can more cheaply ascertain the credibility and capacities of producers and exporters, as well as the corruptibility of local officials and transportation executives. Chinese gangs are better partners for Kun Sa, the long-standing leader in the Burmese/Thai opium trade, historically connected with remnants of the Kuo Min Tang army from pre-1949 China.

In the United States, these gangs have better natural cover. Even creative and entrepreneurial drug-enforcement organizations have had difficulty developing informants and intelligence about Asian distributors. Few agents speak the relevant languages, and even fewer are of Asian origin. It is difficult to blend into the community, which, reflecting its recent immigration and cultural distinctiveness, is generally distrustful of police agencies.

In contrast, the Mafia is familiar territory to enforcement agencies, with its membership and affiliate lists updated as often at FBI headquarters as at John Gotti's Ravenite Social Club hangout. Indeed, there have been occasions in which, as was true for the U.S. Communist Party in the 1950s, FBI undercover agents seem to be as significant in some families as were the members themselves. The communities in which the Mafia recruits and operates are well known to police and provide comfortable terrain for undercover operations; language is not much of a problem anymore.

The Drug Trade and the Unions

The Mafia's failure to play a role in the cocaine market is particularly striking. Most reasonable estimates suggest that this constitutes the largest single illegal market, in terms of gross sales, in recent times and perhaps ever. Credible estimates of U.S. revenues are approximately $40 billion, with as much as $10 billion going to higher-level distributors. No list of the major players has ever included any senior Mafiosi. The failure of the Mafia to participate directly in this market is partly explained by the very high legal risks associated with drug trafficking (a reason offered for the often-broken rule, immortalized in the movie *The Godfather*, for staying away from heroin), but more interesting is the Mafia's failure to serve as the source of dispute-settlement, enforcement, or financing services.

Several factors may explain the Mafia's inability to provide services to cocaine dealers. Colombian drug-dealing organizations have developed their own general reputation for violence. Indeed, the Colombians are known for their unwillingness to follow even the moderately restrictive rules of Mafia murders, e.g., that wives and children are exempt. That probably reflects a shorter planning horizon (the leaders will go back to Colombia once rich) and a belief that the criminal-justice system will not punish them. The historical experience in Colombia itself since 1950 could account for that; the criminal-justice system there has been highly vulnerable to intimidation and corruption, and Colombia has experienced extraordinary levels of political and other violence over the last 40 years.

The Mafia has also suffered a major loss from its racketeering activities in legal markets. The election of a Teamsters reform slate, headed by Ron Carey, capped a decades-long battle with the U.S. Department of Justice. During that time, four Teamster presidents (Dave Beck, Jimmy Hoffa, Roy Williams, and Jackie Presser) were indicted and/or convicted of corrupt activities in connection with the Mafia, particularly the Chicago and Kansas City families. The Mafia's long-standing role in Las Vegas casinos, originally arising from the pariah-like nature of the industry itself, had come to center on its ability to direct the Central States Teamsters pension funds to compliant casino operators. The shift to trusteeships of that fund, again after a remarkably long battle with the Justice Department, greatly reduced the capital available to the Mafia.

Deregulation of the trucking industry, which curtailed the bargaining power of the Teamsters, also played a major role in lowering the value of racketeer control of the union. Trucking companies now had to compete with each other, as well as with other modes of transport, and could no longer pass on wage increases in regulated prices.

The most poignant indicator of decline is evidenced by recent court pleadings. Twelve Philadelphia Mafiosi have asked for public-defender representation, and prosecutors believe that they may indeed be poor enough to justify the request. Even the bar specializing in defense of Mafiosi has apparently hit hard times: "Lawyers who once made a steady diet of this type of work are having to diversify," said a prominent local defense lawyer.

Sources of Decline

Some have suggested that the decline is largely the result of the "Americanization" of the Mafia—the demise of old values of loyalty to the fictive family and the increasing greed and self-centeredness of members. A less colorful, but more plausible, explanation may be found in a combination of three factors.

The altered structure of urban politics and policing. As already stated, the principal original asset of the Mafia, built during the Prohibition era, was its connection to urban political machines. Mayors in Boston, Kansas City, New York, and Philadelphia were all credibly associated with their local Mafia families between 1950 and 1980. Those connections helped the Mafia develop property rights to centralized police corruption. As Thomas Schelling argued in *The Public Interest* in 1967, the Mafia's ability to control illegal markets may have rested largely on its ability to use the monopoly power of the police. The Mafia was, in effect, the collector for corrupt politicians and police, with the limits of the franchise dictated by political resistance in the populace.

By 1970, urban machines were largely gone; Chicago was an important exception into the 1980s. Cities are now mostly governed by much broader coalitions, with strong federal involvement in local government financing. Local corruption, the original justification for passage in 1970 of the Organized Crime Control Act, is now much less systemic. The flight of white ethnic communities to the suburbs and the growth of strong urban black political organizations has also contributed to the decline. Though *The Godfather* movies depicted corrupt, whiskey-guzzling Irish police overcoming their contempt for wine-sloshing Sicilians and making deals with the Mafia, the traditional relationship between blacks and the Mafia has not encouraged the development of trust. For a long time, the Mafia pushed around black gambling operators, and the memory remains.

Local police agencies have become more professional, and the growth of large federal law-enforcement agencies, with concurrent jurisdiction and strong interest in making corruption cases, has inhibited the development of long-term corrupt relationships between Mafiosi and police. Before 1960, the local police effectively had a monopoly of law enforcement aimed at illegal markets; paying off the Miami Police Department was enough to provide total protection of bookmaking there in the 1950s. Federal and state agencies might have jurisdiction, for example, under the Harrison Act (drugs) or the Mann Act (prostitution), but these agencies were small and timid. The famous Harry Anslinger, an aggressive proselytizer for tough drug enforcement and the head of the predecessor to the Drug Enforcement Administration (DEA), had assembled a force of no more than 300 agents when he retired in 1962.

Now, the local police can sell, at best, very partial protection, since state and federal agencies can all make cases against loansharks, drug dealers, or extortionists. To make matters worse for would-be sellers of local protective services, offering up your local protector is one of the few ways for criminals to get relief from long federal sentences. The market for local police corruption has certainly not disappeared, but it is much less systemic than in previous decades. What the Mollen Commission inquiry in New York City uncovered was a group of entrepreneurial police who stole drugs from dealers when they had the chance but then had to sell the stuff themselves. There was no criminal organization able and willing to take advantage of their corruption to develop control of some area or market.

Legal Eagles and Stumbling Felons

Better federal enforcement. The FBI got out of pretentious pinstripes and into badly cut leisure suits in the late 1970s. Long-term undercover investigations, which J. Edgar Hoover had always rejected because of the difficulty of controlling the agents, became frequent. One of the first (UniRac, for "union racketeering") snared Anthony Scotto, a highly visible figure in the waterfront industry with close ties to the New York State political system and, as it turned out, a member in good standing of the Gambino family; that membership was scarcely surprising since he had married the daughter of Anthony Anastasia, of Murder, Inc., fame.

Federal prosecutors became much more sophisticated in their use of the Racketeer Influenced and Corrupt Organizations (RICO) and the Continuing Criminal Enterprise (CCE) statutes. Instead of convicting dons for running gambling enterprises, which was the outcome of many investigations in the early 1970s, RICO allowed them to bring cases with more significant and substantive crimes. John Gotti, the putative Godfather, was sentenced for his involvement in a homicide. The list of charges on which the heads of the five New York families were convicted in 1986 (the "Commission" case, in which, for the first time, the defendants admitted that the Mafia existed and was directed by a commission of the leaders) included three murders.

The federal judiciary, with guidelines in hand, delivered long sentences. For example, taking the *Times* listing as definitive, each of the leaders of the five families in New York in 1985 has received a sentence of at least 15 years; most of them and their principal deputies are in prison for life sentences without parole.

The price of loyalty, the much-vaunted "omerta," has thus become a lot higher. Members who might serve three years rather than inform changed their minds when 15-year terms became common. John Gotti is serving a life sentence because Salvatore Gravano, his longtime deputy and an admitted participant in 19 murders, chose to testify and turn an expected life sentence into a more reasonable five years. The federal government now reports over 100 Mafiosi in its witness protection program, compared to just a handful 10 years ago.

Not surprisingly, the increasing incidence of informants has begun to destroy the families from within; by early 1993, 11 Lucchese family members had been killed in an internal struggle. As Ronald Goldstock, longtime director of the New York State Organized Crime Task Force, commented in 1993: "The fate of anyone who assumes a leadership position in a [Mafia] family is a life prison sentence or assassination by a rival."

Incompetence. The Mafia has continued to recruit from among uneducated, tough felons and requires that they commit serious and brutal crimes to gain admission. This is not a very effective method for finding the best and the brightest of criminal talent, particularly when the shrinking pool of young Italian-immigrant labor has much better legitimate opportunities than in the past. Whereas in the period from 1900 to 1909 over one million Italian males under the age of 45 migrated to the United States, for the 1960s the figure was only 80,000.

Inevitably, some older leaders lost their edge. Mark Haller, the leading historian of American organized crime, reports that Harry Riccibone, a senior member of the Bruno group, was accused by one of his associates of turning into a "philanthropist" because of his unwillingness to act aggressively against his debtors. The current leader of the Genovese family, Vincent Gigante, may be mentally impaired, though some maintain that this is a ruse on his part to ensure that he cannot be tried.

The leaders may be decisive, they may be shrewd at determining when to use force, but they are not strategic in their thinking. Colombian drug distributors are less sophisticated than suggested by highly stylized accounts, such as novelist Tom Clancy's *Clear and Present Danger*, but they do seem to have acquired a few contemporary business practices, particularly with respect to financial services. The American Mafia languishes in suspicion of such sophistication, with nary a computer in sight. . . .

Bring Back the Godfather?

A nostalgia for the Mafia has already emerged in this country. It is associated with a remembrance of orderly illegal markets, when bootleggers and bookmakers only shot each other and understood the dangers of killing the innocent. Alan Block, a Pennsylvania State University historian, estimates that only about 190 gangland murders occurred in New York during the 1930s, a mere bagatelle when compared with the hundreds generated annually by drug markets through the 1980s and 1990s. Unless we want to reinstall systemic, local police corruption and have police intimately involved in the regulation of the business, the Mafia would not be able to do much about the retailing end, where almost all the violence occurs.

Another component of the nostalgia is for the simplicity of having one monolithic enemy, particularly one whose leaders often displayed a certain panache and whose lineages were well known. Alas, to conclude with the Soviet analogy, we will now have to live with the more complicated world of many less well-known gangs. The FBI, like the CIA, must develop the capacity to track the activities of lots of groups, many as meaningless to the American public as the leaders of Azerbaijan. We may be better off dealing with a foe less capable of undermining government, but we will inevitably pay less attention to the struggle, and the agencies themselves will miss the public attention that goes with catching stars.

LA COSA NOSTRA'S NEW ALLIES

Claire Sterling

Despite a steady decline in power over the past few decades, the American Mafia is here to stay, according to author and organized crime expert Claire Sterling. While many commentators believe that international crime groups, such as the Sicilian and Russian Mafias and the Chinese Triads, will supplant La Cosa Nostra as the greatest criminal threats to America, Sterling maintains that La Cosa Nostra's cooperation with these groups may lead to its rejuvenation. In the following excerpt from her book *Thieves' World: The Threat of the New Global Network of Organized Crime*, she examines how the traditionally distrustful relationship between the American and Sicilian Mafias may be evolving into one of mutual prosperity.

"This is gonna be a Cosa Nostra till I die. Be it an hour from now, or be it tonight, or a hundred years from now, when I'm in jail. It's gonna be Cosa Nostra." So John Gotti said before a judge sent him up for life in 1992. The perceived wisdom today is that he was wrong, but the facts suggest that he may have been right.

Cosa Nostra's end, predicted regularly in America for half a century, *ought* to be near. Over a thousand of its members and associates have been indicted or imprisoned since the 1980s. Its entire governing commission has been convicted. The biological solution awaits its geriatric bosses. Practically all its top patriarchs are behind bars for good anyway, including Gotti himself.

Their younger successors are inexperienced, brash, incautiously greedy, several generations removed from the old mafia culture, and bereft of historical memory. Their discipline is poor. Their humus, the Italian-American community, is washing away into the mainstream of American life. Their hold on the streets seems to be weakening since they lease out rackets to others. Their nerve appears to be slipping, in that they kill less than some of their ceaselessly multiplying and recklessly violent rivals. On the other hand, they are killing each other off more persistently than they have done in decades.

"This is the twilight of the mob. It's not dark yet, but the sun is going down," one expert announced.

Reprinted with the permission of Simon & Schuster from *Thieves' World*, by Claire H. Sterling. Copyright ©1994 by Claire H. Sterling Associates, Ltd.

Yet for the FBI, Cosa Nostra is still "the most serious organized crime problem in the United States." The crime ring that has outlived every other in America since the 1890s is still recruiting, still creaming 20 percent off the top of all new construction in New York, still doing nearly everything it has always done, in the areas that have always been its strongholds.

FBI field officers report that Federal prosecutions have "had little impact on Cosa Nostra's overall activity" in Detroit, "no impact" in Los Angeles, "little effect" in Chicago; that its activities "do not appear to have diminished" in Miami and "remain relatively unchanged" in Kansas City; that the Genovese Family has "a huge operation" in New Jersey where its structure "remains intact."

Nationwide, the organization "remains particularly strong in Chicago, New England, southern Florida, Las Vegas, Atlantic City, and New York City," the FBI says.

"In the universe of organized criminal groups, the racketeering activities of La Cosa Nostra are the most protracted and sustained, the most impacted and entrenched, the most expansive and profitable, the most corrosive and deleterious to legitimate sectors of society, the most resistant to enforcement efforts generally, and the most resilient to the aftermath of any single enforcement effort," observes the FBI's New Jersey office.

The Sicilian Mafia

Second only to this seemingly unsinkable organization is its big brother from Sicily. An independent entity in America since the 1960s, Sicily's Cosa Nostra was supposed to have been finished there halfway through the 1980s when its heroin network was cracked in New York's Pizza Connection case. Actually, it has been "growing precipitously," says the head of the FBI's organized crime section, Jim Moody.

It may become a graver menace than its American counterpart, warned Attorney-General William Barr in 1992. "I've said this privately, and I've said it at the cabinet table. We are facing a tremendous challenge from the Sicilian Mafia, one that could dwarf La Cosa Nostra here in the United States. We may be at the beginning of a more serious threat from organized crime than ever before," he told a reporter for the *Legal Times*.

There were clear signs by then that the Sicilian Mafia was rapidly colonizing the American underworld. Its men have been arriving legally; visas are no longer required for Italian nationals. Keeping away from big cities inhabited by the American mob and knowledgeable cops, they have been fanning out over the countryside like KGB moles. They settle into small towns, file for citizenship, go into business, and win the community's respect. Their names and faces are unknown, and they have no rap sheets in America.

The harder the law bears down on the American mafia, the more Sicilian mafiosi arrive. The FBI thought there were a few hundred of them in the late 1980s. By 1991 it was speaking of three thousand, not counting members of the Camorra and 'Ndrangheta [rival groups in Italy], "noted with increasing frequency." By the end of 1992 it was estimating "between ten and twenty thousand members and associates." That is roughly the size of the American mafia itself: two thousand members, some twenty thousand associates. A second Mafia as large as the first, accountable to Palermo, has calamitous implications for the United States. These are the . . . veterans of Sicily's Great Mafia War, interlocked with the world's biggest crime syndicates, brutalized to a degree that frightens even their American cousins. They are already drawing the American mafia into their planetary orbit . . . and they can undoubtedly give it lessons in the art of wielding power.

The Two Mafias Unite

"If you want your Cosa Nostra to be as successful as our Cosa Nostra, you oughtta use Sicilian methods, like killing judges and cops," advised a prize Sicilian trafficker in New York.

Relations between the two mafias have always been mysterious, at times unfathomable. By mutual agreement they have been separate and distinct for some forty years; neither can intrude on the other's sovereign territory. Actually, the Sicilians have occupied several of the Americans' exclusive enclaves since the 1960s and poached all over their criminal preserves.

For the Americans they are the "zips," "geeps," "fuckin' siggies," secretive, predatory, resented, and detested. . . .

Yet the Sicilian Mafia's top emissary to the United States was taken into New York's Gambino Family with "five, six, seven of his crew" in the mid-1970s; a decade later he was elevated to the rank of *capodecina* by John Gotti himself. . . .

Once installed in America, they could not be dislodged. Nor, for all their incursions, could they be molested.

The Sicilians might be feared and disliked, but they were needed— are needed urgently today. American bosses habitually dodge their own ban on drugs by investing money in Sicilian deals. More and more of their soldiers are risking an in-house death sentence to work with Sicilian traffickers. Many Families, running to flab, are in search of more backbone and muscle. For an aging organization tormented by the law and beset by new young rivals, the Sicilians have come to mean fresh blood and the saving strength of ancestral Mafia tradition. Compared to their American cousins, they are still the keepers of the ancient Mafia code, however they may have trashed it. Thus, a growing number of Sicilians "made" at home are getting made in the United States as well. Several have become *capos* in American Families. One has taken over a Family altogether.

Spicy evidence to this effect dropped into the lap of FBI agents in Medford, Massachusetts, in the autumn of 1989. Twenty-one members of Boston's Patriarca Family gathered there on a Sunday to induct four new members. An FBI bug picked up every word as a Patriarca captain administered the ritual oath: *"Io, Carmen, voglio entrare in questa organizzazione . . ."* [I, Carmen, want to enter this organization . . .]

The oath giver, a Sicilian Man of Honor named Biagio DiGiacomo, had to explain from time to time in strangled English. "Put your hands out like this, Carmen, and when I read it to you, repeat after me and then go like this, boom, boom, boom," he said, preparing to draw blood from Carmen's trigger finger. He continued:

"If I said you must kill a police informer, would you do that for me on behalf of our organization?"

"Yes, I would."

"You would do that?"

"I would do that."

"This thing of ours, we would be delighted to have you . . ."

Then DiGiacomo continued in Sicilian: "I swear to enter this organization alive and leave it dead." In English, he went on, that meant, "We get in alive in this organization, and the only way we gonna get out is death, no matter what. It's no hope, no Jesus, no Madonna, nobody can help us if we ever give up this secret to anybody. . . . This thing that cannot be exposed. . . ."

The Patriarca Family inducted several more Sicilians in 1992; bugged repeatedly and mercilessly by the FBI, it is plainly in need of their reviving presence. New York's Lucchese Family has sworn in an unregenerate Sicilian drug trafficker, Enzo Napoli. The Philadelphia Family, an exceptionally riotous lot, has actually come under a Sicilian's rule.

The Sicilians in Philadelphia

The Philadelphia Family has dominated crime and politics in much of Pennsylvania for some seventy years, but it started to fly apart when its longtime boss, Angelo Bruno, was shot dead with a sawed-off shotgun in March 1980. A month later Bruno's consigliere was tortured, stabbed, and shot to death. A few months afterward his chief loan shark was found stuffed into two green plastic garbage bags. At year's end his successor was blown up by a bomb packed with nails.

The perpetrator, Nicodemo Scarfo, ordered the murders of nineteen more members after he took over—this out of forty in all, replaced by his own men. Ruling with a flamboyance and raw violence much like John Gotti's, Scarfo met much the same end. He was tried in 1988 for criminal conspiracy and a continuing criminal enterprise—ten homicides, five attempted homicides, extortion, gambling, narcotics—and jailed for life.

The fact that he left the Philadelphia Family in shambles does not altogether explain why the highest echelons of America's Cosa Nostra sent in a Sicilian Man of Honor to replace him. The reputed new boss, John Stanfa, once drove for Angelo Bruno, but he is still a "zip." Born and made in Sicily, he communicates regularly with Palermo's top bosses and is part of their crowd in the United States. Nevertheless, the Gambino Family sent Stanfa down from New York, John Gotti backed him, and Cosa Nostra's national commission even authorized him to swear in a few more Sicilians. Decisions like these are not made casually.

Philadelphia is where the American mafia is "the *second* most serious problem, *after* the Sicilian Mafia," says the FBI. Sicilian drug traffickers infest the city—indeed, they own the whole northern half of it. Angelo Bruno, Sicilian-born himself, turned over the north side long ago to John Gambino and his brothers in nearby Cherry Hill, New Jersey. It is in Philadelphia that the two mafias may decide to remarry after nearly half a century apart: a union of imperial grandeur for the international underworld and a nightmare for American authorities. . . .

La Cosa Nostra's Rebirth?

"A reorganization and perhaps a return to tradition is taking place in the Philadelphia Family and others as well. . . . What is developing may signal a new trend for the organization and operation of La Cosa Nostra," says the authoritative Pennsylvania Crime Commission. "If Stanfa is successful . . . we may see a powerful confederation of Sicilian Mafia members with the remaining Family veterans. Cosa Nostra may emerge as far more powerful, effective, and insulated from law enforcement. The metamorphosis in the Philadelphia Family may represent the future of Cosa Nostra."

This was the attorney general's bad dream: the emergence of a hydra-headed criminal monster in America that would certainly dwarf La Cosa Nostra as we know it.

Never again, the FBI vowed in 1991. The mafia, as if designed by some diabolical hand, seemed impervious to everything the law could throw at it. The United States could not let that happen again.

Apart from redoubled efforts to eliminate the mafia itself, the main thrust of FBI strategy now was to "ensure that no other criminal organization can ever achieve a comparable level of power."

Heartfelt agreement came from Assistant Attorney General Robert Mueller, testifying on the Hill. "For most of the last thirty years we've played catch-up in eradicating what is still this country's most serious organized crime problem—La Cosa Nostra. We will not repeat that mistake. We cannot stand idly by while newer organized crime groups invade our society," he told a Senate committee in 1991.

But American society was invaded already, by the same forces advancing on Europe, working both continents as one. Though far ahead of others in trying to cope with them, U.S. law enforcement agencies still cannot bridge what is known as the "technology gap" between the crime syndicates' capabilities and their own.

An Organized Crime Wave

To deal with more than a thousand organized gangs is overwhelming—Hispanics, Asians, West Indians, Mexicans, African-Americans, California's Crips and Bloods, motorcycle gangs such as the Pagans, the Bandidos, and Hell's Angels. These can be nationwide, disciplined, heavily armed, and lethal. Jamaican Posses rampage through thirty-five states, pushing nearly half the crack sold in the country. Hell's Angels have thirty-five chapters in the United States and as many again abroad, in Canada, Britain, Denmark, Germany, France, Brazil, New Zealand, Russia, Japan.

But they are no potential Cosa Nostras. Most of them hire out to Cosa Nostra or pay it tribute. Hell's Angels are its "working partners," the FBI declares. Cosa Nostra's Chicago Family employs Mexicans, Puerto Ricans, and Colombians. New York's Families collect a tax from Cubans handling the numbers game in Harlem and Russian crooks in Brighton Beach. The Philadelphia Family collects a street tax from any criminal band trying to work there.

What worries Washington is an alarming invasion by Cosa Nostra's true peers—the Triads, the Yakuza, and the Russian mafia, the largest organizations in the crime business. The Triads have four times as many members and helpers as their American counterparts, the Yakuza five times as many, the Russians over a hundred times as many, more and more of whom are drifting into the United States. Any one of the three in league with either of the two mafias in the United States would be a fright story, and they are all in league with both. Such concentrated criminal strength is beyond anything in American experience—in any country's experience, for that matter.

With a statesmanship yet to be achieved by the United Nations, these titans of the underworld have been sharing resources, personnel, and protective cover for years, peaceably and to their mutual benefit. They all "pay tribute" (taxes) to the American Cosa Nostra, the FBI says. In exchange they "utilize Cosa Nostra connections to penetrate the country's law enforcement and judicial communities through long-established Cosa Nostra contacts." The fact that Cosa Nostra gives them access to its private collection of corrupt judges and cops suggests extraordinary levels of complicity.

CHAPTER 2

ORGANIZED CRIME IN AMERICA: NEW THREATS

Contemporary Issues
Companion

LA COSA NOSTRA'S SUCCESSORS

Peter Maas

Although La Cosa Nostra remains a formidable criminal conspiracy, decades of effort by U.S. law enforcement have reduced the once impenetrable organization to a shadow of its former power. However, asserts Peter Maas, new criminal groups are threatening to take its place; foremost among them are New York City–based Russian and Chinese crime syndicates. One of the FBI's top priorities, Maas writes, is stopping these new criminal threats before they become as organized and widespread as La Cosa Nostra did during Prohibition. Peter Maas has written several books on organized crime, including *The Valachi Papers* and *Underboss: Sammy The Bull Gravano's Story of Life in the Mafia*.

The face of organized crime is changing in America. For 65 years, Cosa Nostra, the American version of Italy's Mafia, had held undisputed sway over criminal enterprises across the U.S. While Cosa Nostra ("Our Thing") remains a dangerous force to be reckoned with, it no longer enjoys the unique dominance it once had. Just as Cosa Nostra asserted its supremacy over Jewish and Irish crime groups in the late 1920s and early '30s, today potent new criminal elements settling here—principally Russian and Chinese—loom ominously on the law enforcement horizon.

In recognition of this threat, the FBI has formed special Russian and Chinese organized-crime squads similar to the ones it has successfully employed in recent years against Cosa Nostra. The Russians and Chinese have yet to achieve full flower in the underworld, and FBI Director Louis J. Freeh means to nip them in the bud.

For decades under the late J. Edgar Hoover, the FBI's official position was that the existence of Cosa Nostra was a myth. "We cannot allow the same kinds of mistakes to be made today," Freeh told Congress. "The failure of American law enforcement, including the FBI . . . permitted the development of a powerful, well-entrenched organized crime syndicate [that required] 35 years of concerted law enforcement effort and the expenditure of incredible resources to address."

The downward turning point for Cosa Nostra began in the 1960s with the dramatic revelations of Joseph Valachi, a "soldier" in the secret brotherhood, who first described its oath of fealty—complete with the drawing of blood and burning the image of a saint—and how it was structured in paramilitary fashion into 25 crime "families" throughout the U.S. It came full cycle with the defection of the highest-ranking Cosa Nostra member ever to testify: Salvatore (Sammy the Bull) Gravano, the No. 2 man in the Gambino crime family. His 1992 testimony put the family boss, John Gotti—known as "The Teflon Don" because of his ability to avoid prison—behind bars for the rest of his life.

As a result—according to James Moody, a deputy assistant director who formerly was chief of the FBI's organized-crime section—the Gambino family, at the time the most powerful in the nation, has been reduced from 35 active "crews," or family units, to 10.

Of the remaining four families in the greater New York area, only the Genovese family has escaped relatively unscathed. Its reputed boss, Vincent (The Chin) Gigante, has thus far evaded prosecution on the grounds that he is mentally unfit to stand trial. He is often seen padding around the streets of Greenwich Village in a bathrobe and pajamas, muttering incoherently to himself. Federal authorities, convinced it's all a hoax, will attempt to try him again in 1996 on multiple charges, including conspiracy to murder. "We've just got to get the courts to realize that he's crazy all right—like a fox," Moody told me. [In 1997, Gigante was fined $1.25 million and sentenced to 12 years in prison on charges of racketeering.]

Down but Not Out

Moody ticked off the current status of Cosa Nostra families elsewhere, beset by broad-based federal statutes—both criminal and civil—under the innovative Racketeer Influenced and Corrupt Organizations (RICO) Act that followed the Valachi revelations in 1963. "In the Boston region now, all we have active is one crew in Rhode Island," said Moody. In Philadelphia: "Almost everybody is in jail." In Cleveland: "Technically, there is no real family." In Detroit: "The family's still there, but I think good things may occur in the future."

In Milwaukee, St. Louis and Kansas City, he went on, the local families "have almost ceased to exist." In Chicago—once a Cosa Nostra crown jewel, with such famous past bosses as Al Capone and Sam Giancana—a new FBI approach of targeting one family crew at a time has proved effective. In Los Angeles and San Francisco, what's left of the families is small potatoes. In "open" Las Vegas, where all the families can operate, the casino business has gotten too big even for Cosa Nostra, although it still hovers on the fringe of things. In Buffalo, New York, however, the family remains "pretty strong," especially with its alleged stranglehold over the local construction union.

While Cosa Nostra families generally are hanging on the ropes, the idea is to keep hammering them. Otherwise, "they'll come back fast,"

Moody noted. "Until we get to the point where a young man decides he doesn't want to be a member because it'll put him in jail for the rest of his life, we haven't won yet."

Russian Organized Crime

Still, the situation is well enough in hand to enable an undermanned FBI to divert agents from its Cosa Nostra squad and others from counterintelligence squads—now that the Cold War is over—to meet a new domestic menace: Russian organized crime.

Its rise has been startlingly swift. The initial influx of Russians— about 300,000—occurred in the late 1970s and early 1980s, when immigration barriers were temporarily lifted to allow persecuted Jews to leave the Soviet Union. A large number of these immigrants, however, turned out not to be Jewish at all and included "second-echelon" criminal elements. They settled primarily in the Brighton Beach section of Brooklyn, which quickly was dubbed "Little Odessa." As with past ethnic waves of new arrivals, these hoodlums began by victimizing their own people. And at first, according to Moody, the FBI considered it a local police problem.

But that would not long be the case. In 1989, the number of visitors' visas to the U.S. from Russia was 3,000. By 1994, just two years after the collapse of the Communist regime, 129,500 such visas had been issued in Moscow, St. Petersburg, and Kiev alone. Now came a flood of high-ranking, hardened, organized criminals—"the first team," as Moody put it.

Moody got an inkling of what lay ahead when he attended a 1991 international crime conference. Its host was the Russian Ministry of Internal Affairs (MVD), which was trying to cope with a sudden onslaught of savage gang warfare in Moscow (one of the bitter fruits of democracy) that made the bloodletting of Chicago in the 1920s look like play school. "You don't understand what these people are like," Moody recalled being told. "They're very tough, very smart, very educated and very violent. They attack police officers. They don't care."

And soon the U.S. was awash with Russian-instigated gangland murders, complex tax and health-care fraud schemes, vicious extortions, money laundering, major drug trafficking and huge auto-theft rings with the cars being shipped back for sale in Russia (Jeep Cherokees are especially favored).

The FBI's Russian squad in New York, led by the supervisory agent Ray Kerr, was formed in May 1994. Due to the cooperation between the FBI and the MVD, Kerr's squad got an immediate break—the kind that FBI Director Freeh was hoping for. The MVD warned the FBI that a man named Vyacheslav Ivankov, whom they believed to be a Russian version of a Cosa Nostra "godfather," had left Moscow for America, where he was to manage and control Russian gangland activities in the U.S. He was placed under immediate surveillance. Along with his residence in Brighton Beach, New York, he took another one in Denver and was spotted meeting Russian organized-crime figures not only there but also in Miami, Los Angeles, Boston, suburban New Jersey and Toronto.

Then, the Justice Department says, Ivankov made a mistake while masterminding an extortion plot against two Russian emigrés who owned a Wall Street investment advisory firm. Ivankov allegedly demanded separate payments of $5 million and $3.5 million, accompanied by threats of mayhem. On April 26, 1995—presumably, the government says, to get the message across—the father of one of the extortion targets was beaten to death in a Moscow train station.

Russian organized crime counts on fear to keep its victims silent, but the two targets had gone to the FBI. A tap was put on Ivankov's phone, and he was overheard discussing the plot, FBI officials say. In June 1995 he was awakened and arrested at the apartment of a girlfriend. At a press conference, the head of the FBI's New York office, Jim Kallstrom, dryly observed: "He muttered something to the agents in Russian. It didn't sound too nice." Then, after being fingerprinted and photographed, the handcuffed Ivankov spat and kicked at reporters and photographers.

As Ray Kerr pointed out, however, "We aren't there yet with the Russians the way we are with Cosa Nostra. We have to learn more about how they are structured, who answers to whom, how many different groups there are here. That's what we're looking at right now."

Chinese *Triads* and *Tongs*

Then there are the Chinese mobsters. The Chinese population is exploding in the U.S., and with it comes China's own brand of organized crime. It arrives in three layers: First are the Hong Kong–based *triads*, secret criminal societies that predate even the Sicilian Mafia. Second are the Chinese-American *tongs*, ostensibly business and fraternal associations in America's various Chinatowns, which have been known to ape the criminal enterprises of the *triads*. Third are the violent Chinese street gangs—with names like Ghost Shadows and White Tigers—which, the FBI believes, both the *triads* and *tongs* use to enforce their rackets.

At the moment, the main trade of the *triads* in the U.S. is the importation of China White, the purest form of heroin yet developed, which has become the fastest-growing drug of choice throughout much of the country. The *triads* and *tongs* also organize the smuggling of tens of thousands of illegal Chinese immigrants into the U.S., who then receive slave wages in garment sweatshops, restaurants and brothels until they pay off fees ranging from $30,000 to$50,000.

In New York, for instance, three *tong* chieftains were accused by the Justice Department of carving up Chinatown into designated zones, using street gangs to oversee gambling, extortion and murder operations. They demand as much as $100,000 to open a restaurant and $20,000 a week to let gambling dens function. To make matters worse, two Chinese-American police detectives in New York pleaded guilty to feeding Chinese gangsters advance information about raids on gambling and prostitution houses.

A bright spot in the fight against organized crime is San Francisco. Long sensitive to Chinese crime, the FBI has two Chinese-American agents who gained Chinatown's confidence and quickly thwarted a Hong Kong *triad*'s incursion into the Bay Area. According to Tom Fuentes, head of the FBI's organize-crime unit in San Francisco, a major investigation also is under way involving shipments of goods hijacked in Russia and sold legitimately in the U.S., the laundered cash then returned to Russia's gangland coffers.

Colombian Drug Cartels

Meanwhile, the Colombian cocaine cartels present a special problem. Unlike the Russians and Chinese, the drug overlords have no intention of settling here, preferring to remain in their native havens, where they reap many millions from the manufacture and delivery of their deadly product. Under intense U.S. pressure, the Colombian government recently arrested six cartel kingpins. Whether this was only window dressing remains to be seen.

The bottom line is that organized crime still represents an enormous peril to the well-being of this nation. The only difference is that today it has become multicultural.

And the expense of fighting it is significant. But, as Louis Freeh said, "Let us learn from the past and pay the price now, before it becomes too costly later on."

ASIAN ORGANIZED CRIME: THE TRIADS

U.S. Senate Committee on Governmental Affairs

In 1992, the U.S. Senate Committee on Governmental Affairs met to discuss a new wave of criminal groups gaining influence in the United States. In its report, *The New International Criminal and Asian Organized Crime*, from which the following selection is excerpted, the committee identifies ethnic Chinese organizations called Triads as some of the most powerful of these new groups. The committee traces the history of the Triads from their seventeenth-century origins through their rise in Hong Kong and describes what is known of the secretive Triads' methods and organizational structure.

Asian criminal groups represent a problem of dramatic proportions, both in the United States and internationally. Indeed, Asian criminal groups are a major new threat confronting law enforcement around the globe. Such groups have become involved in a wide range of organized criminal activities, including narcotics trafficking, money laundering, bribery, business extortion, alien smuggling, home invasion robberies, computer chip theft, and credit card counterfeiting. While warnings have previously been heard about the possible migration of secret criminal triad organizations to the United States from their base in Hong Kong prior to the assumption of control by the People's Republic of China in 1997, the Subcommittee on Investigations of the Committee on Governmental Affairs's investigation revealed that structured triad organizations already exist in the United States and in other countries around the world. . . .

The investigation uncovered little evidence to suggest that either U.S. or foreign law enforcement entities are currently equipped to meet the challenge of this new breed of international criminal. On the contrary, it is clear that the current law enforcement responses are inadequate. Problems confronting U.S. law enforcement agencies include lack of foreign language expertise, inadequate knowledge of Asian cultures and customs, and limited success in gathering or sharing criminal intelligence. . . .

Excerpted from *The New International Criminal and Asian Organized Crime*, a report prepared by the U.S. Senate Permanent Subcommittee on Investigations of the Committee on Governmental Affairs, December 1992.

Historical Overview

Ethnic Chinese organized crime groups in the United States are of three kinds: Triads, criminally-influenced tongs, and street gangs. Triads are secretive criminal fraternities that are primarily headquartered in Hong Kong and Taiwan. Criminally-influenced tongs are business associations located in many U.S. cities which engage in lawful as well as unlawful activities. Street gangs often operate under the influence or sponsorship of tongs, but may also operate independently. Both tongs and street gangs are often influenced by what can be referred to as "triad subculture."

Modern triads trace their history to secret political societies formed in China during the 17th Century to overthrow the Ching Dynasty and to restore the Ming Dynasty to power. The term "triad," later coined by British authorities in Hong Kong, is based on the triangular symbol found on flags and banners of the early secret societies. The symbol represents the three essential elements of heaven, earth, and man.

Because the early triads were attempting to topple the ruling elements of the day, and had, in fact, been persecuted in the past, they developed secret forms of identification and communication. Triads today remain obsessively secretive and closed criminal fraternities. The triads also developed highly ritualized initiation ceremonies meant to instill a strong sense of secrecy, and more importantly, loyalty to other triad members. Thirty-six oaths, most dealing with loyalty to the triad, traditionally are part of these initiations. Each oath ends with a promise of death if the oath is broken.

The existence of triads is most extensively documented in Hong Kong, where the number of triad members is estimated to be in the tens of thousands, and to a lesser extent in Taiwan. While there is clear evidence that triad members have engaged in criminal activities in the United States, the extent of triad structure and operations in the United States is disputed among law enforcement. Perhaps the best evidence of triad structure being transplanted to the United States has been the recent ascendency of the Hong Kong–based Wo Hop To Triad as the dominant Asian organized crime group in San Francisco.

Organizational Structure

Triad societies all display some degree of hierarchy, and a typical triad has members organized by rank. Each rank carries a title and a numerical value, based on triad ritual. The leader of a triad is known as the "Dragon Head," and carries the rank "489." Other "office bearer" positions also exist, including "438," which is the second highest rank in a triad, and may be held by several different officials. If a Deputy Leader is appointed, he will hold the "438" rank, as well as an "Incense Master" or "Vanguard," who are in charge of triad rituals and initiations. The "426" or "Red Pole" is a fighter official responsible for enforcement. The "432" or "Straw Sandal" handles liaison and communication for the triad. The "415" or "White Paper Fan," is in charge of planning and administration. All other triad members are known as ordinary members or soldiers, and hold the rank of "49." The relationships among individual triad members are based on ties between "Dai-Lo's" (big brothers) and "Sai-Lo's" (little brothers), where the Sai-Lo's give loyalty, support and sometimes money to their Dai-Lo, in exchange for protection and advice.

Although hierarchical in nature, triads tend not to be strictly controlled from the top, in contrast to more familiar crime groups such as La Cosa Nostra. Instead, triad members frequently branch out into their own criminal enterprises. While the triad leadership does not always initiate and direct the activities of all the triad members, triads clearly serve as international networking associations that facilitate such activity. Moreover, monetary profits from criminal activity of triad members often flow to the top in indirect ways, such as through gifts. This practice prompted one knowledgeable official to describe triads as "criminal Amways."

As one member of the Hong Kong–based 14K triad testified:

> I was not required to pay any percentage of profits to the 14K leadership. Triads do not work that way. Triad members do favors for each other, provide introductions and assistance to each other, engage in criminal schemes with one another, but triads generally do not have the kind of strictly disciplined organizational structure that other criminal groups like the Italian mafia have. For example, a triad member would not necessarily be required to get permission from the dragonhead of his particular triad in order to engage in a particular criminal undertaking—even if the particular deal involved an outsider or even a member of another triad. On the other hand, on the occasion of traditional Chinese holidays such as Chinese New Year, triad members traditionally give gifts to their "big brother" or "uncles" who often are office bearers in the triads.

Further testimony regarding relationships among Chinese crime groups came from Johnny Kon, a convicted heroin smuggler and triad member. He noted the importance of the Chinese concept of "Guan Shi" in facilitating criminal relationships:

> Members of the Big Circle get power from "Guan Shi," which is a relationship among people. Through such relationships, Big Circle members can call on triad members or other Big Circle members for help.

Triad membership is thus a valuable asset to the new international criminal. Triad membership facilitates criminal activities in a manner similar to the way membership in business associations facilitates the activities of a legitimate businessman. Thus, even though triads, as organizations, may not control a wide range of criminal activity, it is important for law enforcement officials to understand, investigate, and develop intelligence about triad organizations, because individual triad members are invariably involved in a wide range of criminal activity.

Although the criminal activities of triad members can be thought of as constituting both domestic and international activities, even domestic activities such as illegal gambling, extortion, and prostitution often have an international element. For example, prostitutes are imported or smuggled, sometimes against their will, over national borders, while proceeds from illegal domestic activities such as gambling are often laundered internationally. International activities include narcotics trafficking, money laundering, counterfeiting currency and credit cards, and alien smuggling.

"Triad subculture" often permeates Chinese criminal groups in the United States. In other words, some Chinese criminal groups in the United States, although not triads themselves, are influenced by triad culture and traditions, characterized primarily by ritualism, obsessive secrecy and loyalty.

The triads of Mainland China migrated to Hong Kong and Taiwan when the Communists took over Mainland China in 1947. Even though it is now a criminal offense to even be a member of a triad in Hong Kong, Hong Kong is the undisputed capital of modern day triads. . . .

The Chinese Connection

Ethnic Chinese Triad members are heavily involved in heroin trafficking. The French Connection, the old heroin smuggling route from Turkey to New York by way of Marseilles, has been replaced by the Chinese connection. Heroin from Southeast Asia begins in the poppy fields of the Golden Triangle area of Myanmar (formerly Burma), Laos, and Thailand and continues through Hong Kong, Mainland China, Taiwan or other routes, to the United States with the ultimate destination usually New York City.

At the Subcommittee's August 4, 1992, hearing, David Cohen of the Central Intelligence Agency's Counternarcotics Unit, testified that worldwide opium production has more than doubled since 1985 and that two-thirds of that total originates in Southeast Asia. Cohen reported that opium production in the Golden Triangle is currently at record levels. Growing areas appear to be spreading as China has once again become an opium producer. Vietnam has also become a source for opium production. . . .

Illegal gambling has long been a core criminal activity of Asian criminal groups. In the United States, illegal gambling operations are a major revenue source for Chinese crime groups. The same is true for Chinese crime groups in other countries, including the triads, who control illegal gambling in Hong Kong. . . .

Asian organized crime presents an increasingly formidable challenge to law enforcement throughout the world. The extension of Asian organized crime from its origins in the Far East to the United States and elsewhere has been clearly documented. Asian crime groups have proven themselves to be dynamic, sophisticated, and internationally connected.

Law enforcement in both the United States and abroad must take the necessary steps to recognize, pursue, and prosecute Asian criminal figures. New approaches are necessary, and such approaches must seek to dramatically increase the level of international coordination. A failure to do so will only serve to further endanger Asian-American communities and ultimately to threaten the safety and well-being of all citizens.

THE RUSSIAN MAFIA IN NEW YORK

Scott Anderson

Russian organized crime groups centered in the Brighton Beach area of Brooklyn, New York, have been hailed as the newest and most dangerous criminal conspiracy in America, writes Scott Anderson. But their power, he maintains, has been exaggerated by both law enforcement and the news media. Russian organized crime consists mostly of petty fraud, extortion, and minor violence, rather than large-scale and sophisticated operations, he says. To illustrate the grim reality of Brighton Beach's underworld, Anderson chronicles the rise and fall of Vyacheslav "Yaponchik" Ivankov, a Russian mobster who, according to Anderson, was not the powerful godfather that the media and the FBI depicted him to be. Anderson is a freelance writer based in New York City.

No matter what their age or ethnicity or criminal specialty, all gangsters seemed to possess the same essential outlook on life—"In all matters, I come first"—and to present the same basic public persona: a dead-fish stare; a haughty, contemptuous manner; a predatory aura that tended to keep "civilians" out of their way.

It was these universal signs of the underworld that first led me to notice the two Russian gangsters on the F train out of Manhattan. The men were in their early thirties, pokerfaced, their powerful builds cloaked in expensive fur coats. They stood with arms crossed, their backs against a closed subway door, and carried on an intermittent sideways conversation in Russian while methodically sizing up everyone who entered their immediate orbit. It wasn't these details that tipped me off—hyper-vigilance, after all, is a common phenomenon on the New York City subways—but the requisite touches of underworld dandyism: permed hair, gold chains visible past the fur collars, the profligate use of cheap aftershave.

Russians were not an unusual sight on the Brooklyn-bound F train. The line ends at Coney Island, adjacent to the waterfront community of Brighton Beach, New York. Since the late 1970s, some 50,000 Russians have settled in this area—primarily Jewish refugees in the early days, but increasingly a polyglot of other ethnic groups from the former Soviet Union—making it the largest Russian émigré neighborhood in the Western Hemisphere and earning it the nickname "Little Odessa." I had chanced upon the ebb and flow of this community at various times on the F train—the middle-aged women going to their early morning janitorial jobs in Manhattan, a few hours later the carefully groomed secretaries with their romance novels and Reeboks, in the evening the Orthodox Jews in their long black coats and fedoras returning from the garment and jewelry districts. The gangsters, however, were something new, and after that first sighting I began to see more and more of them. My curiosity was piqued; in the summer of 1994, I decided to explore their world.

America's Newest Mafia

Just in time too. From the sound of it, the Russians were taking over American organized crime. In magazines and newspapers across the United States, there had been an explosion of articles about the burgeoning Russian émigré mafias: they were establishing prostitution rings and protection rackets, hiring themselves out on murder-for-hire schemes, collaborating with the more venerable Cosa Nostra to make inroads into the heroin trade. Most terrifying of all were reports that they were in the research and development phase of an international black market in nuclear material, stolen from the fire-sale emporium that the Soviet Union had become. The American headquarters for this *Organizatsiya*, journalists and law enforcement officers seemed to agree, was Brighton Beach.

The specter of nuclear holocaust notwithstanding, the rise of the Brighton Beach godfathers appeared to be a fairly typical immigrant success story, one previously played out by the Italians, the Irish, the Chinese, and a half-dozen other ethnic groups that had settled in enclaves in America's larger cities. In the early days of Little Odessa, the Brighton Beach criminals had been two-bit thugs largely preying on their own, running numbers rackets, pyramid schemes, and loan-sharking operations.

No one took much notice until Marat Balagula, the owner of the Odessa Restaurant in Brighton Beach, put the Russian émigré underworld on the map in a big way. In the mid-1980s, Balagula teamed up with members of various Cosa Nostra crime families to pull off an elaborate gasoline distribution scheme that cost the government over $42 million a year in lost tax revenue.

When Balagula was finally locked up in 1989, Russian crime figures had already been introduced to the world of high finance and "real" mafiosi. The collapse of the Soviet Union and a second wave of Russian emigration to the United States in the early 1990s made the situation even worse. Whereas the early émigrés had been primarily Jews granted political asylum, now virtually anyone could obtain a Russian exit visa and slip into the country as a tourist; along with tens of thousands of bona fide refugees came an estimated 2,000 convicted criminals. Although Marat Balagula was out of the picture, it appeared that there was now a small army of excellent students to take his place.

"Spreading out from their base in Brighton Beach," Robert Friedman wrote in the January 1993 issue of *Vanity Fair*, "the Russians have pulled off the largest jewelry heist, and insurance and Medicare fraud, in American history, with a net haul exceeding $1 billion. They are importing heroin into the U.S. from Southeast Asia as well as from poppy fields around Chernobyl. . . . Through their control of gasoline terminals and distributorships in the New York metropolitan area and elsewhere, Russian mobsters evade as much as $5 billion a year in state and federal taxes, a portion of which goes as tribute to the Italian Mafia." Other journalists painted an equally ominous picture. "More and more Russian Mafiosi and their hired thugs are pouring into the United States," reported Andrew Meier in *Image* magazine in December 1993, "and expanding their murderous network into new markets at a rapid clip."

The statements of American law enforcement officials involved in tracking the Russian gangsters were even more alarming. "The Russian criminals are networking and developing much faster than any group I've seen in the United States," Jim Moody, the head of the FBI's organized crime section, announced at a Moscow news conference in 1993. "They're often highly educated, and now that they can get to the U.S. more easily, they've hit the ground running."

Believe the Hype

"You better believe the hype," an investigator for California's Soviet Organized Crime Intelligence Team had told Meier. "The Russians aren't coming anymore. They're here."

In meeting this new threat, the American government had gone "proactive." In January 1994, the Justice Department announced that it was placing the Russian mafia on the highest investigative priority status, on the same level as the Cosa Nostra and the Colombian cocaine cartels. The FBI opened a Moscow liaison office and formed specialized Russian Organized Crime (ROC) squads in New York and Los Angeles, complementing the new Russian-crime task forces being hastily established by a half-dozen state and local governments. A U.S. Senate subcommittee heard frightening testimony from a parade of experts on the growing power of the Russian crime syndicates.

For a bit of guidance on finding my own niche in all this, I sought out one of the preeminent authorities on the Brighton Beach gangsters. From his office on Fifth Avenue in Manhattan, Alexandre Grant, news editor of *Novoye Russkoye Slovo*, the largest Russian-language newspaper in the United States, has had a bird's-eye view of the changing face of Brighton Beach. . . .

Grant brought out a folder of news clippings and 8 x 10 black-and-white photos, his chronicle of the rise and fall of a score of Brighton Beach thugs. In some of the photos, sullen men glowered into the camera—mug shots of still-active players—while photos showing smiling, relaxed men tended to mark those who had gone by the wayside, studio portraits selected by families to run on the *NRS* obituary page.

One photograph caught my attention. It was of a stern-faced, bearded man in his forties, with a strong jaw and prominent nose, staring directly into the camera. But his eyes were his most arresting feature. Beneath extremely thin eyebrows, they sloped dramatically downward. I was reminded of paintings of Genghis Khan.

Vyacheslav "Yaponchik" Ivankov

"Yaponchik," Grant said. "His real name is Vyacheslav Ivankov, but everyone calls him Yaponchik—Little Japanese—because he looks Oriental. They say he is trying to organize the Brighton Beach mafias into one syndicate."

Grant dug through his sheaf of news clippings and handed me an AP news article from December 1993: "Moscow Underworld Boss Puts Down New Roots—In Brooklyn."

It seemed that with Little Japanese I had lucked into a key functionary in the *Organizatsiya* hierarchy. Arrested for robbery and sentenced in 1982 to fourteen years in a Siberian prison, the AP article explained, Ivankov had built a personal power base there and become a *vory v zakone* (thief in law), "an obscure old Russian term for a ceremonially installed criminal leader who decided disputes and divided spoils according to the thieves' 'law.'"

Released in 1991, Ivankov somehow managed to obtain both a passport and an American visa; he then settled in Brighton Beach—a source of great concern to police on both sides of the Atlantic.

"Dozens of 'thieves in law' run gangs across Russia," the AP reported, "but Yaponchik . . . has stood out among them. A leader of his stature controls a large region and possibly thousands of criminals through a dozen or so underbosses, [Russian] police say."

A weird nickname, a face out of Central Casting, a mysterious honorific, and a grand evil scheme to boot—Yaponchik had it all. When I asked Grant how to find him, however, the editor sighed. "He will not talk. I have tried, but he's always refused to say anything to the press. He's still pulling the triggers and at the levers, and the criminal law of the *vory v zakone* is to have no contact with the press. When he retires, maybe, but not now." But Grant could see that his cautions were lost on me.

"He likes to eat in the Brighton Beach restaurants," he offered. "A lot of people say they have seen him walking on the boardwalk.

If you want to find him, go to Brighton Beach.". . .

Little Odessa

I set out to explore Brighton Beach. I usually began these explorations by taking the F train out to Coney Island and cutting through the seedy amusement park, past the forlorn-looking rides and roustabouts, to the boardwalk. Walking east along the shore, I would come to a point where the crowds of sunbathers and strolling teenage couples dissipated, a brief stretch where I had the boardwalk almost to myself, before reaching the edge of Brighton Beach and the beginnings of a very different crowd: elderly Russian women packed hip-to-hip on benches, wearing scarves and long dresses even at the zenith of summer, knots of men hunched over card tables and domino games, a sudden profusion of outdoor cafés with names in Cyrillic script.

I arrived as a tourist, certainly, but a special sort: the tourist-journalist, the morbid voyeur drawn to the darkness of a place even on a sunny afternoon. In those early days, Brighton Beach was like a vast museum to me, the repository of a hidden history, and I came to know where a few of the more interesting artifacts were. On the corner of Sixth Street and the boardwalk, I watched as workmen put the finishing touches on Naum Raichel's new Winter Garden Restaurant. Raichel was a Russian émigré who had gone to prison here in 1987 for extortion. Through the restaurant's large windows were neat rows of tables, chandeliers, and pleated napkins sticking out of wine glasses. Just a few days earlier, two unknown men had confronted Raichel around the corner and fired three bullets into his chest and stomach. . . .

But invariably I focused on the sidewalk before the Cafe Arbat, where Oleg Korataev's body had been left, or on the stolid facade of the National Restaurant, where one morning in May 1991 a gunman stepped into the foyer during the breakfast rush, passed beneath the gaudy chandelier and the framed photographs of Jackie Mason against the brocaded wallpaper, and entered the crowded dining room to put eight bullets into Emil Puzyretsky. This particular killing had already entered the realm of local folklore; I tended to doubt the stories about the waiter continuing to serve omelettes during the shooting but tended to believe those that told of extremely cooperative National patrons moving tables and chairs for the gunman as he scoured the carpet for his spent bullet casings. . . .

Gradually I began to meet raffish elements of the community, a succession of young men—most with crew cuts and tattooed biceps—who offered to act as my guide through the Brighton Beach underworld. These prospective guides were expansive in discussing the past deeds of the *Organizatsiya*—or, at least, in recycling the old rumors—but chary when it came to describing the current scene. . . . Whenever I mentioned my desire to meet Ivankov [there would be] a brief moment of consternation, a thoughtful gazing into space, and then the casual, confident shrug—"Yes, it is no problem; I can take you to Yaponchik." Always underlying these offers was the tacit understanding that such an endeavor would require money—possibly a very considerable sum of money—but none of my newfound friends wished to sully our relationship with details.

As with any foreign culture, the longer I stared at the Brighton Beach underworld, the more opaque it became. Beyond the folklore and sensational newspaper accounts—and the dramatic re-enactments in my own imagination—many of the killings that had occurred there began to take on a decidedly small-time quality the more I investigated them: a falling-out among petty thieves, a bar fight gone bad. And while the body count might have been alarming to someone in Iowa, say, it hardly constituted an epidemic by New York City standards.

What's more, if there was any signature to a Brighton Beach hit, it appeared to be a rather eerie streak of incompetence. Victims had a way of lingering on in hospital beds for days—or not dying at all. Where in all of this, I began to wonder, was the smooth hand of a professional *Organizatsiya*? And then there was the riddle of Yaponchik. If the authorities knew Ivankov was in New York, why was he being allowed to operate with such impunity? Why, with so many sightings of him in the nightclubs and on the boulevards of New York—sightings of such frequency that at times it seemed the man had cloned himself—were the authorities never able to find him?

Forget the Hype

"Because no one's looking for him," Peter Grinenko said. "He's not wanted for anything. All Ivankov's doing is working a hustle, and he's not going to get busted for that, because everyone wants to believe it. You want me to tell you about Ivankov and the *Organizatsiya*? Okay, I'll tell you: it's all bullshit."

It wasn't a very convincing statement coming from Grinenko; with his massive barrel chest and small angry eyes, he looked a lot like a mafioso himself. Except that Grinenko, a native Russian speaker, had been a New York City detective for twenty-three years and was now a part-time investigator for the Brooklyn district attorney, specializing in Russian crime cases. He was also something of a pariah on the Russian émigré crime-fighting circuit. It was easy to see why: within moments of our first meeting, he had launched into an angry diatribe—liberally scattered with scatological references—on various state and local law enforcement agencies, whole branches of the federal government, journalists in general.

"What you've got in Brighton Beach," Grinenko said, "are a bunch of two-bit hustlers. You've got junkies ripping each other off, you've got a few punks fighting over their little rackets, and you've got a whole mess of people—old ladies, doctors, housewives—ripping off the state. This is organized crime?"

As one of the only native Russian speakers on the New York City police force, Grinenko started getting pulled onto Brighton Beach duty with the first wave of Soviet emigration in the late 1970s. Over the years, he has been at least peripherally involved in nearly every major law enforcement operation launched in the émigré community.

"And after every operation," he said, "I look at what the newspapers say and I can't recognize it. Two fuck-ups get arrested at JFK [airport] with a couple of kilos of heroin, and suddenly everyone's talking about how the Russians are setting up the next Cali cartel. Last year, a dozen guys get busted with some [illegal] slot machines, and it's 'the Russian mafia is taking over the gambling industry.'"

Grinenko held up a finger a few inches from my face. "Now, there's one kind of crime that the Russkies are very good at, better than anyone else in the world: fraud. And that's what Ivankov is." He chuckled derisively. "Let me tell you about Ivankov's big life of crime." Ivankov, Grinenko said, stole a car in 1980 and tried to extort ransom for it. "When he went to collect, he was busted. That was Ivankov's big crime. This guy is a mafia godfather? Forget about it.". . .

From Con Artist to Godfather

In the Brighton Beach émigré community, I began to see, were many who had been shaped by seventy years of misrule, who had learned to lie, cheat, and steal in order to survive. I now understood the Brighton Beach "tour guides" as newly hybridized men—half socialist, half capitalist—frantically seeking to find their way in a strange new world where everything was a potential commodity, everyone was a potential mark, a bountiful land that offered endless opportunity for those with the gall to exploit it. I had been just such a mark, for I had come to Brighton Beach as a buyer—in the market for Little Japanese and the *Organizatsiya*, thieves in law and gangland informants—and they had done their best to sell me.

Here, I felt, was finally the answer to the Yaponchik riddle. He had remained a legendary figure because it was lucrative to do so.

With a certain smugness, I watched the Yaponchik myth continue to grow. In February 1995, the *Washington Post* put his photograph on its front page and used his story to illustrate the "extraordinary growth of Russian organized crime." The following month, CNN joined in with an alarming "Special Assignment" report on the newcomers to the American underworld, linking the Russians to "extortion, prostitution, insurance fraud, guns, heroin, money laundering, murder for hire." At the climactic moment, the old, familiar photograph of Yaponchik filled the television screen.

"From New York to Los Angeles to Miami," the reporter intoned, "this is the man from Moscow who [federal] agents say has come to take control of the Russian mob: Vyacheslav Ivankov."

He was also, quite suddenly, becoming a personality. In the pages of the *Washington Post*, Ivankov was "a man who tended carefully to his appearance, favoring a dapper little kerchief tucked neatly in his suit pocket," the master criminal who had escaped capture and prosecution with "fast cars and smart lawyers." On CNN, the ubiquitous Alexandre Grant offered that Ivankov liked music, drank in moderation, and was "very good with girls.". . .

"Certainly he's the biggest [Russian mafia] figure that we've seen or heard of yet here in the United States," Drug Enforcement Administration (DEA) administrator Thomas Constantine told CNN, an analysis reiterated by Alexandre Grant: "Ivankov now is number one."

The only thing missing in all this was the same component that had been missing all along: hard facts. No one writing or broadcasting the Ivankov story had actually interviewed him or independently verified his criminal background. Rather, they were simply parroting the vague pronouncements of the FBI and other federal agents who, in turn, appeared to be recycling information supplied by the Russian Ministry of Internal Affairs, or MVD, an offshoot of the old KGB. If nothing else, this suggested a remarkable change of heart by both the American media and government in the post–Cold War era: in the five years between 1990 and 1995, the Soviet intelligence services had gone from symbolizing all that was dark and treacherous in the Soviet Union to being trustworthy sources for both news stories and federal investigations.

I made these observations with a faintly sanctimonious pleasure, rather like the man who has already been duped in a game of three-card monte shaking his head at the craven stupidity of new victims. But then something unexpected happened: Yaponchik emerged from the shadows at last.

Yaponchik's Fall

The long, strange story of Vyacheslav Ivankov finally reached its denouement in the offices of Summit International, an investment-advisory company based in New York. As with the rest of the Yaponchik story, however, there was nothing simple about the conclusion.

Despite its prosperous-sounding name, Summit International was a decidedly modest operation established by two Russian émigrés, Alexander Volkov and Vladimir Voloshin, who had found their market niche in servicing the flight of capital from the chaos of Russia. In November 1994, the company officers were visited by two Moscow "businessmen," Roustam Sadykov and Maxim Korostishevsky, who had come to collect 60 percent of a $2.7 million investment made by a third party, now deceased; for their cooperation, Volkov and Voloshin could keep the other 40 percent and be free of any future "aggravation."

But the Summit executives balked at the offer. For the next several months, they stalled for time, enduring a series of increasingly angry and threatening calls and visits from the Russian visitors. Things turned ominous on the afternoon of February 21, 1995. Shortly before a scheduled 5:30 meeting with their pursuers, Volkov and Voloshin panicked and fled the Summit offices. From behind the plate-glass window of a store across the street, they watched Sadykov and Korostishevsky arrive with a man they recognized from newspaper photographs: Vyacheslav Ivankov. That was enough for the Summit executives. Fearing for their lives, they hastily packed up their families and fled to Miami. They also went to the FBI.

"They were very frightened, very concerned," recalled Raymond Kerr, the special agent in charge of the FBI's ROC squad—or C-24—in New York. "With Ivankov appearing on the scene, they sensed they were in serious trouble."

The FBI, which had been intermittently watching Ivankov since early 1993, now intensified their effort. By the end of March 1995, they had placed a wiretap on Ivankov's cellular phone and were cataloguing the involvement of a half-dozen lesser-known Russian émigrés—"mutts," in FBI parlance—in the attempted Summit shakedown.

It appeared that Ivankov had signed on with a particularly hapless bunch. Despite his persistent admonitions to be circumspect, his co-conspirators were in the habit of discussing their plans on the phone. All showed a rather quaint willingness to believe the Summit officers' promises of settlement even as the officers stayed on the move and broke one scheduled appointment after another. After Volkov failed to show at yet another meeting, this time at Manhattan's Russian Samovar restaurant on April 19, 1995, Sadykov complained about him to the Samovar waiters, saying that he was stranded in the United States because Volkov owed him thousands of dollars. Even Ivankov began to complain.

"I have lots of people around me and things to do," he told Sadykov at one point. "I did not want to be on the phone all the time. I'm being pulled in all directions."

In late April 1995 the patience of the would-be extortionists apparently ran out. On a Moscow train station platform, Vladimir Voloshin's elderly father was set upon by thugs and severely beaten; he died from his injuries within the week. To the Summit officers, this was a brutal indication that their protracted cat-and-mouse game was over. On the evening of May 25, 1995, they were taken to the Troika Restaurant in Fairview, New Jersey, where Sadykov waited in an upstairs office with a bit of dispiriting news: instead of 60 percent of the $2.7 million, he now wanted 100 percent of $3.5 million. Before the night was out, the Summit executives had signed a promissory note, agreeing to pay Sadykov that amount in nine installments over the next two months.

As if this wasn't going to be painful enough, the terms soon changed again. On June 5, 1995, Volkov and Voloshin were summoned to another meeting, this one presided over by Ivankov. Ivankov explained that the first payment was to be made not in a week's time but by 2:00 P.M. the following day. For the undercover FBI team working the case, it was time to move.

"This might not have been the way we would have preferred to take this case down," explained Raymond Kerr, the agent in charge of the operation, "but our hand was forced because of threats to some people."

The wait had been well worth it for investigators. Throughout the shakedown effort, Ivankov had remained carefully in the background—never personally confronting the Summit officers, conspicuously absent from the conclave at the Troika—and investigators had compiled only a thin string of circumstantial evidence against him. That all changed with the June 5 meeting. At the last moment, Yaponchik had stepped into the open and handed his pursuers the rope they had so desperately sought.

At 7:00 A.M. on Thursday, June 8, 1995, arresting FBI agents pounded on the door of a Brighton Beach apartment to be greeted by a bleary-eyed Ivankov, clad in underwear and a black T-shirt. In contrast to his reputation in the media for courtliness and charm, the fabled Yaponchik kicked and spat at reporters when led into court for a preliminary hearing. . . .

Sending a Message

This was enough to warrant a triumphant press release:

"In a major move against a growing Russian organized crime structure in the United States, the FBI today arrested Vyacheslav Kirillovich Ivankov, allegedly one of the most powerful Russian crime leaders in this country. . . . The FBI described the arrests as a significant step toward stemming the efforts of major Russian criminal organizations and a key example of the newly-developed law enforcement cooperation between Russia and the United States."

From his spacious corner office on the twenty-eighth floor of 26 Federal Plaza in New York, FBI assistant director James Kallstrom has a spectacular view not only of upper Manhattan and portions of New Jersey but, on a clear day, the Long Island Sound and the Connecticut coastline. In the conference corner of the room, there is a low coffee table upon which sits a piece of highly polished brown granite with a small metal label: "Alfred P. Murrah Federal Building, April 19, 1995."

As the special agent in charge of the New York regional office, Kallstrom first started seeing the Russians show up on law enforcement radar in the early 1990s. "We saw a problem and the potential for that problem to get worse, and that is why we moved so quickly to establish a Russian squad. Our philosophy was to contain it, to not let it gain a foothold the way [the Cosa Nostra] did in the Fifties and Sixties."

A big, affable man in his early fifties, Kallstrom takes a rather long view on the battle against organized crime in émigré communities, seeing it as a hearts-and-minds campaign to win over the populace.

"We're in the information business," he said. "Theoretically, we could just sit here and answer the phone and get all the information we need if the people who knew would tell it to us. Well, we don't get it all that way, so we have to do other things. You go to Brighton Beach, or to any émigré community where people are less familiar with the way things are done in the United States, where they're not sure they can trust law enforcement, and you can see crime thriving in those areas. The real challenge we face is Americanizing them to the extent that justice can work. By taking out Ivankov, a major criminal back in Russia, we are putting the word out that we will take action, that the system of justice here prevails."

But was Ivankov, in fact, a major criminal back in Russia? I asked. Kallstrom motioned to the other FBI agent at the meeting, ROC squad commander Raymond Kerr.

"That's certainly the way it was told to us," Kerr said. "A representative of the MVD told us exactly that, that Ivankov was sent here to organize the Russian criminals in North America, not just the United States but North America.". . .

James Kallstrom nodded.

"The arrest of Ivankov is much more important than the case itself—geometrically more important than the case itself—because it sends a message into that community. We need the honest citizens out there to tell us what the hell is going on, and that has already started happening since we got Ivankov. Now there are people in those communities who understand we will take action, because they have seen the giant fall."

The Man and the Myth

A funny choice of words, for the first thing that struck me when Ivankov was led into Judge Carol Amon's chambers in the U.S. District Courthouse in Brooklyn on the morning of June 23, 1995, was how tiny he was: about five foot four and maybe 150 pounds. No one I had spoken to, nothing I had read, ever mentioned that. Standing alongside his celebrity lawyer, the tall and rail-thin Barry Slotnick, I was reminded less of Genghis Khan than of Mutt and Jeff.

Still, he was an imposing figure: compact, muscular, the peculiar, downward slope of his eyes given an added severity by his crew cut and close-cropped beard. Sitting alone as he waited his brief turn before the judge, he seemed to withdraw into himself, staring into space with a slight, distracted frown, as if trying to remember something. Only occasionally would he glance at the gallery, acknowledging with an almost imperceptible nod the waves of the two attractive Russian women who attended all the preliminary hearings. Several times he caught me staring at him and briefly stared back, without curiosity, before gazing into space again.

I suppose I was hoping for some telltale sign that would finally reveal who Ivankov was. He looked like a criminal, of course—anyone dressed in prison blues does—but I still harbored doubts about his godfather status. Rather than be assuaged, these doubts had only grown since my meeting with the FBI, since I read their account of the Summit extortion case.

Just how intimate a role had Yaponchik played in the plot? The shakedown attempt had begun in November 1994, but Ivankov didn't physically appear on the scene until three months later. The "contract" signed at the Troika was for payments to Sadykov, not Ivankov.

While it seemed clear that he had played some role in the conspiracy, this merely raised a larger question: why? Why had this master *vory v zakone*, the warlord of a vast criminal empire, worked so hard and put himself at such risk for the 10 or 15 percent commission he would collect on a piddling $3.5 million deal?

Image Is Everything

But watching Ivankov in Judge Amon's courtroom, I finally saw that all along I had been asking the wrong questions, that viewing everything from the perspective of a journalist—searching for facts and documentation and plausibility—I had missed what was important in the Yaponchik story. An entirely different perspective was required, for I had entered a shadow world where cops, journalists, and gangsters exist and maneuver in a complex symbiosis. In this world, there was no separating myth from reality; myth and reality were the same thing.

Ivankov *was* a mafia godfather because it served everyone's interest that he be one. It gave the media a frame, a way to personalize stories about a complex issue. It gave the FBI a symbol to take down, a tool with which to convince the Russian émigré community that justice would prevail. It gave the Summit extortionists the necessary fear factor with which to shake down their victims. And, not least of all, it gave Ivankov the necessary status and cachet to be called upon as muscle in the first place.

MEXICO AND THE DRUG TRADE

Thomas A. Constantine

Mexican crime syndicates smuggle in most of the drugs that enter the United States, asserts Drug Enforcement Administration (DEA) administrator Thomas Constantine. In the following selection, excerpted from his March 1997 testimony before the Senate Foreign Relations Committee, Constantine states that these Mexican groups have become as powerful as Colombia's Cali and Medellin cartels were in the 1980s and early 1990s. Constantine describes the Southwest Border Initiative, the federal law enforcement's response to the drug trafficking that occurs across the U.S.-Mexico border. However, he maintains, the greatest obstacle to law enforcement's efforts to combat the Mexican drug trade is corruption within the Mexican government.

I am not exaggerating when I say that the sophisticated drug syndicate groups from Mexico have eclipsed organized crime groups from Colombia as the premier law enforcement threat facing the United States today.

Many phrases have been used to describe the complex and sophisticated international drug trafficking groups operating out of Colombia and Mexico, and frankly, the somewhat respectable titles of "cartel" or "federation" mask the true identity of these vicious, destructive entities. The Cali organization, and the four largest drug trafficking organizations in Mexico—operating out of Juarez, Tijuana, Sonora and the Gulf region—are simply organized crime groups whose leaders are not in Brooklyn or Queens, but are safely ensconced on foreign soil. They are not legitimate businessmen as the word "cartel" implies, nor are they "federated" into a legitimate conglomerate. These syndicate leaders—the Rodriguez Orejuela brothers in Colombia to Amado Carrillo-Fuentes, Juan Garcia-Abrego, Miguel Caro-Quintero, and the Arellano-Felix Brothers—are simply the 1990's versions of the mob leaders U.S. law enforcement has fought since shortly after the turn of the twentieth century.

But these organized crime leaders are far more dangerous, far more influential and have a great deal more impact on our day-to-day lives

Excerpted from the statement by Thomas A. Constantine, "Mexico and the Southwest Border Initiative," made before the Senate Foreign Relations Committee, March 12, 1997.

than their domestic predecessors. While organized crime in the United States during the 1950's through the 1970's affected certain aspects of American life, their influence pales in comparison to the violence, corruption and power that today's drug syndicates wield. These individuals, from their headquarters locations, absolutely influence the choices that too many Americans make about where to live, when to venture out of their homes, or where they send their children to school. The drugs—and the attendant violence which accompanies the drug trade—have reached into every American community and have robbed many Americans of the dreams they once cherished. . . .

At the height of its power, organized crime in this nation was consolidated in the hands of few major families whose key players lived in this nation, and were within reach of our criminal justice system. All decisions made by organized crime were made within the United States. Orders were carried out on U.S. soil. While it was not easy to build cases against the mob leaders, law enforcement knew that once a good case was made against a boss, he could be located within the U.S., arrested and sent to jail.

That is not the case with today's organized criminal groups. They are strong, sophisticated and destructive organizations operating on a global scale. Their decisions are made in sanctuaries in Cali, Colombia, and Guadalajara, Mexico, even day-to-day operational decisions such as where to ship cocaine, which cars their workers in the United States should rent, which apartments should be leased, which markings should be on each cocaine package, which contract murders should be ordered, which official should be bribed, and how much. They are shadowy figures whose armies of workers in Colombia, Mexico and the United States answer to them via daily faxes, cellular phone, or pagers. Their armies carry out killings within the United States—one day an outspoken journalist, one day a courier who had lost a load, the next, an innocent bystander caught in the line of fire—on orders of the top leadership. They operate from the safety of protected locations, and are free to come and go as they please within their home countries. These syndicate bosses have at their disposal airplanes, boats, vehicles, radar, communications equipment, and weapons in quantities which rival the capabilities of some legitimate governments. Whereas previous organized crime leaders were millionaires, the Cali drug traffickers and their counterparts from Mexico are billionaires.

It is difficult—sometimes nearly impossible—for U.S. law enforcement to locate and arrest these leaders without the assistance of law enforcement in other countries. Their communications are coded; they are protected by corrupt law enforcement officials. Despite pledges from the Government of Mexico to apprehend the syndicate leaders, law enforcement authorities have been unable to locate them and even if they are located, the government is not obligated to extradite them to the U.S. to stand trial.

In Mexico, as is the case wherever organized crime flourishes, corruption and intimidation allow the leaders to maintain control. These sophisticated criminal groups cannot thrive unless law enforcement officials have been paid bribes and witnesses fear for their lives. . . .

It is frustrating for all of us in law enforcement that the leaders of these criminal organizations, although well known and indicted repeatedly, have not been located, arrested or prosecuted.

Colombia's Cali Cartel

We cannot discuss the situation in Mexico today without looking at the evolution of the groups from Colombia—how they began, what their status is today, and how the groups from Mexico have learned important lessons from them, becoming major trafficking organizations in their own right.

During the late 1980's the Cali group assumed greater and greater power as their predecessors from the Medellin cartel self-destructed. Where the Medellin cartel was brash and publicly violent in their activities, the criminals who ran their organization from Cali labored behind the pretense of legitimacy, posing as businessmen just carrying out their professional obligations. The Cali leaders—the Rodriguez Orejuela brothers, Santa Cruz Londono, Pacho Herrera—amassed fortunes and ran their multi-billion dollar cocaine businesses from highrises and ranches in Colombia. Miguel Rodriguez Orejuela and his associates composed what was until then the most powerful international organized crime group in history. They employed 727 aircraft to ferry drugs to Mexico, from where they were smuggled into the United States, and then returned to Colombia with the money from U.S. drug sales. Using landing areas in Mexico, they were able to evade U.S. law enforcement officials and make important alliances with transportation and distribution experts in Mexico.

With intense law enforcement pressure focused on the Cali leadership by brave men and women in the Colombian National Police (CNP) during 1995 and 1996, all of the top leadership of the Cali syndicate are either in jail or dead. The fine work done by General Serrano and other CNP officers is a testament to the commitment and dedication of Colombia's law enforcement officials in the face of great personal danger and a government whose leadership is riddled with drug corruption.

Since the Cali leaders' imprisonment, on sentences which were ridiculously short and inadequate, traffickers from Mexico took on greater prominence. The alliance between the Colombian traffickers and the organizations from Mexico had benefits for both sides. Traditionally, the traffickers from Mexico have long been involved in smuggling marijuana, heroin, cocaine into the United States, and had established solid distribution routes throughout the nation. Because the Cali syndicate was concerned about the security of their loads, they brokered a commercial deal with the traffickers from Mexico, which reduced their potential losses.

This agreement entailed the Colombians moving cocaine from the Andean region to the Mexican organizations, who then assumed the responsibility of delivering the cocaine into the United States. In 1989, U.S. law enforcement officials seized 21 metric tons of cocaine in Sylmar, California; this record seizure demonstrated the extent and magnitude of the Mexican groups' capabilities to transport Colombian-produced cocaine into the United States. This huge shipment was driven across the Mexican/U.S. border in small shipments and stored in the warehouse until all transportation fees had been paid by the Cali and Medellin cartels to the transporters from Mexico. Now, trafficking groups from Mexico are routinely paid in multi-ton quantities of cocaine, making them formidable cocaine traffickers in their own right.

The majority of cocaine entering the United States continues to come from Colombia through Mexico and across U.S. border points of entry. Most of the cocaine enters the United States in privately owned vehicles and commercial trucks. There is new evidence that indicates traffickers in Mexico have gone directly to sources of cocaine in Bolivia and Peru in order to circumvent Colombian middlemen. In addition to the inexhaustible supply of cocaine entering the U.S., trafficking organizations from Mexico are responsible for producing and trafficking thousands of pounds of methamphetamine, and have been major distributors of heroin and marijuana in the U.S. since the 1970's.

Major Traffickers from Mexico

A number of major trafficking organizations represent the highest echelons of organized crime in Mexico. The leaders of these organizations are under indictment in the United States on numerous charges. The Department of Justice has submitted Provisional Warrants for many of their arrests to the Government of Mexico, and only one, Juan Garcia Abrego, because he was a U.S. citizen, has been sent to the U.S. to face justice. The other leaders are living freely in Mexico, and have so far escaped apprehension by Mexican law enforcement, and have suffered little, if any inconvenience resulting from their notorious status. I believe that in order to fully expose these syndicate leaders, it is more beneficial to refer to them by their personal names than by the names of their organizations.

Amado Carrillo-Fuentes. The most powerful drug trafficker in Mexico at the current time is Amado Carrillo-Fuentes, who allegedly has ties to the former Commissioner of the Institute for the Combat of Drugs (INCD), Gutierrez-Rebollo. His organized crime group, based in Juarez, is associated with the Rodriguez-Orejuela organization and the Ochoa brothers from Medellin, as well. This organization, which is also involved in heroin and marijuana trafficking, handles large cocaine shipments from Colombia. Their regional bases in Guadalajara, Hermosillo and Torreon serve as storage locations where later the drugs are moved closer to the border for eventual shipment into the United States. . . .

Miguel Caro-Quintero. Miguel Caro-Quintero's organization is based in Sonora, Mexico, and focuses its attention on trafficking cocaine and marijuana. His brother, Rafael, is in prison in Mexico for his role in killing DEA Special Agent Kiki Camarena in 1985. . . .

The Arellano-Felix Brothers. The Arellano-Felix Organization (AFO), often referred to as the Tijuana Cartel, is one of the most powerful and aggressive drug trafficking organizations operating from Mexico; it is undeniably the most violent. More than any other major trafficking organization from Mexico, it extends its tentacles directly from high-echelon figures in the law enforcement and judicial systems in Mexico to street-level individuals in the United States. The AFO is responsible for the transportation, importation and distribution of multi-ton quantities of cocaine and marijuana, as well as large quantities of heroin and methamphetamine, into the United States from Mexico. The AFO operates primarily in the Mexican states of Sinaloa (their birth place), Jalisco, Michoacan, Chiapas, and Baja California South and North. From Baja, the drugs enter California, the primary point of embarkation into the United States distribution network. . . .

The Southwest Border Initiative

The Southwest Border Initiative (SWBI) is Federal law enforcement's joint response to the substantial threat posed by Mexican groups operating along the Southwest Border. The SWBI, now in its third year of operation, is an integrated, coordinated strategy that focuses the resources of DEA, FBI, the United States Attorney's Office, the Criminal Division, the U.S. Border Patrol, the U. S. Customs Service and state and local authorities on the sophisticated Mexican drug trafficking organizations operating on both sides of the U.S./Mexican border.

Through this initiative we have identified the sophisticated Mexican drug trafficking organizations operating along the entire U.S. border. These groups are transporting multi-ton shipments of cocaine for the Colombian groups, as well as heroin, methamphetamine and marijuana. Imitating the Colombian groups, the Mexican organizations are highly compartmentalized, using numerous workers to accomplish very specific tasks, such as driving load cars, renting houses for storage sites, distributing cocaine, and collecting profits. Through the compartmentalization process, each worker performs a distinct task and has no knowledge of the other members of the organization.

We are attacking the organizations by targeting the communication systems of their command and control centers. Working in concert, DEA, FBI, U.S. Customs Service and the U.S. Attorney offices around the country conduct wiretaps that ultimately identify their U.S.-based organization from top to bottom. This strategy allows us to track the seamless continuum of cocaine traffic as it flows from Colombia through Mexico to its eventual street distribution in the United States. However, even though this strategy is extremely effective in dismantling the U.S.-based portions of the organizations, we are frustrated by not being able to use this same information to reach the organization's bosses in Mexico and their current counterparts in Colombia. Criminals such as Carillo-Fuentes and Arellano-Felix personally direct their organizations from safe havens in Mexico and until we garner the complete cooperation of law enforcement officials in Mexico, we will never be truly effective in stopping the flow of drugs from their country.

The Southwest Border Strategy is anchored in our belief that the only way of successfully attacking any organized crime syndicate is to build strong cases on the leadership and their command and control functions. The long-term incarceration of key members of these organizations' command and control will cause a steady degradation of their ability to conduct business in the United States, and with the assistance of foreign governments, the long-term incarceration of the leadership will leave the entire organizations in disarray. The Cali syndicate once controlled cocaine traffic in the world from a highly organized corporate structure; with the incarceration of the Cali leaders we see the cocaine trade in Colombia has become far less monolithic and several independent unrelated organizations are controlling the exportation of cocaine to the U.S. and Mexico. This change is a direct result of the incarceration of the Cali leaders and their inability to fully control their organizations from prison. . . .

Corruption and Intimidation: Tools of the Trade

Traditionally, organized crime has depended on the corruption of officials and the intimidation of potential or actual witnesses, as well as violence against anyone who stands in the way of business. The Medellin and Cali traffickers were masters of corruption, intimidation and violence, and used these tools effectively to silence and coerce. . . .

Historically, corruption has been a central problem in DEA's relationship with Mexican counterparts. In short, there is not one single law enforcement institution in Mexico with whom DEA has an entirely trusting relationship. Such a relationship is absolutely essential to the conduct of business in that, or any other nation where organized crime syndicates traffic in narcotics.

I would like to provide some recent examples of the corruption which we encounter all too frequently in Mexico:

- In January 1997, the Mexican Army raided the wedding party of Amado Carillo-Fuentes' sister. When they arrived at the scene, Mexican Federal Judicial Police were guarding the party. The

MFJP had alerted Carillo-Fuentes about the planned raid, and he was able to escape.

- The Arellano-Felix organization routinely bribes government officials to obtain information from prosecutors' offices, including information on potential witnesses.
- Despite the firing of over 1200 government officials for corruption charges by Mexican President Ernesto Zedillo, no successful prosecutions of these individuals has taken place.
- In March 1996, DEA Task Force Agents arrested two individuals who identified themselves as police officers from Sonora, Mexico. Eleven hundred pounds of marijuana were found on the scene and the police admitted they worked at the stash house.
- In July 1996, a Mexican Army Division arrested nine Mexican Federal Judicial Police Officers and seized 50 kilograms of cocaine and $578,000 in U.S. currency. The defendants were acting under the direction of the Commandante for Culiacan, Sinaloa, at the time.

While a great deal of the corruption plagues the law enforcement agencies in Mexico, the Mexican military and other institutions are also vulnerable to the corrupting influences of the narcotics trade. The Mexican Government has replaced police with military officials, who are not fully trained in all of the aspects of narcotics investigations. This situation is far from ideal. Political officials are also not immune to narcotics corruption; DEA has documented instances where public officials have allowed drug traffickers to freely operate in areas under their control. Corruption is the most serious, most pervasive obstacle to progress in addressing the drug trade in Mexico. . . .

Prospects for Progress

The primary program for cooperative law enforcement efforts with the Government of Mexico is a proposed series of Bilateral Task Forces (BTFs). The U.S. and Mexico signed a memorandum of understanding in 1996, outlining the framework for the United States Government and the Government of Mexico to conduct joint investigations against targeted drug organizations. These Bilateral Task Forces were established in Juarez, Tijuana and Monterrey. [However,] the task forces in Tijuana and Juarez have been limited in their ability to collect intelligence and seize drugs, and they have not met their most important objectives of arresting the leaders of the major syndicates and dismantling their organizations. . . .

Since coming to office, President Zedillo has promised that he would take action against organized criminal groups in Mexico. It was announced on March 11, 1997, that President Zedillo had named Mariano Herran Salvatti to replace General Guiterrez-Rebollo as Director of the INCD. Mr. Salvatti, a long-time lawyer and magistrate, reportedly passed a background investigation and a polygraph prior to being named to the post. This is the first step utilized by most law enforcement agencies to professionalize their ranks and if sustained over a long period could be the beginning of the creation of a credible agency.

President Zedillo has also moved to make significant changes to the law enforcement process by sponsoring the Organized Crime Bill to provide the tools needed to successfully attack the criminal syndicates and formed the Organized Crime Task Force and the Bilateral Task Forces. However, even with the improved process, the infrastructure of the mechanism itself is so decimated by corruption that short term results are very doubtful.

The real test is in the mid- and long-term. Unless some meaningful reforms are made in the law enforcement systems—and Mr. Herran Salvatti's appointment may well be the step—such as targeting and apprehending major organized crime figures in Mexico, that nation, and unfortunately our own, will continue to fight an uphill battle as drugs will continue to flow into cities and towns across the United States. To date, our inability to successfully attack the major organized crime groups in Mexico as we have in the United States and Colombia is a direct result of our inability to arrest the leadership of these groups.

President Zedillo has acted against corrupt officials, and has stated that he is committed to professionalizing Mexican law enforcement. Yet the bottom line remains: until the major organized crime figures operating in Mexico are aggressively targeted, investigated, arrested, sentenced appropriately and jailed, both Mexico and the United States are in grave danger.

THE FUTURE OF ORGANIZED CRIME IN AMERICA

William Kleinknecht

In the following excerpt from his book The New Ethnic Mobs: The Changing Face of Organized Crime in America, *William Kleinknecht assesses the various organized crime groups operating in America and speculates on the futures of each. He predicts that Chinese criminal groups will grow in power but will never become as dominant as La Cosa Nostra once was. Black and Hispanic groups will continue to be players in the drug trade, he contends, while the future of Russian organized crime is unclear. Kleinknecht believes that La Cosa Nostra's influence will dwindle but not disappear. Moreover, he maintains, organized crime will continue to thrive in the United States; the Mafias of tomorrow will simply be more multicultural.*

In the opening of his 1927 book, *The Gangs of New York,* underworld historian Herbert Asbury breathed a sigh of relief that the "gangster" had receded into the American past. "Happily, he has now passed from the metropolitan scene, and for nearly half a score of years has existed mainly in the lively imagination of industrious journalists, among whom the tradition of the gangster has more lives than the proverbial cat," Asbury wrote. "Hopeful reporters continue to resurrect him every time there is a mysterious killing in the slum districts or among the white lights of Broadway." Asbury obviously had in mind gangs like the Five Pointers and the Eastmans, the veritable armies of young ruffians that once battled for the streets of Lower Manhattan, not the white-collar thugs that we regard as gangsters today. But given that he was writing in the middle of Prohibition, when the progeny of America's great brawling gangs were assembling into a national crime syndicate, his obituary for the American gangster still strikes something of an odd chord.

Asbury's mistake points up the hazards of trying to map the future of organized crime, but it has not prevented all manner of writers, academics and law-enforcement officials in the succeeding decades from predicting that the American gangster would shortly become an endangered species. This has been especially true of *La Cosa Nostra*. The Italian mob's reign has been so long, and its control of the underworld and many legitimate industries so well documented, that many observers perhaps find it hard to accept that such a medieval institution could continue to flourish in postmodern America. How else do we account for the misplaced optimism of so many in predicting the Mafia's demise?

Such speculation began cropping up in the mid-1970s, when black and Hispanic gangsters first flexed their muscles in the ghetto. Francis Ianni, Donald Goddard and a number of newspaper and magazine journalists speculated that not only were there new faces in the underworld—it's hard to argue with that proposition—but that the old faces were beginning to disappear.

The requiems for the Italian Mafia became louder in the 1980s, when the Reagan administration waged war on organized crime, toppling Mafia bosses around the country. With each major prosecution, FBI officials and prosecutors would sound a death knell for the Honored Society. After winning convictions in the famed Pizza Connection heroin case in 1987, Rudolph Giuliani, then the U.S. attorney in Manhattan, became perhaps the best-known proponent of the extinction theory. "Five or six years ago, nobody would have believed that we could convict the head of the Sicilian Mafia in New York," he said in 1987. "If we continue our efforts, there's not going to be a Mafia in five or ten years." G. Robert Blakey, a University of Notre Dame professor and organized-crime expert, went even further in 1990: "They are dead or finished almost everywhere. Their strongholds in Boston, Philadelphia, Atlantic City, Cleveland, New Orleans, Chicago and New York are all gone or under siege." Journalists have been just as quick to pick up on this theme. Selwyn Raab, the *New York Times'* well-sourced organized-crime reporter, seemed to write an article every couple of years about the Mafia's infirmity. His boldest report on the subject, published on October 22, 1990, began with this sentence: "Battered by aggressive investigators and weakened by incompetent leadership, most of America's traditional Mafia families appear to be fading out of existence. . . ."

Predicting the Future of Organized Crime

Accompanying these rosy predictions about the Mafia's setting sun has been widespread speculation about what crime groups will take the place of the Italians at the forefront of organized crime. Over the years, the conventional wisdom about what crime group is "emerging" most quickly has been subject to wide variations. Ianni and the other pioneering ethnic-succession theorists seemed sure that blacks and Hispanics—the new kings of the ghetto—would be the new royalty in organized crime. By the early 1980s, James Moody was telling a Senate subcommittee that motorcycle gangs were the most potent of

the new crime groups. Then the President's Commission on Organized Crime devoted an entire hearing to Asian organized crime in
1984, and the Chinese were tagged as the most threatening of the
new groups. Between 1994 and 1996, the Chinese have gone out of
fashion. The attention of law enforcement and the media is now fixed
on the Russian Mafia.

None of these shifts in public concern has been based entirely on
reality. Motorcycle gangs are just as active in this country now as they
were in the early 1980s, but one no longer hears them ballyhooed as a
criminal threat. Chinese gangs were already well entrenched in extortion and gambling in the Asian community by 1970, and perhaps even
then could have been seen as the mostly likely successors to the Mafia.
But they had not yet been "discovered" by federal law enforcement
and the media. Despite his insight into the changing face of the underworld, Ianni seems not to have even been aware of the Chinese mob.
On top of all this, the author will argue below that the mid-1990s have
shown that much of the speculation about the Mafia's decline has
been wrong. When we add all these facts together, we see that, at least
to some degree, the nation's focus on organized crime shifts more with
the changing *Zeitgeist* than with the realities of the street.

What, then, is the real future of organized crime in this country? This
author will not pretend to have any greater clairvoyance on that point
than others who have tried to answer that question over the years. But a
careful look at what is really occurring in the nation's underworld can
help sweep aside some of our more glaring misconceptions.

Chinese Gangs, *Tongs*, and Triads

When one surveys the new landscape of American organized crime,
the Chinese clearly stand out. Chinese gangs, *tongs* and triads together are second only to the Italian Mafia among domestic crime groups
in the sophistication and reach of their crimes. Like their Italian
counterparts, Chinese gangsters are the progeny of a criminal conspiracy that is centuries old and whose traditions include an inviolate
oath of secrecy that has changed little over hundreds of years.

This triad tradition gives Chinese crime groups in this country a
strong international connection that not only helps them smuggle
heroin across the globe but gives them a ready source of new recruits,
especially since Asians continue to immigrate to this country in large
numbers. That gang members are members of triads or *tongs* also gives
them important alliances with similar groups in cities across the
country. Indeed, none of the other emerging crime groups has the
national scope of the Chinese. Dominicans may move drugs across
the Northeast, but the trade is not governed by a central figure who
shares in the proceeds of every crime that is committed. The Blood
and Crip gangs that exist in cities across the country share at best a
loose affiliation with the mother gangs in Los Angeles. With the Chi-

nese crime groups, however, such affiliations are real and enduring. The Ghost Shadows chapters in New York, Boston, Chicago, New Orleans and other cities are all affiliated with the same national On Leong president. When the Wah Ching was at the height of its power, Vincent Jew was the boss of the Chinese rackets from Los Angeles to Portland, Oregon, and that fact was recognized in every *mah-jongg* parlor on the West Coast. Meetings between Chinese gang leaders from around North America have been well documented.

Chinese crime groups also have an exceptionally broad criminal base in their communities. Black gangs exist almost entirely to sell drugs. Without cocaine and heroin, Dominican organized crime would not exist. But in their own communities, Chinese crime groups control casino gambling, bookmaking, loan-sharking, extortion, the infiltration of legitimate businesses, credit-card fraud, video poker machines, alien smuggling, heroin smuggling, food-stamp fraud, and a wide array of other crimes. No other crime group save for the Mafia has such a diverse portfolio.

Chinese gangsters are also deeply wired into the civic life of American Chinatowns. Their sponsors are often the most powerful business interests in the Chinese community, an alliance that gives them a patina of respectability even in the eyes of Chinese who may not approve of their activities. When the Chinese merchant hands over an extortion payment to a gang member, he is not just doing so out of fear for his life. He is obeying a neighborhood code that has been in place since the first railroad workers established American Chinatowns in the 19th century.

Finally, Chinese crime groups in New York share another trait with the city's Mafia families—they are nearly indestructible. Just as the same five mob families have controlled New York's Italian crime since the 1930s, the criminal map of Chinatown has not changed since the early 1970s. The oldest three gangs—the Ghost Shadows, the Flying Dragons and the Tung On—have held down the same turf all these years despite the efforts of law enforcement to dislodge them. Authorities had proclaimed the Ghost Shadows finished after Nicky Louie and 24 others were locked up in the 1985 RICO prosecution. And yet federal authorities brought another racketeering case against the Shadows in 1994, which shows that the gang had little trouble rebuilding after its leaders were taken off the street. In the latest case, the Shadows' chief gambling-house operator, Moy Bong Shun, was charged with paying off a detective in the Police Department's public morals squad to warn him of police raids. To their credit, prosecutors were careful this time not to predict an end to the Ghost Shadows.

Limited Influence

In these respects, the conventional wisdom about Chinese organized crime is correct—it is an insidious criminal virus that will afflict the country for years to come. But Chinese gangsters wield not even a fraction of the influence that the Italian Mafia has had in 20th century America, and it is doubtful that they ever will. Thirty years after they arrived on the American scene, Chinese gangs remain largely an immigrant phenomenon with little influence outside the Chinese community. To be sure, the heroin that Chinese import from the Golden Triangle affects a broad segment of society, but Chinese gangsters otherwise limit their crimes to their own people. The Italian Mafia has been about far more than just neighborhood rackets. Italian gangsters have controlled national labor unions and entire legitimate industries. They have been able to fix elections and hit every consumer in the pocket with the extra costs they have built into construction and trash hauling. It is highly unlikely that even two or three decades from now the Chinese will be able to achieve that kind of influence.

The Chinese are an Eastern people in a Western nation. Even second-generation Chinese criminals seem to lack interest in insinuating themselves into the non-Asian community. With a few exceptions, Chinese crooks have not shown an ability to make the kinds of friendships in the political clubhouses that gave the Mafia unfettered access to the halls of power. . . .

Chinese organized crime is likely to remain an immigrant's game. Chinese-Americans are an upwardly mobile people whose children are overrepresented in elite high schools and good colleges. Those Chinese who are Americanized enough to help the crime syndicates branch out beyond the Asian community are unlikely to do so in any great numbers. The Chinese emphasis on hard work and education is likely to undermine the spread of Asian organized crime more effectively than federal racketeering laws. Even people who spend their early 20s in gangs like the Ghost Shadows and the Flying Dragons often end up as legitimate restaurant owners by the time they are in their 30s. (By contrast, once you are in a Mafia family, you never quit.) And it is almost unheard of for the children of Chinese gangsters to end up in the rackets themselves. There don't seem to be any Michael Corleones or Junior Gottis in Chinatown. Chinese gangsters may well go the route of their Jewish rather than their Italian counterparts. If the mass immigration of Chinese should come to a halt, the Chinese gangster may disappear in a blaze of assimilation after a couple of decades.

Black Gangsters

Sadly, the same cannot be said of black gangsters. With more than half of the nation's African-Americans mired below the poverty line, the black ghetto seems destined to be an enduring feature of the inner city. And if the black underclass is not going to go away, neither is the problem of ghetto crime. For the near future, the drug trade will continue to be the only road to wealth for many inner-city youths whose backgrounds leave them ill prepared for college or the job market. Drugs will not go away. Guns will not go away. And neither will the problem of the black gangster. He is too much a creation of the pathology of the ghetto to disappear any time soon. Indeed, his kind are more likely to multiply. In a few short years, the children of mothers swept up in the crack epidemic of the 1980s will reach their teenage years. These are the children behind all those tales of drug-induced abuse and neglect, the children who stayed home alone in firetraps while their mothers went to the crack house, the children bounced from one foster home to another, unwanted, unloved and ill prepared for life. Come the dawn of the 21st Century, these children will be on the streets.

With the ghetto swarming with aspiring Al Capones, the Black Mafia dreamed of by Joe Gallo, Nicky Barnes, Aaron Jones and so many others cannot be counted as an impossibility. [In 1971, Gallo and Barnes tried unsuccessfully to unite New York City's black mobsters; Jones led Philadelphia's Junior Black Mafia to notoriety in the 1980s.] Certainly the black underworld as it currently exists, with millions of dollars in drugs changing hands on ghetto streets every day, will not get any kinder or gentler. The black gangsters will continue to fit prominently into the matrix of organized crime.

In the near future, drugs will no doubt remain the staple of black organized crime. The big question is whether black gangsters who retail drugs in New York and other cities will remain subservient to the Hispanic wholesale suppliers. The Colombian and Chinese suppliers have chosen to deal with Dominicans, Cubans and Mexicans, giving them a higher place in the pecking order of the underworld than black Americans. . . . But in Detroit, a city with a minuscule Hispanic population, some black drug dealers have established connections directly with the Colombians. Blacks in other parts of the country are likely to tire of dealing with middlemen and forge their own links with Colombians, or Chinese, or whoever else is controlling the flow of drugs in the 21st Century.

The brash and violent drug gangsters of the ghetto may not be the Mafia successors that Ianni envisioned twenty years ago. They may never reach the level of organization that links them to the city-wide power structure and insinuates them into the legitimate economy—the true test of criminal supremacy. They may never free themselves entirely from dependence on wealthier and better-connected crime groups. But as long as there is an underclass, as long as there are American cities, American blacks will be a force in organized crime.

Hispanic Groups

That Hispanic crime groups will also have a future in organized crime is a good bet. But their role is harder to predict. Cuban and Dominican gangs are the most organized of the Hispanic crime groups, but they have about them an aspect of impermanence. Cubans have seen rapid upward mobility in the last two decades. Many have abandoned the Cuban ghettos in Union City and West New York as more of them have saved enough money to move to suburban Bergen County, New Jersey. Cuban crime boss José Miguel Battle's chief source of income in the New York area is the illegal numbers game, an activity that is threatened in the long term by the proliferation of legal betting opportunities like the legalized state lottery, Indian reservation casinos and expanded Off Track Betting.

Cubans are no longer a big presence in the inner-city areas of New York and New Jersey. And except in Florida, they have never had much of a population concentration elsewhere in the country. Indeed, Cuban gangsters have managed to have a presence in the underworld of cities like Philadelphia and Detroit only by working with other Hispanic groups. Cubans will increasingly dominate organized crime in the Miami area, supplanting the Mafia groups from around the United States and Canada that used Florida as a playground in the past. But the future of Cuban organized crime elsewhere in the country hardly seems significant.

Dominicans, too, have an uncertain future in the rackets. Their spread in the American drug trade has been meteoric in the last 15 years, and they can be expected to continue playing a greater role in the movement of cocaine and heroin, especially in their new capacity as importers and major wholesalers. Young men from the poverty-ridden Dominican Republic will continue to make the journey to the streets of Washington Heights [in Manhattan] in search of fabulous wealth. But it is doubtful that Dominicans will take the next step and build well-structured, hierarchical crime groups with highly diverse criminal portfolios—that is, that they will begin to resemble the American Mafia. Most Dominican drug kingpins seem to have little interest in building a future in this country. They spend their lives as immigrants with one foot in the Dominican Republic, sustained by the dream that they will return to enjoy the good life in their native country when they have made enough money in New York. A good share of the millions of dollars made every week on the streets of Washington Heights is wired directly to the Dominican Republic. Those money-wiring houses lining every major thoroughfare of Harlem, Washington Heights and Inwood are there for a reason. That could leave the ultimate future of Hispanic organized crime to Puerto Ricans and Mexicans, whose rapidly proliferating gangs give them the same potential for growth in the criminal underworld as American black groups. But given their failure so far to organize stable, self-perpetuating crime groups, any criminal visionaries in the Puerto Rican and Mexican communities may not have an easy time building a Latin Mafia.

Other Groups

The future of the Russian Mafia is difficult to predict because it is so new in this country and relatively little is known of its operations. Russian immigrants are few in number compared to Asians and Hispanics. And since so many Russians coming into this country are well educated and upwardly mobile, it is likely that the Russian community will not remain long in the inner city. On the other hand, the fuel-tax evasion scam has shown how much damage can be done by a handful of Russian mobsters. And with organized crime so clearly on the rise in Eastern Europe, we could end up seeing a steady influx of Russian thugs for years to come. If many of them come here with the ambition of Vyacheslav Ivankov, a nationwide Russian crime syndicate could be the result—if it is not already secretly taking shape. And if the close working relationship that has developed between Russian and Italian mobsters continues, the Russian Mafia could end up as the natural heir to *La Cosa Nostra*. At the very least, the two groups could solidify their partnership and become a lasting combine. It was, after all, a Jewish-Italian combine that founded the first national crime syndicate.

In predicting tomorrow's dominant criminal ethnicity, one must also consider the possibility that new groups will arrive on the scene. For example, the Japanese *Yakuza* is powerful criminal force that so far has been restricted to Asia, making only limited forays into the United States. There are also immigrant crime groups that operate quietly in parts of the country that are outside the media spotlight but have the potential to become a national problem. The best example of these is the Iraqi mob in Detroit.

A Multicultural Mob

We come finally to the question of how rapidly the Italian Mafia is likely to decline and whether it will ever follow the Irish and Jewish mobs by disappearing altogether. That the Mafia is no longer the power it was for the first three decades of the postwar period cannot be disputed. The Mafia has lost control of many of the national labor unions, including the Teamsters, that were perhaps its greatest source of influence. Gangsters no longer have undisputed control over the docks through the International Longshoremen's Association, although many of the ILA's locals are still influenced by the mob. What is more, the federal government has begun the process of weeding the Mafia out of legitimate industries ranging from seafood wholesaling and other food distribution companies to garbage hauling and concrete companies. . . .

The Mafia is in a very gradual decline. It may fade away in Cleveland, St. Louis, Denver and other cities, but it will not be eliminated in Chicago and its eastern strongholds for decades to come. And as long as it is powerful in New York, it will be a key player in the nation's organized-crime business. The difference is that it will not be the sole arbiter of big-time crime. It will increasingly become simply one among several powerful crime groups plundering the nation.

The view, then, is hardly optimistic for the nation. Tomorrow's chief racketeers will not be Italian, Chinese, black, Hispanic or Russian. They will be all of the above. Even more than today, organized crime will be a diffuse threat that challenges law enforcement from a host of different nationalities, regions and activities. None will be as singularly powerful and impenetrable as the old Mafia groups, but there will be so many more of them that police will find themselves hankering for the old days of Mafia control.

More ominously, these crime groups are showing an increasingly propensity for joining forces. In New York's so-called Blue Thunder heroin case, Bonanno family mobsters were accused of buying heroin from Chinese suppliers and distributing it in partnership with a Puerto Rican drug gang. Mafia figures sell Chinese the video poker machines that gangs like the Flying Dragons force on helpless merchants. Russian mobsters have been partners with the Mafia in fuel-tax scams. Italians have operated gambling joints with Albanians in the Bronx and Westchester County, New York, and they have numerous partnerships with Cubans in the illegal numbers game. What is more, just about any crime group that sells cocaine—the Italians and the Russians included—gets it from the Colombians. The Italian and Irish mobs have been partners in South Boston bookmaking for a couple of decades. In January 1995, Boston's Mafia boss, Francis (Cadillac Frank) Salemme and the city's Irish rackets boss, James (Whitey) Bulger, both went on the lam after they were charged together in a 37-count racketeering indictment. . . .

Law Enforcement

The performance of law enforcement over the next few years to some degree will determine how big an impact the new diversity in organized crime will have on our lives. And the FBI and other agencies in the last half-decade have clearly begun overcoming the bureaucratic inertia that hampered their initial response to the changing face of the underworld. The biggest successes have grown out of the task forces that local and federal agencies have put together in the last few years. In New York, the task-force approach has achieved especially dramatic results. The New York City Police Department's major-case squad and the U.S. Bureau of Alcohol, Tobacco and Firearms have joined with the FBI in a series of hammer blows against Chinese organized crime. In 1994 and 1995, the task force brought major racketeering cases against the Ghost Shadows, the Flying Dragons, the Fuk Ching, the White Tigers, the Tung On gang, the Tung On *tong* and the On Leong *tong*'s leader. Of Chinatown's major groups linked to organized crime, only the Hip Sing *tong* and the Fukien American Association have escaped prosecution. Similar task forces have cracked down on the Ping On and Chinese Freemasons in Boston and the Wo Hop To triad and Hop Sing *tong* in San Francisco, as well as Vietnamese gangs in San Jose and Boston. Authorities have also used the task-force approach to target dozens of violent gangs around the country, including the Mexican Mafia in Los Angeles, the Latin Kings in New York, the El Rukns in Chicago, Best Friends in Detroit, the Abdullahs in Atlantic City, and the Junior Black Mafia in Philadelphia.

But law enforcement alone is hardly the solution to our nation's organized-crime problem. One of the things drawing the world's criminals to the United States is our incredibly rich market for narcotics. Drugs remain the single biggest factor driving the underworld, and federal officials have rightly made the elimination of that illegal market a top priority. But they have gone about it the wrong way. The drug war of the Reagan and Bush administrations was an abject failure. It made the same wrong assumption that the U.S. government made during Prohibition—that you can somehow prevent gangsters from supplying Americans with a commodity that they badly want. If the demand exists for drugs, all of the resources of the FBI, DEA, CIA and U.S. military put together are not going to stop them from being imported. . . .

Organized crime is a logical outgrowth of a society that was founded on the violence of the frontier and that has made worship of the dollar its highest principle. As long as we are a society that rests on greed, that neglects its poor and that promotes materialism in its media, organized crime in all of its aspects—no matter what language it speaks—will continue to plunder our nation.

CHAPTER 3

ORGANIZED CRIME IN RUSSIA

Contemporary Issues
Companion

Russia's "Mafiyas"

Stephen Handelman

Shortly after the collapse of the Soviet Union in 1991, organized criminal groups emerged throughout Russia, contributing to a rash of murders and gang violence. Their extortion and fraud schemes compounded the confusion brought about by the sudden transition to a free market economy and continue to pose a serious threat to Russia's political and economic future. In the following selection, Stephen Handelman describes how corruption, lawlessness, and Russians' unfamiliarity with capitalism have contributed to the growth of these "mafiyas." Handelman is a former Moscow bureau chief for the *Toronto Star* and author of the book *Comrade Criminal: Russia's New Mafiya.*

Since the breakup of the Soviet Union in late 1991, nearly every major city in Russia has seen a rise in crime. From St. Petersburg to Vladivostok, the police are grappling with an epidemic of murder, robbery and mayhem. In September 1992, mobsters even fired a portable anti-tank grenade launcher at a private medical clinic on the busy Kutuzovsky Prospekt in Moscow—probably, say the police, because managers of the clinic had resisted some extortionist demand.

The Ministry of Internal Affairs recorded more than one million "serious" crimes in the first seven months of 1992—a 40 percent increase over the same period in the previous year. Internal Affairs specialists have identified at least 2,600 separate crime groups across the country during 1992. Most are small gangs of racketeers, but investigators say nearly 300 of these are large syndicates.

In 1992, investigators prevented a powerful crime group based in the Russian autonomous region of Chechen-Ingushetia from swindling the Russian State Bank out of 25 billion rubles (then about $1.2 billion). Through bribes, the syndicate planned to get bank tellers in Moscow and other cities to accept false credit notes presented at their windows. Several million rubles in cash had already been collected before the police, alerted by suspicious bank officials, moved in. If the scheme had been carried out, investigators said at the time, Russia's monetary system would have collapsed.

Although police professionals have no doubt they are facing

sophisticated crime syndicates similar to their counterparts in the West, the word "mafiya" remains a catchall term for a society emerging from the enforced security of a police state and now adrift in a world where nobody seems to bother with rules.

First widely used in the 1970's—to describe the corrupt networks of party officials and black-market bosses—the word, as far as the average Russian citizen is concerned, can be applied to petty hoodlums terrorizing shopkeepers as well as to the (greedy) shopkeepers themselves, to members of crime syndicates as well as to the (corrupt) government officials cracking down on them, to people who kill for a living as well as to those who make a killing on the free market. Even President Boris Yeltsin, faced with a citizenry angered by spiraling prices following the lifting of price controls, lashed out at "mafiya-type structures" that were trying to derail his economic program.

For most Russians, whose wages have not kept pace with high prices and high inflation, today's free market is no different from, and in many ways worse than, the black market under the Communists' command economy. For decades Russians had to deal with a Government that banned private enterprise at the same time that it turned a blind eye to the private marketplace, where most Russians obtained the goods they could not get at state stores. The black-market dealer could be your next-door neighbor who had an extra supply of caviar from his brother in Minsk or he could be the professional salesman who received a shipment of quality fur hats from "suppliers" in the state factory.

The black market fostered furtiveness and dishonesty as much as it served the needs of the Soviet consumer, and that is an enduring legacy. Crime groups have found it easy to exploit the relaxation of government regulations by appealing to the greed of bureaucrats, customs officials and industrial managers.

With the partial lifting of restrictions on trade with foreign companies, some crime groups have obtained strategic metals and other raw materials cheaply from bureaucrats and industrial managers. Using false customs forms, they sell the shipments abroad, often well below the world price. Not only does Russia lose the customs revenue, but it has ceded control of key natural resources to these entrepreneurs.

Every commodity—from gold to petroleum—obtainable on the private market is smuggled abroad, usually through ports in the Baltics, by organized groups who have bribed their way past government officials and defense-industry managers. Police in Western Europe have even intercepted Russian gang members trying to sell a nuclear warhead.

During October 1992, Russian customs authorities reported the following haul of goods destined for illegal shipment abroad: 25 tons of bronze, 6.5 kilograms of marijuana, 51 railroad cars stocked with rolled steel, 6 wagons containing aluminum ingots, 45 wagons of liquid sulfur and 59 cisterns of crude oil.

"Wild Democracy"

The audacity of Russia's post-Communist criminals has left law-enforcement officials groping for explanations. Yuri Mizum, the soft-spoken former police chief in one of Yekaterinburg's largest districts who now teaches at the Urals College of Security, says many politicians and security officials are part of the problem, because of their inability to abandon decades-old strictures against private enterprise.

"When cooperatives were permitted in the mid-80's, at the start of perestroika, authorities saw no need to provide them with any special protection," he says. "We were all taught to regard private property as somehow illegitimate anyway. The police stayed away from these businesses like the plague, and offered them no help, so of course when they were threatened by black marketeers, they had no alternative but to go along. Now, it's too late."

Many also tie the current lawlessness to a lack of understanding of what constitutes democracy. "A whole class of people appeared who understood democracy as being able to do whatever they wanted," says Aslambek Aslakhanov, chairman of the Russian parliamentary commission on crime. "That caused complete *bezpredel*, an epidemic of seizing anything in sight, getting rich at any cost. In this sort of wild democracy, anybody who wants to make something of himself finds it hard to be honest and incorruptible."

But if some Russians no longer play by the old rules, the existing legal system may be as much to blame as "wild democracy." The Soviet criminal code, which still remains on the books, was better suited to catch political dissidents than to inspire respect for law and order. "Our laws were always aimed at defending the totalitarian state, not the individual," admits Aslakhanov.

Russians, as a result, are now living in a legal jungle. Presidential decrees and legislative acts have expanded the boundaries of Russian life—from the right to buy and sell property to the freedom to set up banks and private businesses—but the notoriously inefficient Soviet courts have no legal basis for interpreting these decrees, much less enforcing them.

The police say they cannot, for instance, formally tackle organized criminal activity, since under the present law only individuals can be held criminally culpable. Aslakhanov, a former senior policeman who is now in charge of drafting a criminal code, says the country needs, among others, a law setting up a professional, nonpartisan civil service, a law granting immunity to witnesses, and a law against official corruption and conflict of interest.

In the meantime, enterprising individuals and groups have been quick to capitalize on the legal muddle. At a 1992 news conference in Moscow, Andrei Dunayev, a deputy minister of Internal Affairs, admitted that "organized criminal structures now operate in almost every region of Russia," but he declined to say how much of the Russian economy was under mafiya control. Pointing out that his ministry had no way of gathering such figures, he said, "Even our specialists find it difficult to determine the legal from the illegal—to determine, for instance, what is profiteering and what is honest trade, or determining what is fraud and what is an honest mistake."

Businessman or Criminal?

What concerns law-enforcement experts in Yekaterinburg and other Russian cities is the blurring of the line between criminal and legitimate business operations. "The legalization of private enterprise was a wonderful opportunity for crime groups to accumulate capital and influence by investing in legitimate businesses, and to become legitimate themselves," says Col. Leonid Zonov, retired chief of the Serious Crimes Division in Yekaterinburg and now an adviser on crime to the Russian Government. "With their old criminal connections, and their muscle, they overwhelm any competition. Eventually, you can't tell the criminals from the businessmen."

To compound the problem, assumptions are widespread that the crime groups are not only protected, but also in some cases instructed by government officials and the police. Major Vladimir Koltsov, of Internal Affairs in Yekaterinburg, says he believes corruption has already penetrated some of the highest levels of the government and security forces.

"There are professional killers roaming around in this *bezpredel*," he says, "but our country is so divided that police in one region who know of a criminal conspiracy affecting another area will not bother to inform their colleagues. That's what really worries me."

But even if the order to clean out corruption came, the police would be ill equipped to fulfill it. "We simply don't have the means to act," says Zonov. He cites poorly armed police, still known as militia, tracking their suspects on public transportation because of the lack of police vehicles. "Our militia get paid between 7,000 and 8,000 rubles a month"—about $22—"and you won't find many fanatics who will put themselves on the line for that kind of money to fight organized crime." Especially when the mafiya is armed with machine guns, hand grenades and even hand-held rocket launchers available on the black market or sometimes directly from military garrisons.

A Changing Underworld

Rows of shabby, high-rise workers' apartment buildings make Yekaterinburg indistinguishable from dozens of gray Russian towns. What sets this city apart is an event that took place in 1918. It was in a merchant's house, now destroyed, that Czar Nicholas II and his family were murdered by the Bolsheviks.

Just as that act of regicide has blighted their past, Yekaterinburgers now see the mafiya destroying their present, a view shared even by those directly involved in the gangs. A few nights after I arrived in the city, a squat man who appeared to be in his late 30's and who had blue prison tattoos on his hands reluctantly agreed to meet me outside the former municipal Communist Party headquarters. He was accompanied by a group of young hoodlums, who exuded sufficient menace for pedestrians to give them a wide berth.

The man with the tattoos introduced himself as Bolt, adding that he was a senior lieutenant of a gang that controlled the illicit supply of vodka and cigarettes to downtown stores. He readily admitted he had never spoken to a journalist before. The group consented to the meeting only after a go-between had approached its boss, currently in prison for reasons no one bothered to explain. It was clear Bolt and his friends now felt at loose ends.

"No one shows us the same respect anymore," Bolt complained. "You get all these big shots who think they own the town, people coming in from Moscow. All our traditions don't seem to matter." He sounded almost wistful as he recalled an earlier time when everyone knew his place. "We kept order here in our own way. The party people left us alone and we left them alone." But now, he said, the old sources of income—from protection and smuggling rackets, the selling of black-market goods—were drying up. The large syndicates were expanding operations in all sectors of the local economy, and Bolt and his fellow hoodlums were forced, as he put it, to "sell their fists" to the same crime lords who were putting them out of business.

Bolt claimed that these crime lords were in the thrall of corrupt politicians in Yekaterinburg, adding, with all the wounded pride of a civic-minded citizen, "They pour mud on the town." He was pessimistic about the future, predicting more violence. "It's terrible what's going on now," he added. "Human values are being lost."

Bolt's lament for the old criminal order is a paradoxical comment on Russia's current problems. The underworld is one of Russia's few durable social institutions, prevailing, like the Russian Orthodox Church, over persistent attempts at its destruction. In the chaotic years following the 1917 revolution, armed gangs left a trail of murder and robbery throughout the countryside, but they also served as a secret ally of the state. Bolsheviks used the bank-robbing talents of crime gangs to raise the money they needed to survive during their years underground. And by sponsoring the black market in the 1970's, the mafiya provided the lubricant that made the inefficient Soviet economy run.

By the time the Soviet Union was broken up, according to investigators, there were more than 700 gangs and clans, organized along ethnic or family lines, in the country. They were each headed by a boss, called *vor v zakone* (thief-in-law). . . .

Koltsov, who plans to retire from the police to serve as a director of the new security service, says the mafiya is far from being as powerful

as it thinks it is. . . . "If we can get tough laws and, much more important, tough enforcement, we still have a chance."

Winking at Organized Crime

Can Yeltsin's reformers crack down on organized crime without
endangering the state's passage from Communism to capitalism?

The fall of the old regime has put vast amounts of wealth and
resources up for grabs. Russia's lack of experience with a free-market
economy and the crippling ambiguity of its legal system virtually
guarantee that only the most ruthless will be willing to take the risks
involved.

Some Russians argue, therefore, that a period of lawlessness is part
of the price every society pays for radical economic change. Pointing
to examples as disparate as the development of the American West
and the transformation of Latin American economies, they suggest
that without a certain amount of robber-baron-style entrepreneurship, the consumer goods in most Russian cities would disappear.

"The mobs have put millions of rubles that used to be concealed in
the black market into circulation," says Sergei Plotnikov, a reporter for
the Yekaterinburg newspaper *Na Smenu* (*Transition*). "That money is
now subject to taxes, so why should officials try to stop it, especially
when there's no money coming in from the central government?"

But winking at organized crime, as officials in many Russian
regions now do, could lead to a different political nightmare. During
my visit to Yekaterinburg, it was clear that the town's economic boom
had opened a gulf between the very rich and the very poor. One afternoon, I attended a fashion show at the local theater sponsored by the
sportswear outlet of the [local crime] syndicate. The invitation-only
audience was a cross-section of Yekaterinburg's post-Communist elite:
the women with their bouffant hairdos, flashy jewelry and tight
dresses; the men in their well-cut suits.

A few blocks away, however, factory workers in ragged clothes,
barefoot beggars and obviously malnourished children waited silently
in the town's filthy central railway station.

Vocal Russian conservatives regularly harp on the contrast between
the opulent life styles of entrepreneurs and the crushing poverty of
"decent people," citing that as a reason for slowing down or reversing
economic reform. The link made by the conservatives between the
high crime rate and the get-rich-quick mania—a connection also
made by the public—helped force the 1992 resignation of the Russian
Prime Minister, Yegor T. Gaidar, an ardent advocate of Western-style
capitalism.

Some Russians warn a powerful "Red-Brown" alliance of disgrun-
tled members of the former Soviet establishment and xenophobic
right-wing parties is already collaborating on programs that would rid
the country of its free-market entrepreneurs, criminal or not.

"If people begin to equate freedom and democracy with crime and anarchy," says Tamara Lomakina, editor of *Na Smenu*, "they will support political forces who say they can eliminate the *bezpredel* by strong-arm measures. There is really only one political force in this country that is strong enough to do that right now, together with the army." She paused. "I mean the fascists."

THE RISE OF THE RUSSIAN MAFIA

Claire Sterling

The Russian Mafia is now the world's most dangerous criminal organization, surpassing even the Sicilian Mafia, says Claire Sterling, an investigative reporter and the author of the book *Thieves' World: The Threat of the New Global Network of Organized Crime*. The origins of the Russian Mafia, she explains, lie in the institutionalized corruption that existed under the Soviet regime. Together, criminals and corrupt politicians exploited Russia's transition to a free market economy, writes Sterling, and now they control much of the Russian economy. According to the author, the weakened Russian government can do little to oppose Russia's vast organized underworld. The Russian Mafia engages in all manner of illegal activities, Sterling warns, and its influence is spreading to the West.

There are fifty ways of saying "to steal" in Russian, and the Russian mafia uses them all. It is the world's largest, busiest and possibly meanest collection of organized hoods, consisting of 5,000 gangs and 3 million people who work for or with them. Its reach extends into all fifteen of the former Soviet republics, across eleven time zones and one-sixth of the earth's land mass. It intrudes into every field of Western concern: the nascent free market, privatization, disarmament, military conversion, foreign humanitarian relief and financial aid, even state reserves of currency and gold. And it has begun to creep toward the rest of Europe and the United States—"looking at the West as a wolf looks at sheep," a Russian crime specialist told me.

A Mafia Without Equal

The Russian mafia is a union of racketeers without equal. Unlike the mafia in Sicily, which it admires and copies as a standard of excellence, it has no home seat or central command. There are no ancestral memories or common bloodlines. Nevertheless, its proliferating clans are invading every sphere of life, usurping political power, taking over state enterprises and fleecing natural resources. They are engaged in extortion, theft, forgery, armed assault, contract killing, swindling, drug running, arms smuggling, prostitution, gambling, loan sharking, embezzling, money laundering and black marketing—all on a monumental and increasingly international scale.

Rising from the ruins of the Soviet empire, the new mafia has far outclassed the one that flourished under Leonid Brezhnev. The mafia was Brezhnev's solution for a stifling centralized economy; it provided illicit goods and services by stealing from the state, buying protection, smuggling, cheating, bullying and bribing its way into the Kremlin. It was *korruptsiya* [corruption] Communist-style, a shared monopoly of power between politicians and crooks. Liberated Russia deserved better. But the old politicians are still largely in place, yesterday's crooks are today's free entrepreneurs and *korruptsiya*, spreading uncontrollably as things fall apart, has become the curse of a stricken nation. "Corruption," Boris Yeltsin exclaimed in 1993, "is devouring the state from top to bottom."

In 1991, the year the Communists fell, the All-Union Research Institute of the Soviet Interior Ministry estimated that half the income of an average government functionary was coming from bribes, compared with only 30 percent before 1985. During the late 1980s the Soviet prosecutor-general's office indicted 225,000 state officials for embezzlement, including eighteen who worked for the government's Department to Combat Embezzlement. By 1991, 20,000 police officers were being fired yearly for collusion with the mafia—double the rate under Brezhnev. That same year, Alexander Gurov, head of the Soviet Interior Ministry's Sixth Department to Combat Organized Crime, estimated that four out of five agents in the ministry's militia were on the take.

These were merely symptoms of a malignant growth pervading the economy, the banking system and the body politic. It is common knowledge that millions of ordinary citizens steal state property, trade on the black market, swindle each other and buy or sell protection. Obviously they aren't all tied to the mob: Russia is so chaotic and broke that few people can stay honest and survive. Yet if not all lawbreakers are mafiosi, the mafia swims among them like a great predatory shark, recruiting some, exacting payoffs from others, frightening away rivals. Insatiable and seemingly invulnerable, it swallows factories, co-ops, private enterprises, real estate, raw materials, currency and gold: one-quarter of Russia's economy in 1991, between one-third and one-half by 1992.

Between 1989 and 1991, communism's twilight years, the mafia's take shot up from less than 1 billion rubles to 130 billion—the size of the Soviet national deficit. "In the next few years, its [gross] will reach 200 billion rubles," Gurov said in 1991. "Organized crime will then control 30 to 40 percent of the country's GNP [gross national product]."

Meanwhile, the mafia's kill rate has climbed to a world record.

Once, Soviet leaders taunted America for its sixty-odd murders per day—a mark of capitalist depravity. By 1993 murders in the Russian republic alone ran to more than eighty per day. Many of the dead were victims of drunken brawls, armed robbery and gang warfare, but contract killings were increasingly popular: there were 1,500 in 1992. In 1993 ten directors of the country's largest commercial banks were murdered, presumably for failing to extend still more outrageous loans than those they had granted already. And a disturbing number of victims were policemen: nearly 1,000 between 1989 and 1992, according to Interpol Moscow.

By the start of 1992, soon after the Soviet Union's borders opened up, all of its institutions were gone, including those for law enforcement. The Soviet-wide Sixth Department, created by Mikhail Gorbachev three years earlier to fight organized crime, was dismantled along with all other nationwide bodies. No central authority remained to coordinate police intelligence, order arrests, control 36,000 miles of border or oversee the movement of people, money and goods. The only organization fully operational in the new Commonwealth of Independent States was the mafia.

The Russian mafia is richer by far than the forces of the law and much better equipped in weapons, communications systems and transport. Members are admitted only with a sponsor, and only after proving their valor by killing somebody on order, preferably a friend or relative—exactly like their Sicilian counterparts. Once in, they risk its death penalties, communicate in a private jargon and flout the tattoos marking their eternal membership: a spider web for drug traffickers, an eight-point star for robbers, a broken heart for district bosses.

The mafia is organized in something like a classic criminal pyramid. First, at the base, are common street hoods, under gang leaders who run their territory like military boot camps. Moscow, for instance, is controlled by twenty criminal "brigades"—some tribal, others regional, others specialized by trade—totaling more than 6,000 armed thugs. Everybody in the city in some kind of business (restaurants, food markets, gas stations, flower stalls, newsstands, casinos, beggars' corners at the Kremlin) is "under somebody" who collects a monthly payoff. The *Dolgoprudnaya*, who drive around in Volvos with heated seats, control the best protection rackets. The *Lyubertsy* run prostitution. The *Solntsevo* run slot machines. The *Ingushy* smuggle contraband leather and skins to Italy. The Azerbaijanis control the drug trade. Then there are the Chechen, with their own army of 600 killers in Moscow. Natives of a self-proclaimed sovereign enclave in the northern Caucasus, the Chechen are the most notorious and versatile of Russia's mafiosi. They will do almost anything imaginable that is illegal.

A level up from the gangs are a "supply" group and a "security" group. The supply group serves as a conduit, ensuring that directives from above are carried out below. The security group is comprised of

respectable citizens—journalists, bankers, artists, athletes, politicians—
who provide intelligence, legal aid, social prestige and political cover.

Thieves-Within-the-Code

On top of the pyramid are the godfathers, the indomitable *vory v
zakone* (thieves-within-the-code); they preserve a "thieves' ideology,"
administer justice and plot strategy. There are 700 known godfathers
at large or in prison. Guiding rather than governing, they provide
most of the brains for their subalterns. They are not absolute rulers
over violently unruly and fiercely competitive gangs. Rather, "each
sphere of influence is under their control," according to I. Pavlovich,
deputy chief of the Russian Interior Ministry's Sixth Department.
Pavlovich says they meet periodically, settle territorial disputes,
decide on operations and make policy. Their power inevitably surpass-
es the fragile Russian government's. Their edicts are instantly trans-
mitted, unmistakably enforceable and almost universally obeyed.

Two stories illustrate how the mafia has of late transformed itself
into a formidable force. First, in January 1991 the most powerful
thieves-within-the-code gathered from all over the country to discuss
a financial emergency. Valentin Pavlov, premier of the crumbling
Soviet empire, had suddenly withdrawn all 50- and 100-ruble notes
from circulation. His plan, he said, was to stop the illegal flow of
rubles out of the country and prevent "a river of dirty money" from
coming in. Everybody in the mafia kept illicit cash reserves in these
notes, which at the time were the largest denominations issued.

"My operational report showed that these thieves-within-the-
code—the supermen, the big-time mafiosi—got together to discuss
ways of selling off or exchanging the banknotes for new ones or getting them out of the country," Gurov later said on national T.V. "The
thieves-within-the-code decided where the rubles had to be exchanged
or smuggled out. Then they gave permission to set aside a quarter of
the entire sum for bribing the administration."

The underworld mobilized overnight. "Black-market currency sharks
vanished from Moscow," Gurov declared. The ruble notes were rushed
to corruptible state factories and banks in remote regions to be
exchanged under the counter. The Konkuret co-op, with only 1,000
rubles in its account, changed 190,000 rubles in 50s and 100s into
smaller denominations at the local bank. A Novosibirsk shop taking in
10,000 rubles per day "contrived to hand in" 240,000 rubles. Hundreds
of millions of rubles were washed with little trouble. Unlike the poor,
who lost their lifetime savings because they had been hiding their
rubles under their mattresses to dodge the tax collectors, the mafia
came out very well.

Then, a few months later the godfathers met again to consider
Gorbachev's 500-day program for transition to a free market. They
liked it. A free market in the USSR meant not only mobility, relaxed

borders and dollars from abroad, but a chance to mount the most colossal criminal buyout in history. For all the wreckage of Russia's economy, it still had the world's richest natural resources. Once privatization got under way, according to Tatjana Kurjaghina, then the Interior Ministry's top social economist, the whole country would be up for sale.

Though few realized it at the time, the Russian mafia was about to make a big strategic leap: from merely feeding off the economy to owning it. To prepare for privatization, however, the godfathers needed to stall the entire government program until January 1992, and they had to impose a new peace among Moscow's eternally warring clans. A truce that they had worked out in 1988, at Dagomys on the Black Sea, had ended in an orgy of bloodshed after barely a year. But the first stage of privatization was an imperative call to order. The logic of peace was unarguable: once inner harmony was restored, the godfathers divided zones of influence and went after the 6,000 enterprises coming up for auction in Moscow. The rules for privatization were fluid, corrupt officials were easily come by and most Russians had no money to speak of. Within weeks, the Russian news agency *Tass-Krim Press* reported that the mafia had "privatized between 50 percent and 80 percent of all shops, storehouses, depots, hotels and services in Moscow."

Today, according to Yeltsin adviser Piotr Filipov, who heads the Center for Political and Economic Analysis, Russia's mafia controls 40,000 privatized enterprises and collects protection money from 80 percent of the country's banks and private enterprises.

Drug Trafficking

The mafia also controls the drug trade. Nature has endowed Russia and its fellow republics with a prodigal source of narcotics. According to Alexander Sergeev, head of the Interior Ministry's anti-narcotics unit, the ex-USSR produces twenty-five times more hashish than the rest of the world; cannabis grows wild on 7.5 million of its acres—in Kazakhstan, Siberia, the Far Eastern republics, the lower Volga River Basin, the northern Caucasus and southern Ukraine. Luxuriant poppy fields sprawl across Kazakhstan, Uzbekistan, Turkmenistan and Tajikistan.

When Soviet controls were severe, organized crime overlooked this potential bonanza: the chance to create and feed a huge addict population and export for dollars. When communism fell, however, things changed. By 1992 family-sized poppy fields yielding two crops per year were under heavy armed guard. New plantations in Uzbekistan increased by 1,000 percent. Around 200,000 acres were planted in Kyrgyzstan. The number of opium growers in Kazakhstan's Chu Valley tripled. Poppies were planted over 1,000 square kilometers of empty radioactive terrain around Chernobyl. Vladimir Burlaka, St. Petersburg's anti-narcotics chief, estimated that the 1992 crop would be worth $5 billion.

Meanwhile, heroin couriers were moving up from the Golden Crescent through Tajikistan, Uzbekistan and Turkmenistan. They carried forged papers and radio telephones and had paramilitary protection as they crossed the breadth of Soviet territory bound for Odessa, Finland, the Baltic states, Poland, Western Europe and America. The drug mafia was taking over horizontally and vertically, from production and processing to transport, distribution and marketing. Free of centralized surveillance, it moved largely unhindered across the crazy quilt of internal Commonwealth borders, ignoring ethnic tensions.

Underground laboratories were also starting to produce synthetic drugs, such as "Krokodil" and "Chert" (devil), that were 1,000 times stronger than heroin and cheaper than homegrown natural drugs. The most lethal, methyl-fentanyl—diluted in proportions of 1 to 20,000—was made exclusively in Russia.

Soviet cities had always been a drug market of sorts, and it expanded as soldiers got hooked on heroin during the Afghanistan War; but galloping addiction set in only after traffickers mounted their assault around 1985. From then on the addict population doubled yearly. By 1992 Russia had at least 1.5 million addicts and occasional drug users, Sergeev says. (The figure was all the more startling for the carefully preserved fiction that Communist Russia had no addicts whatsoever. In fact, some Russian experts thought the "real" figure was "at least three to four times higher.") Also in 1992 the drug mafia's profits increased nearly fourfold, from 4 billion to 15 billion rubles—this before its first harvest of modernized, commercialized crops.

Sergeev says that Russian mafiosi have been trafficking heroin with Westerners, the Sicilian mafia especially, for nearly a decade. In 1992 they were delivering heroin to Sicilian mafiosi in New York, selling amphetamines elsewhere in the United States and moving cocaine in Vienna, Budapest and Frankfurt. They were said by Interpol Poland to have reached "precise agreements in Warsaw with big German and Dutch cocaine traffickers and Colombia's Cali cartel." That same year a shipment of pure Colombian cocaine shaped into 34,000 pairs of Peruvian-made plastic sandals was spotted in Moscow, heading for Warsaw.

Despite this, and to avoid Yeltsin's displeasure, the U.S. State Department did not list Russia among forty-eight producer or transit countries in its 1992 International Narcotics Strategy Report. No Western government publication did. In another year, though, they would.

Looking West

In the summer of 1992 Moscow Interpol's deputy chief, Anatoly Terechov, complained, "Less than half our joint ventures work. Only a quarter deal with their declared activities. Two or three out of five are financed with money of dubious origin. Many . . . are fictitious. Often they're one-man operations to swing hard currency deals. . . . At least 500 of our mafia groups use them to link up with international crime—in the United States, Italy, Germany, Austria, France, Canada, Poland. . . ."

Six months later Yeltsin himself adjusted this estimate upward. "At least 1,000 mafia groups have contacts with international organized crime," he said.

The American and Sicilian mafias were the first in, by way of what was to be the biggest black-market currency swap ever: a plan to trade $7.8 billion for 140 billion rubles, enabling the Westerners to buy Russia's natural resources for rubles and sell them in the West for 300 to 400 times more in dollars. (The plan was aborted in January 1991, but similar dollar-for-ruble scams followed.) With the Americans and the Sicilians entrenched, the Russians are moving out into the rest of the world—and they're heading West.

"It's wonderful that the Iron Curtain is gone," says Boris Uvarov, chief serious crimes investigator for the Russian prosecutor-general, "but it was a shield for the West. Now we've opened the gates, and this is very dangerous for the world. America is getting Russian criminals; Europe is getting Russian criminals. They'll steal everything. They'll *occupy* Europe. Nobody will have the resources to stop them. You people in the West don't know our mafia yet; you will, you will."

TWO VIEWS ON THE RUSSIAN MAFIA

Phil Williams

In the following selection, excerpted from the introduction to his book *Russian Organized Crime: The New Threat?*, Phil Williams sums up the best- and worst-case scenarios that commentators have expressed concerning the organized crime phenomenon in Russia. At one extreme, explains Williams, are warnings that the Russian crime groups are among the most powerful in the world, pose a serious danger to the international community, and will either take over Russia or force the government to adopt authoritarian measures. At the other end of the spectrum, he writes, are those who think the Russian Mafia is helping its citizens with the transition to a free market economy and will likely fade away as economic reform progresses.

During the 1990s transnational criminal organizations of all kinds have received increased scrutiny from law enforcement agencies, intelligence analysts, and academic researchers. While there are many differences of both interpretation and assessment regarding a whole range of issues, divisions are particularly acute in the area of Russian organized crime. Assessments of the seriousness of the challenge from Russian organized crime diverge remarkably. At one end of the spectrum are those who consider Russian organized crime a dangerous successor to the threat posed to Western values and Western societies by the Soviet Union. Adherents of this view provide what is, in effect, a worst case estimate of the Russian organized crime threat. At the other end of the spectrum are those who not only believe that the threat from Russian organized crime is greatly exaggerated in many Russian and Western commentaries, but also argue that, in present circumstances, organized crime has certain positive functions in Russian society and the economy. Members of this group, providing what is in essence a best case analysis, contend that Russian organized crime has attained considerable prominence only because of the particular set of economic and political conditions that currently exist throughout the Commonwealth of Independent States (CIS). The

Reprinted by permission from *Russian Organized Crime*, by Phil Williams, published by Frank Cass & Company, 900 Eastern Avenue, Ilford, Essex, England. Copyright Frank Cass & Co. Ltd.

corollary is that as these conditions change then organized crime is likely to diminish in importance.

Shortcomings to Both Arguments

In some respects these contrasting assessments can be understood as the new variant of the Cold War debate between hawks and doves. As in this previous debate, however, neither the worst case nor the best case assessment is wholly compelling. Many proponents of the worst case assessment tend to be more concerned with highlighting and publicizing what they see as a new threat to Western security rather than with a systematic analysis of the phenomenon of organized crime in Russia; while those at the other end of the spectrum depreciate the seriousness of the challenge posed by Russian organized crime either to transition processes in Russia or to other states. The problem with the worst case assessment is partly one of exaggeration—a tendency to draw facile conclusions from partial evidence—but even more one of over-simplification. Not only do the members of this group tend to seize on particular aspects of the problem and give them a salience that is unwarranted, but they describe the issue in terms such as 'crimefest' and 'kleptocracy' that have maximum emotional impact but minimum analytical utility or rigor.

On the other side, those who believe that the problem has been greatly exaggerated are generally much more analytical in their approach. Partly in an effort to redress the balance in a debate that, at the popular level at least, tends to be dominated by the worst case assessment, the best case advocates downplay the adverse consequences of Russian organized crime. The argument here, however, is that both approaches have serious shortcomings. The worst case thinkers are too mesmerized by the threat from Russian organized crime to assess it critically; while the best case analysts are too enamored of the free market economy to accept its limitations. Moreover, there is a central irony in this debate: the worst case assessment may be more accurate but not for the reasons that its proponents suggest; the best case perspective is less compelling but, because of its more analytical approach, highlights the need to go beyond rhetorical slogans and engage in a systematic and rigorous analysis. . . .

The Worst Case Assessment

The worst case assessment of Russian organized crime can be seen as the direct heir to the conservative assessment of the Soviet Union threat during the Cold War. For those who still cling to the belief that the Soviet collapse was a ruse, Russian organized crime is an enormously convenient if very natural target. There are several features of Russian organized crime that are emphasized in the worst case approach:

1. Its highly predatory nature. As Claire Sterling has noted: 'Russia is so chaotic and broke that few people can stay honest and survive.

Yet if not all lawbreakers are mafiosi, the mafia swims among them like a great predatory shark, recruiting some, exacting payoffs from others, frightening away rivals. Insatiable and seemingly invulnerable, it swallows factories, co-ops, private enterprises, real estate, raw materials, currency and gold: one-quarter of Russia's economy in 1991, between one-third and one-half by 1992'.

2. The highly structured nature of the challenge. Although there are few observers who, when pressed, would deny that there are important divisions within Russian organized crime, there is nevertheless a tendency among certain commentators to treat it as a highly cohesive force that is largely dominated by past KGB operatives, as well as some current members of the security services, who have transferred their skills to personal profit while retaining their malevolence to the West and its institutions. In addition, considerable importance is given to the role of the 'thieves professing the code' who are generally portrayed as the Russian equivalent of Mafia 'godfathers'. The thieves are seen as the organizers of the criminal world and as the leaders who develop the overall strategy that gives direction and form to criminal activities.

3. An emphasis on the excellence of Russian organized crime. Russian criminal organizations are seen as surpassing Colombian drug cartels, Chinese Triads, or the various branches of the Italian Mafia. They are portrayed as more ruthless, more skillful, and more successful than organizations that are better known and more deeply entrenched. As well as the KGB influence this is attributed to the experience of the criminal organizations in circumventing a totalitarian political system. As Claire Sterling, once again, observed, 'The Russian mafia is a union of racketeers without equal. Unlike the mafia in Sicily, which it admires and copies as a standard of excellence, it has no home seat or central command. There are no ancestral memories or common bloodlines. Nevertheless, its proliferating clans are invading every sphere of life, usurping political power, taking over state enterprises and fleecing natural resources. They are engaged in extortion, theft, forgery, armed assault, contract killing, swindling, drug running, arms smuggling, prostitution, gambling, loan sharking, embezzling, money laundering and black marketing—all on a monumental and increasingly international scale'.

The Nuclear Threat

4. Another component of the worst case analysis is the emphasis placed on the linkage between Russian organized crime and nuclear material trafficking. It is sometimes implied and sometimes stated unequivocally that the Russian mafia is trafficking in nuclear materials, and that Russian organized crime may well have developed an alliance with pariah states or terrorist organizations. This tends to be particularly powerful in the public debate as it combines elements of

the familiar Cold War paradigm relating to the nuclear danger with the new 'red Mafia'.

5. Another element in this assessment of Russian organized crime emphasizes the close links between Russian organized crime and criminal organizations from other nations, especially the Italian Mafia and the Colombian drug trafficking organizations. Claire Sterling has suggested that these links are developing into a 'pax mafiosa', a series of criminal conglomerates that are threatening global security and stability. Support for this assessment is provided by a succession of what are described as summit meetings between the leaders of national organized crime groups, including most notably one in Prague in October 1992.

6. The worst case assessment also emphasizes the political consequences of Russian organized crime. Not only is it argued that Russian organized crime could derail the process of democratization and create such a backlash that ultra-nationalists or communists who want to reimpose some kind of authoritarian rule are likely to come to power, but it is even suggested that the Russian state itself could fall under the domination of organized crime. The fact that the number of criminal organizations in Russia has increased from 3,000 in the early 1990s to over 8,000 at the end of 1995 is seen as indicative of the growing power of Russian organized crime and the severity of the threat it poses to the Russian state and the democratization process. Indeed, in some variants of the worst case analysis the struggle has already been lost and Russia has already become a criminal superpower.

While not all those who adhere to the worst case analysis would necessarily accept every detail of this picture as presented above, there is certainly a consensus on the seriousness of the threat both domestically and, increasingly, internationally. At the other end of the spectrum are those who, in effect, deny that Russian organized crime poses a real threat to national or international security. In this view— promulgated by some economists and some criminologists—organized crime in Russia is far from the negative phenomenon portrayed in the worst case assessment.

The Best Case Assessment

In some respects, the best case assessment of Russian organized crime is more difficult to crystallize than the worst case analysis. Part of the reason for this is that those who have made such an assessment do it in a more analytical way than many of their more pessimistic counterparts. Nevertheless, it is still possible to discern several major themes that are central to the best case analysis:

1. A consistent theme of the best case analysis is that Russian organized crime currently fulfills certain positive functions in Russian economic and social life. In particular, it is argued, organized crime has become a substitute for government, particularly in the matter of con-

tract enforcement. Jim Leitzel, for example, a specialist on Russian economic reform, has argued that the main problem in Russia is that the reform process is incomplete, with the continued absence of contract law, continued government monopolies, and continued ambivalence to private economic activity. The first of these is particularly important: 'If the state is unable to enforce private contracts business people must look elsewhere. Organized crime can provide the contractual security that business people need to enter into deals in the first place'. In a similar vein, one Russian analysis noted that 'Russia's criminal world . . . has become the only force that can give stability, that is capable of stamping out debts, of guaranteeing the banks repayment of loans and of considering property disputes efficiently and fairly. The criminal world has essentially taken on the state functions of legislative and judicial authority'. In other words, organized crime offers the protection and contract enforcement that are not provided by the state but that are crucial to the functioning of a market economy. The implication of this is that rather than organized crime infiltrating business, business will often seek out organized crime to fulfill the needed functions of contract enforcement. Indeed, according to this analysis, 'in the last year or two, serious criminal groups have not "cornered" anyone, that is, they do not forcibly thrust their protection on anyone; they have more than enough requests of this kind.". . .

This argument is given credence by those who emphasize that something similar occurred in Sicily. Diego Gambetta, in particular, has argued that the Sicilian Mafia grew up in response to a weak state, and the concomitant absence of a legitimate body to enforce business contracts and property rights. With an economy permeated by a basic lack of trust, protection becomes essential. The Mafia provides this protection. This is a process, it is argued, that is fundamentally different from extortion in which businessmen pay simply to avoid being beaten up, robbed or killed by those who are selling the protection. In other words, organized crime is providing a necessary function that is crucial to the functioning of a market economy where there is a lack of regulation and enforcement. Moreover, it does so in response to requests for assistance. Protection is something that businessmen voluntarily choose rather than something they have forced upon them. In short, the introduction of private property and private business in Russia has led to a demand for protection which the state has been unable to meet—and that organized crime is meeting instead.

2. The second component of the best case analysis is that organized crime simply represents the ultimate form of capitalism, a form that is unregulated by either law or morality, and therefore is particularly efficient at capital accumulation. In this view, criminal organizations are among the most progressive forces in the former Soviet Union since they are among the strongest supporters—and are certainly one

of the main beneficiaries—of the privatization process. Furthermore, as the profits from organized crime and drug trafficking are reinvested in the legitimate economy, they will provide a considerable boost to the development of the market economy. In other words, every transition is a rough one and what we are seeing is the Russian equivalent of the nineteenth century robber barons who played such an important role in the industrialization of the United States. At a time when the market remains imperfect and there is a lack of clarity about what kind of behavior is permitted and what is prohibited, entrepreneurial activity, to be effective, has to be ruthless. In these circumstances, it is hardly surprising that entrepreneurship and criminal activity are closely linked.

3. The third component of the best case assessment is that the situation is likely to improve since organized crime is a transient phenomenon that is the product of particular conditions. As the conditions change, organized crime will become weaker rather than stronger. This argument has again been articulated most effectively by Leitzel, who argues that although organized crime fulfills several positive and necessary functions in the economies of states in transition, its 'sphere of influence' is likely to dwindle to 'normal' Western levels as reform proceeds. As the state gradually fills the role currently occupied by organized crime then the opportunities available to criminal organizations will diminish. Similarly, as the reform process is completed, government monopolies disappear, and private economic activity becomes the norm so, the argument goes, organized crime will find fewer avenues for advancement. And as the opportunities for organized crime contract, so will its power. The concomitant is that criminal organizations will gradually be assimilated into the legitimate economy and its leaders become respectable legitimate businessmen, the source of whose wealth is less important than the wealth itself. The power of the market is such that the prevalence of organized crime will diminish as the market becomes free.

The Middle Ground

Neither of these highly discrepant views is without merit. The big problem with the worst case assessment is that it engages in threat inflation through over-simplification. The problem with the best case assessment is that the focus primarily on the economic aspects of organized crime ignores the potential for its consolidation, the development of symbiotic links with political and economic elites, and the capacity of organized crime to perpetuate the conditions that initially gave rise to it and allow it to flourish. The best case is too sanguine, with an over-emphasis on the positive contribution of Russian organized crime and insufficient attention to the deleterious nature of much organized criminal activity throughout the CIS.

ORGANIZED CRIME'S ROLE IN THE RUSSIAN ECONOMY

Marshall I. Goldman

Marshall I. Goldman traces the history of organized crime in Russia from the earliest days of the Soviet Union through its collapse. The Russian Mafia, he argues, gained much of its strength because of the way in which economic reform was instituted under Mikhail Gorbachev. Presently, the Mafia in Russia distorts the nation's economy through its activities, mainly by maintaining monopolistic control over markets, says Goldman. Therefore, he contends, efforts to weaken the Mafia should focus on opening markets and relaxing governmental economic restraints. Goldman is a professor of Russian economics at Wellesley College in Massachusetts and the associate director of Harvard University's Russian Research Center.

The level of penetration of crime in Russia is unprecedented. An article on the front page of *Izvestiia* on January 26, 1994, reported that the Russian Mafia now controls 70 to 80 percent of all private business and banking. The Russian Mafia seems even more pervasive than its Sicilian counterpart. Most important, the Russian Mafia poses a major impediment for healthy economic recovery. That does not mean that with a strong Mafia there can be no growth. Indeed there is. But it tends to be a distorted kind. Too much is spent on protection and security and not enough on breaking up monopolies and opening up markets.

The buildup of a Mafia also illustrates the problems of trying to reconfigure a society that has been subjected to seventy years of communism and overly strict control. It brings to mind the fish that live in the bottom of the deepest part of the ocean. They are semiblind. When they are brought to the surface they explode because they do not have a chance to decompress. The East Europeans and the Chinese were able to avoid many of Russia's problems with the Mafia because they moved gradually or because they already had many market-type institutions in place. But Russia, like the deep-sea fish, is exploding because it has not had time to build up the institutions it

Excerpted from "Why Is the Mafia So Dominant in Russia?" by Marshall I. Goldman, *Challenge*, January/February 1996. Reprinted by permission from M.E. Sharpe, Inc., Armonk, NY 10504.

needs to cope with market processes.

What is particularly fascinating about the all-encompassing nature of the Russian Mafia is how quickly they took over the economy. Although there has always been corruption and crime in Russia, even in Stalin's time, by today's standards, the extent of criminal influence prior to 1987 was relatively moderate. By contrast, the Mafia in Russia today controls and affects not only traditional criminal activity such as prostitution and drugs but much of the general economic activity as well.

Some have called this outbreak of crime and corruption inevitable, a natural part of the move to capitalism. Michael Scammell wrote in the *New York Times* (December 26, 1993) that this is simply robber-baron capitalism, and we really should not be surprised by it. To the contrary, that is not the case at all. That is not to say that we in the United States were immune to the Michael Milkens of the 1980s or the robber barons of the nineteenth century. But it is fascinating to look at such countries as China, Hungary, Poland, and the Czech Republic and see that the pattern that developed there is very different. In other words, they also emerged from communism and switched to a market system, and while they are not immune to gangs or corruption, there is nowhere near the scale of crime we see inside Russia and the former Soviet Union.

Some important questions arise from such a comparison. Is what occurred in Russia unique? What, if anything, was done in the reform process to exacerbate the problem? An argument can be made that to some extent the Russian reformers made the Mafia movement worse than it needed to have been.

The Soviet State

Let us begin when the Soviet Union was a strong Stalinist state. There was a very strong government as well as central control of the economy. Generally, it was very inflexible. When things are inflexible there is a need for arbitrage, for some kind of balancing off, to compensate for oversights of the central planners. Joseph Stalin focused on heavy industry and neglected consumer goods. As indicated earlier, this gave rise to an illegal, informal market that provided the goods and services the state sector considered unimportant and did not produce in adequate quantities. This in turn gave rise to the underground economy. The Russians called it *nalevo* (everything to the left).

It is important to remember that the Mafia in Russia predates the Mikhail Gorbachev and Boris Yeltsin eras. Nonetheless, it was relatively muted because the Stalinist government was so strong. If you violated the law it was an economic crime. Economic crimes were punishable by death. That dissuaded a lot of people, but not everybody. The penalties were severe, but the potential rewards were enormous. As a result, some people were tempted despite the draconian penalties.

When Stalin died, conditions and regulations gradually became less severe and less highly enforced, particularly under Leonid Brezhnev. By the latter years of Brezhnev's life, things had become much more lenient and tolerant. The climate was typified by his daughter (who was running around with a diamond smuggler who happened to be a circus clown) and her husband, Yuri Churbanov, who after the marriage was appointed Deputy Minister of the Interior. Before long, Mr. Churbanov began to solicit bribes from the Mafia in Uzbekistan. Under Brezhnev, legal enforcement in general became quite relaxed, yet the underlying economic structure remained inflexible. As disorder increased, Mafia-like groups sought to establish their own kind of order. This explains why the Mafia influence at the time was at a high point, at least until the Yeltsin era.

There was another factor at work. Because of the pervasiveness of the state, both politically and economically, it became socially and morally acceptable—politically correct if you will—to cheat the state. That was not new for Russia. Such attitudes antedate communism; they go back to the nineteenth century and earlier. As one of my Russian friends said, "What is intolerable today in Russia is not corruption, that's historic, it is the violence." If you read Nikolai Gogol or Leo Tolstoy, you know that the *chinovniki* (the bureaucrats) made their living by cheating. In *The Inspector General*, for example, the whole story reflects the acceptance of this kind of corruption. Historically there has been an underlying ethic that all but lionizes those who cheat the state. The difference today is that some worry that violence may also become part of the ethic.

When Brezhnev died, he was succeeded by Yuri Andropov, who had been the head of the KGB. He knew where the criminality was, and he had a rigid sense of legality. Consequently, he cracked down in a strict way, to the great anxiety and concern of the Mafia. No wonder they were pleased when Konstantin Chernenko took over after eighteen months or so! He died in March 1985, and Andropov's protégé, Mikhail Gorbachev, was made General Secretary. Gorbachev immediately cracked down again. Along with his campaign against corruption, Gorbachev also introduced his programs of perestroika and glasnost. Unfortunately, he had no clear conception initially of what the aim of such programs should be, except that he wanted to shake up Soviet society. But when a leader shakes up a society that has been very rigidly controlled, inevitably there are bound to be surprises. That is because in the process of transition from a strong to a weak state, lines of authority become undermined, and there is almost certain to be enormous confusion.

Confusion and Disorder

An analogy may help to explain why such a radical transaction can be so disruptive. When I was a child I went to a carnival that had a death-defying act. It consisted of a motorcyclist who would run his machine around the inside of a large wooden cylinder. He would build up enough speed so that eventually he became parallel to the ground, thereby defying gravity. In a sense, the Soviet system prior to Gorbachev was like that. Like the motorcyclist, the pre-Gorbachev leaders seemed to defy gravity. Yet there were relatively few problems as long as the Soviet Union maintained its momentum. On occasion, the motorcyclist would hit a bump and lose speed. Then he would fall because he could not really defy gravity. Similarly, the minute there is a radical halt in the affairs of a centrally planned system, the whole system is likely to fall into turmoil.

That is what began to happen when Gorbachev started perestroika and moved the Soviet system in a different way. The most radical change came in May 1987, when for the first time Gorbachev announced he was going to allow private trade, private businesses, and cooperatives. This was terribly confusing for the police. They no longer could decide in an instant if a business was legal or illegal. Their confusion was compounded by the fact that only the year before, in 1986, Gorbachev had taken just the opposite stance; he had banned all private trade. In order to sell anything, the seller had to prove that he himself had produced what he was selling. But how could anyone prove that he had produced the tomatoes he was selling? Trade was disrupted. The police had a wonderful time and cracked down with great glee. But after a few months Gorbachev reversed his course completely. No wonder there was enormous anxiety and public confusion!

What is intriguing, of course, is that both before and simultaneously with Russia, some other countries in Eastern Europe as well as China were making a similar transition. But they did it without this kind of trauma. How? In large measure it was because when the Chinese and the Poles—and, for that matter, the Hungarians and the Czechs— began their reforms, they did it by removing rather than imposing barriers to entry. Anyone who wanted to could open up a private business.

The Chinese, of course, began with agricultural reform that allowed the peasants to set up their own farms. What was important was that anybody who wanted to could break out of the collective farms (the communes). By 1982, almost everyone in China was operating their own farm (albeit on leased land). Most communes gradually disappeared. The government also allowed people to set up private businesses, even if it was no more than a corner stand. They relaxed other economic controls gradually; there was no shock therapy in China.

The East Europeans chose a different strategy. The difference in Eastern Europe was that most countries there had tolerated some private business activities all along. In the case of Poland, for example, 80 percent of the farms had never been collectivized; the peasants resisted it. The Polish peasants were not very efficient, but their farms were private and competitive. The private trade sector was not as large, but an estimated 15–20 percent of activity was in the hands of private traders. Moreover, when shock therapy was introduced in Poland in 1990, anybody who wanted to go into business was allowed, even encouraged, to do it. There were few restrictions.

Restrictions on Market Entry Helped the Mafia

This was very different from Russia. When Gorbachev said in May 1987 that he was going to allow private and cooperative business for the first time, he nonetheless imposed limits initially on those who decided to set up their own businesses. He was fearful that if private business was open to everybody, the state sector would collapse. And so he did it by stages. He initially limited the private sector to pensioners and students. Later he allowed the rest of the population to participate. To an economist, this was a restriction on entry, and such restrictions usually lead to problems.

The Gorbachev strategy inadvertently spawned a surge in the influence of the Mafia. Because of the entry restriction there were great opportunities for arbitrage. There were enormous disparities between state controls and market pressures. As a result, those few people who were allowed to open their own businesses often became millionaires overnight. In one instance, a small group of people began to make pantyhose. Pantyhose had generally been regarded by state planners as too unimportant to produce much of it. Taking advantage of the enormous unsatisfied demand, the new manufacturers became so rich that after about six months of production they closed down because they feared nobody would believe they had made their money honestly. They and others like them made so much money, they stood out. It was understandable that after having been deprived of wealth of this magnitude for seven decades they began to spend it. But there were also groups of thugs and racketeers who saw what was going on and realized that with a little muscle they could take a share of that wealth. Before long, the racketeers and the Mafia began to move in and, in a matter of months, they came to control 70 to 80 percent of the private sector. By the time Gorbachev and Boris Yeltsin opened the private sector up to everybody, the Mafia had a stranglehold and grew faster than the private sector. . . .

Many Russian government officials continue to insist that the government is needed to allocate property. Admittedly we have zoning laws in this country as well, but in the case of Russia, the buyer must often deal directly with the government in negotiations because the government continues to own most of the land. By contrast, in the West we assume the market will be used to allocate most of the nation's property. To the extent that the market is carrying out such functions, there is less room for bribes and corruption. It is probably impossible to eliminate all corruption. We still have to deal with regulatory officials like building inspectors, but for the most part, if the price of the property is freely and fairly determined by the buyer and the seller, there will be less reason or incentive to offer bribes. . . .

Consequences of Mafia Activity

What is the consequence of all this activity? As mentioned earlier, the Mafia encroaches on 70–80 percent of all business activity and is increasingly active in the government sector as well. It demands 10–20 percent of the gross revenue of business operations, not just the profit. Thus, whether or not a firm makes a profit is immaterial; the Mafia insists on its money even when there are losses. This means the costs of doing business are raised to at least 10–20 percent more than they otherwise would be.

The Russian Mafia is growing faster than business. It is stronger, in fact, than the government. If there is a commercial dispute, the parties are more likely to go to the Mafia for help; the government's enforcement abilities are usually ineffective. After all, the government even has difficulty collecting its taxes; the Mafia has no such trouble.

There is yet another impact on the economy. Because the Mafia has a strong interest in maintaining disequilibrium in the economy, it seeks to restrain markets, maintain monopolies, and obstruct economic reform. These monopolies seek to distort the economy and keep prices up and entry down. For example, various Mafia groups refuse to allow most of the country's private farmers access to farmers' markets. Even though only 5 percent of the country's farms are private, these farmers are viewed as a threat to the Mafia's monopoly control. Frustrated by their inability to find outlets for their output, a growing number of these newly privatized farms have been forced to close. In fact, by late 1994, the number of private farmers giving up their farms exceeded those opening new ones. . . .

Pressure on foreigners is increasing. Estée Lauder, the cosmetics firm, opened up a retail store in Moscow in 1991. In 1993, the Russian manager forced the Americans out. The same thing happened to the American owners of the Subway Sandwiches franchise in St. Petersburg. . . .

Attempts at Reform

Is there a solution to this kind of problem? Because the Mafia is so pervasive, the solutions, if there are any, will not come easily. There may come a time when the general public becomes so angry that it rises up and throws out the existing government and demands a stronger one. Such a reaction, however, does not seem imminent. That is partly because the Russian people are slow to respond. In describing Russians, we always say that they tend to be much more patient, much more tolerant of abuse, than other nationalities. Sometimes that is good because otherwise there would be more violence. But in some sense, if the Russians were more responsive they might suffer fewer abuses.

So what can be done? Appointing special commissions and giving more money to the police will help, but it will not solve the problem in Russia any more than it will in the United States. Opening new jails may help, but it also is not going to be the solution. Instead, something must be done to eliminate the underlying economic stimulus to crime. This is how the United States curbed the influence of the mob in the 1930s. We reduced Al Capone's power by confronting him with more competition. We ended prohibition and legalized the sale of alcohol. Almost overnight, there were too many outlets to control.

In a similar way, that was exactly what happened in Poland and China. There simply was no way the Mafia in those countries could control the number of farmers and retailers. The private sector grew faster than the Mafia. Yeltsin almost adopted this approach. On January 29, 1992, he said that anyone could sell anything he or she wanted on the country's street corners. Soon the streets were filled with women standing shoulder to shoulder selling a bottle of shampoo, a bottle of vodka, or a piece of silverware. There were so many, the Mafia could not control them. This made them angry because it looked like they might lose their monopoly hold on the markets. By contrast, they were able to maintain control of the more established street sellers who returned to the same location each day and sold from card tables. The Mafia had no trouble forcing them to pay tribute. The average "tax" was fifty dollars a month. When I asked some of those selling from card tables in St. Petersburg how the Mafia was able to keep track of them, I was told that the Mafia sent out checkers twice a day to conduct a census to see who was there and who was paying them money.

If the sellers have no card table but instead sell from their coat pockets or a knapsack, they can easily melt into the crowd and are therefore much harder for the Mafia to control. In response to the opportunity presented by Yeltsin in January 1992, new mobile entrepreneurs filled the streets around the Bolshoi Theater and Detskii Mir department store in Moscow, standing in a shoulder-to-shoulder phalanx with their wares in their hands. Not surprisingly, the Mafia did all it could to fight these new opportunists and decided that one way to force them off the streets was to create a public backlash. The streets were left uncleaned and unlike the rest of Moscow soon became unsightly.

Eventually this had the desired effect. Ordinary Russians were angered that a cultural symbol like the Bolshoi Theater had been turned into a flea market. Allowing sellers there was *ne kulturnyi* (uncultured). As a consequence, in May 1992, the controls were reinstated, the women traders were driven off the streets, and once more prospective sellers had to obtain licenses, which put them right back into the hands of the bureaucracy and Mafia.

Something similar has even happened to the kiosks that began to appear throughout Moscow in 1993. Mayor Yuri Luzhkov decreed they were unsightly and ordered that selling outlets should be largely restricted to stores located in buildings. In mid-1994, he and the city council decreed that almost half of Moscow's outdoor kiosks must be closed down. That is one reason many entrepreneurs report that it is harder today to open up a private business than it was two or three years ago. This restriction on entry serves to strengthen, not weaken the Mafia's control.

Open the Markets

How can Russia introduce a large number of new competitors? Yeltsin will again have to decree that anyone who wants to can begin selling without formal approval. Those who want to sell should be required to do no more than send in a postcard to the regulating authorities. Undoubtedly there will be resistance. After all, even Prime Minister Victor Chernomyrdin declared in January 1994 that "Russia will not become a bazaar economy."

If the Chinese had taken a similar attitude, instead of growing at rates of 12 or 13 percent a year and with noncentral-government factories generating more than 60 percent of the country's industrial production, China would probably be where Russia is today. Instead, Chinese traders were allowed to stand on the street corners; eventually they moved to tables, and then to stores, and then on to wholesale operations, and finally to manufacturing. They began, however, with a bazaar economy. If it is beneath the country's dignity to begin that way, the process will take much longer and may give rise to malignant institutions like the Mafia. . . .

An effort should also be made whenever possible to challenge Mafia domination in order to show that it is vulnerable. Cartels ultimately fail, and so too, sooner or later, will the Russian Mafia. But it may require strategic targeting. For example, it would be impressive if the Mafia's control over Sheremetievo Airport could be broken. Mafia control explains why it is impossible to find transportation into Moscow from the airport for less than $60. There have been instances where Mafia-coordinated drivers have been able to charge as much as $100. There is a public bus route, but it is inconvenient and it does not go to the center of Moscow. To break through the Mafia's cartel and show that it is vulnerable, an effort should be made to provide frequent bus service, just as Carey Transportation or Grayline Bus Service do at most American airports. Realistically, it is unlikely that many private companies will undertake such an effort in Russia. They would open themselves to retaliation. The solution instead would be for the Russian army to establish such a service—in a convoy, if necessary. Once the Mafia is challenged and shown to be vulnerable, the odds are that private vendors will then be more willing to take over from the army.

There must also be a return to a certain amount of government control, especially the introduction of effective anticrime measures. As indicated earlier, this in itself will not be enough, but it can help. At the same time, more control does not necessarily mean increasing government regulation. For example, it is essential that licenses, regulations, and permits be reduced to a minimum. The minute there are regulations on a building, for example, the building inspectors will be there with open palms. This also means an end to the continual introduction of new taxes on what seems to be a week-to-week basis. Such regulations and taxes offer too much room for bribery and illegal influence peddling. . . .

The Mafia Is Entrenched

The Russian Mafia has become so ubiquitous that it will not be easy to dislodge it. This means that, short of a harsh political crackdown, its effects will be felt for the foreseeable future. As a consequence, economic reform in Russia will be handicapped and distorted. Eventually some of the dominant Mafia groups may seek to pass on their gains to their children. This could bring with it a reduction in violence and a semblance of normality. The odds are, however, that even if more benign, the Russian Mafia will make it difficult for Russia to attract the investment, both domestic and foreign, enjoyed by less afflicted societies.

To repeat, the Russian Mafia will not be easy to dislodge. There even is fear now that the Mafia may come to dominate the political scene. Because Russian law provides immunity from criminal prosecution for elected members of legislative groups, approximately eighty candidates with criminal records declared their candidacy for the December 1995 parliamentary elections. Victory was all but assured as potential rivals were either bought off or physically threatened off the ballot.

This plus their economic inroads means that short of a draconian political crackdown, the Mafia's effects will be felt for the foreseeable future.

RUSSIAN GANGSTERS BENEFIT RUSSIA'S ECONOMY

Edward M. Luttwak

While organized crime certainly has negative effects on Russia's economy, it provides many benefits as well, writes Edward Luttwak, a senior fellow at the Center for Strategic and International Studies in Washington, D.C. According to the author, the mobsters in Russia are simply entrepreneurs doing what they must in order to survive hard economic times. Furthermore, Luttwak maintains, the Russian economy benefits much more from some Mafia practices than it does from the currently ineffectual government. The Russian Mafia provides many services that the government cannot, he says, and in some cases may be private business's only defense against corrupt bureaucrats and police.

It is now conventional wisdom that "mafia" extortion and official corruption of every sort are inflicting much damage on the Russian economy. In one widely cited estimate, crooked officials and plain gangsters are said to have sent some $100 billion into foreign bank accounts since 1990, thus depriving the Russian economy of more hard currency than the sum total of post-1990 Western aid. The unappealing beneficiaries of the new economic order range from violent thugs with platinum-blond molls and BMWs to sleek ex-Communists in Armani suits with Vienna bank accounts, Manhattan apartments and good friends in the Kremlin.

Far more numerous are the less obviously criminal and much less glamorous "biznessmen"—thousands of them—who traffic in state-owned raw materials; who help thieving state managers transfer public property to personal ownership; who collaborate with foreign adventurers to smuggle consumer goods in and weapons out; or who simply buy and sell without bothering to pay taxes.

The intense popular resentment of both gangsters and tycoons certainly threatens Russia's economic liberalization very directly. At the next opportunity, a majority—not just a substantial minority as in the 1996 parliamentary elections—may decide to vote for go-slow Communists or even hard-line Stalinists. But while the political threat is

Reprinted from "What the Mafia's Good For," by Edward M. Luttwak, *The Washington Post National Weekly Edition*, February 12–18, 1996, by permission of the author.

real enough, the conventional wisdom that the mafia is bad for Russia is, in purely economic terms, all wrong.

To begin with, it overlooks the natural evolution of the capitalist animal. The fat cows that populate advanced economies—stable, highly capitalized firms that offer good employment, pay their taxes, invest in new plants, develop technologies and contribute to charities and culture—were not born as such. They started out as lean and hungry wolves that accumulated capital by seizing profitable market opportunities—often by killing off competitors in ways that today's antitrust regulators would not tolerate—and by cutting costs in every way possible—not excluding all the tax avoidance they could get away with.

Yet there are times when conditions are too harsh even for the wolves of commerce. When countries and their economies undergo truly drastic transformations, as Germany, Italy and Japan did because of the destruction of World War II—and as Russia is now doing—only the most ruthless hyenas can survive and prosper.

The years after 1945 saw the emergence of many of the dynamic industrial firms that now fill the landscape of Emilia-Romagna in Italy, most Japanese real-estate fortunes that long ago diversified into industry and finance and not a few of the businesses that propelled West Germany's rise to prosperity. Black-marketeering, predatory buying, sub-standard manufacture, and efficient stealing (but the polite expression was to "organize") enabled these hyena-entrepreneurs to accumulate the capital that enabled them to become honest wolves, and eventually productive cows.

Had the respective police forces been effective enough to round up all the hyenas and lock them up, the economic recovery of West Germany, Italy and Japan would have been much slower, and many of the successful entrepreneurs of the 1950s and 1960s would never have been able to get their start.

Productive Theft

All this is true of the Russian economy—only more so, because in Russia simple theft can be relatively productive. It is often forgotten that the still-intact Soviet Union produced more electricity per capita than Italy (5,986 kilowatts vs. 3,650); more steel per capita than the United States (557 kilos per person vs. 382); more mineral fertilizer than Japan (119 kilos vs. 12); and a respectable 70 kilos of meat per capita (as compared to 32 for Japan, 63 for Italy, 96 for West Germany and 120 for the United States). Yet, at the same time, the Soviet standard of living was almost incomparably lower than those of France, Italy, Japan, West Germany or the United States.

Why? The huge cost of Soviet military ambitions was one partial explanation. But the larger answer is that by 1989 the Soviet economic system was no longer just inefficient. In many ways, it was positively destructive. Perfectly good Uzbek cotton that had real value—it could be sold on the world market—was made into shirts so poorly cut and so ugly that not even Soviet consumers would buy them. Hence all the spinning, weaving, dyeing, cutting and sewing actually removed value from the raw material, turning virgin cotton into the equivalent of scrap rag for papermaking.

The same was true of Soviet leather, wool, wood, plastics and of all sorts of other inputs that went into Soviet light industry. Likewise, the steel and cement not reserved for military use that ended up in Soviet building projects was, in effect, lost for several years because the pace of construction was so extraordinarily slow (five to seven years even for standard housing). And quite a lot was lost forever, as unsheltered cement bags solidified and steel rods rusted away.

In such a counterproductive economy, stealing can be highly productive. Theft certainly increased the overall standard of living of the Soviet Union. Cotton and other light-industry raw materials diverted from official channels could be made into useful products by domestic or illegal craft workers. Construction materials stolen from the interminable official projects provided the means to build many houses and dachas with illegal or do-it-yourself labor. Gasoline removed from state trucks that often drove about uselessly could provide much-needed fuel for private car owners. And the stolen fertilizer and farm tools used to cultivate private plots produced much of the Soviet Union's food supply.

The Mafia's Indispensable Services

Inevitably, thieves and consumers could only be brought together by a functioning illegal market. That market, in turn, could only be operated by criminals who were sufficiently organized to do the job, i.e., the mafia. Because bureaucrats and policemen had to be paid off at every stage of acquisition, transportation and distribution, it followed that the mafia had to collect "protection," i.e., its own unofficial taxes. This was a crypto-capitalist system that emerged in view fully ready to function in sector after sector, in place after place, as the economic liberalization progressed after 1990. Many, if not most of the Russians, who bitterly complain about the mafia today had greatly relied on its indispensable services during Soviet times.

This is not to say that the pervasive criminalization of the Russian economy does not impose real costs. It does.

The purchasing power of an impoverished population is further reduced, because "protection" fees increase prices. Efficient private-enterprise firms suffer from the unfair competition of less efficient rivals backed by corrupt officials. And, as anywhere else, tax evasion must ultimately be offset by inflationary money-printing or higher taxes inimical to growth.

But in one crucial respect, organized crime remains a very beneficial force: It is the only counterweight to the great number of firms backed by corrupt officials that now engage in ruthless monopolistic practices.

At the local level, ex-Soviet officials who now own shops, restaurants, hotels, and workshops do not hesitate to use their old party connections to drive competitors out of business—by arranging the imposition of huge taxes and fines, by hygiene inspections followed by shutdown orders and by the arbitrary possibilities of obtaining redress from the overburdened Russian courts, which have barely started to deal with commercial and fiscal matters. Only the local criminal mafia may be able and willing to resist the ex-party mafia (if the two are not one and the same) and at a price, of course.

On a larger scale, genuinely private industrial firms—usually joint-ventures with foreign partners—are now often confronted by the extortionate pricing of officially-backed suppliers, especially for natural gas, oil, coal and electricity. Liberalization has created many natural monopolies, but there is still no functioning anti-monopoly system, nor any mechanism to regulate utility prices. Again, the only possible counterweight is organized crime.

Even the outflow of capital for which the mafia is blamed (though legitimate business is just as guilty) is now being reversed. The U.N.'s Economic Commission for Europe has released its statistics for foreign direct investment in the Russian Federation. The grand total, at $3.3 billion, amounts to very little, of course, and is the best evidence for the nationalists' claim that the world is indifferent to Russia's economic plight. Most revealing, however, is the country-by-country breakdown of flight capital.

By far the biggest single source of direct investment in Russia is Switzerland with more than $1 billion. The United States, for all the talk of big oil company investments, accounts for only $750 million in foreign investment. Third on the list is Singapore with $230 million. One wonders who are the upstanding Swiss and Singaporean businessmen courageously betting on Russian economic recovery—until one recalls that banks in Switzerland and Singapore are the favorite destinations of Russia's mafia and other flight capital. It seems that after sanitizing their money, and giving it a safe foreign identity, Russians—mafia included—are more willing to invest in Russia than all the famous German, Japanese or Korean corporations whose investment promises have been so widely trumpeted.

One day, Russia will acquire a functioning system of commercial law, administrative and fiscal courts that can actually protect citizens from the demands of arbitrary, corrupt government officials, and can even impose anti-monopoly safeguards. Only then will it be safe to unleash the police against the mafia, to stop the social and political damage it is certainly inflicting. In the meantime, organized crime is the only force interposed between the new economic boyars and the defenseless consumers and entrepreneurs of Russia.

THE RUSSIAN MAFIA IS NOT ENCOURAGING CAPITALISM

Annelise Anderson

In the following selection, economist Annelise Anderson takes issue with claims that Mafia activities in post-Soviet Russia are similar to the "rough-and-tumble" capitalism of America in the 1800s. There was no organized crime in the early United States, argues Anderson, and the belief that the American frontier was violent and lawless is inaccurate. There are other differences between today's Russia and America's frontier West, she writes, such as the extent of government corruption. Anderson maintains that the current situation in Russia will not simply evolve into capitalism; left to itself, the Mafia will instead act to reduce competition and inhibit economic growth. Anderson is a Senior Research Fellow at the Hoover Institution on War, Revolution and Peace, a think tank based at Stanford University in California.

Some Russians and Americans hold the view that crime in Russia, especially organized crime, is simply an "early stage" of capitalism, implying that conditions in Russia today are like those in some earlier era in the United States, perhaps the era of the frontier West or that of the so-called robber barons. "Some Russians argue," Stephen Handelman (1993) says, "that a period of lawlessness is part of the price every society pays for radical economic change. Pointing to examples as disparate as the development of the American West and the transformation of Latin American economies, they suggest that without a certain amount of robber-baron-style entrepreneurship, the consumer goods in most Russian cities would disappear."

"Russia right now is a bit like America west of Dodge City in the mid-1800s," according to George Melloan (1992). "Today's corruption" writes Michael Scammell, a professor of Russian literature at Cornell, "seems to be characteristic of a period of profound change and upheaval, when Russian society is in the stage (to paraphrase Marx) of the primitive accumulation of capital." A Russian friend told Scammell that "the situation should be compared not with profit-making in today's America but with the rough-and-tumble of America

Adapted from "The Red Mafia: Legacy of Communism," by Annelise Anderson, in *Economic Transition in Eastern Europe and Russia: Realities of Reform*, edited by Edward P. Lazear, with the permission of the publisher, Hoover Institution Press. Copyright 1995 by the Board of Trustees of the Leland Stanford Junior University.

of a century ago, and the new entrepreneurs should be compared with the robber barons of those days" (Scammell 1993).

But the Russian mafia phenomenon and other peculiarities of economic life in Russia have little similarity to conditions in the nineteenth-century United States or to any "early" stages of capitalism.

The Rule of Law, Not Gangs

An important characteristic of the United States from its formation (and before) was a respect for the rule of law. "For eighteenth-century Americans, like the English writers they admired, liberty demanded the rule of law" writes historian Pauline Maier (1978). Furthermore, property law and contract law had been developing in Great Britain for centuries, and the legal system of the United States drew heavily on British common law. William E. Nelson (1975), in a study of the legal system in Massachusetts between 1760 and 1830, found substantial changes in the law on relationships between debtors and creditors and in contract and property law, generally in the direction of facilitating commerce and competition as Massachusetts became less agrarian and more industrialized. But these developments proceeded in an orderly way through legislation and court cases on the basis of colonial and common law.

As the settlers moved West they sought to adopt the legal codes established in other states and create legal institutions in the new territories and states. Nevertheless, law enforcement was stretched thin on the frontier and the Western states. Sometimes local officials could not handle the problems confronting them, and help from the statewide law enforcement authorities, depending as it did on the state's priorities, was not always available. There were interstate criminal gangs as early as the eighteenth century and, especially in frontier areas, horse theft and counterfeiting of private bank notes; after the Civil War gangs robbed trains and banks (Brown 1969).

The response to this "absence of effective law and order in a frontier region" was not the gang as a primitive state but a uniquely American response: the vigilante group of citizens who took the law into their own hands. Richard Brown notes that members of these groups were leading citizens in their communities and often well-known public figures. He sees their purpose as establishing in frontier regions the community structure of older areas "along with the values of property, law, and order." Some of these groups functioned well; others did not.

Brown differentiates the vigilante group from the lynch mob—"an unorganized, spontaneous, ephemeral mob which comes together briefly to do its fatal work and then breaks up." In fact it was not until the mid–nineteenth century that lynch mob came to imply illegal hanging or killing. Before that, from its origin in the late 1760s, it had meant whipping or other physical punishment for real or alleged crimes without due process of law. Nevertheless, like the vigilante groups, the motivation of lynch mobs was anticrime and supportive of what was understood to be the law except in the South, where it was racially motivated and the black victims had often committed no offense.

Thus there was no mafia phenomenon in the early United States. No "gangs as primitive states" emerged. Scholars are also beginning to question the popular assumption that the Western frontier was violent and lawless. A study of two typical frontier mining towns (Bodie, California, in the 1870s and 1880s and Aurora, Nevada, in the 1860s) by Roger McGrath (1989) found that robbery, theft and burglary were rare and that bank robbery, rape, racial violence, and serious juvenile crime were nonexistent. A considerable number of homicides occurred, but most were the result of fights between willing combatants—men who were "brave, strong, reckless, and violent."

It was not until the early twentieth century that "centralized, citywide criminal operations under the control of a single 'syndicate' or 'organization' began to take shape in New York." Urban criminal gangs appeared in the decades before the Civil War but were "limited in significance and restricted to ethnic 'slum' neighborhoods" (Brown 1969).

Bribery and Government Corruption

Bribery was not an institutionalized practice in the early United States, but neither was it rare. The Constitution identified bribery as one of the reasons for impeachment (the others being treason and the catchall, other high crimes and misdemeanors). Revelations of bribery brought forth public outrage, and laws were passed relating to conflict of interest and bribery. John T. Noonan (1984) recounts the history of bribery and antibribery legislation in the United States as well as the writings of journalists and novelists about bribery, the general thrust of which is that the public found bribery and corruption severely objectionable. By the 1960s the United States, "unlike any previous society," had "statutes comprehensively extending the criminal law of bribery to almost every class and occupation." With the Foreign Corrupt Practices Act of 1977, the United States "for the first time in the history of the world . . . made it criminal to corrupt the officials of another country."

It is possible to compare the extent of antibribery legislation in Russia with that in the United States at different times in history, but quantifying the extent of bribery is another matter. Certainly bribery was extensive in the United States in the era of big-city machine politics. "Where the voters, the legislature, or the newspapers of New York needed to be won, [corrupt political boss William] Tweed was a bribegiver. Where the city had a say, Tweed took. . . . Bribery is central," says Noonan.

But any comparison or any attempts at quantification is overwhelmed by the fact that in the early United States and even until the

Second World War, government expenditures—at all levels—were small relative to the size of the economy, and regulatory controls minor, so that whatever the level of corruption, its effect on the economy was limited. Most of the economy proceeded unhindered by authorities at either the federal, state, or local levels.

Changing technology and economic growth provided opportunities for business fraud and dishonesty in the nineteenth and early twentieth centuries. Changing technology is always a source of new kinds of crime, but law enforcement and legislation continually adapt to changing technology. Today the challenge comes from computers and electronic property. The question is not a "stage" of capitalism but the ability to respond to change with appropriate legislation and law enforcement—and appropriate judicial decisions—by building on existing concepts of contract, property, and commercial law. Again, commitment to the rule of law and substantial consensus on what the law should accomplish have characterized the United States since its founding. It is also far easier to deal with business fraud if the authorities are not themselves involved in corrupt practices.

Other Points of Contrast

The early United States differed from Russia today in a number of other important ways.

The Banking System. The banking system of the early United States had its ups and downs but on the whole served developing farming and commercial interests well. Banks were privately owned, although regulated by state legislatures. In Russia, by contrast, few banks are truly privately owned. Most are partially or entirely owned by state-owned enterprises, the central bank, or ministries, which have powers left over from their role in the communist era. Writing about how things work, Bill Thomas and Charles Sutherland (1992) say this about Russian banks: "Bankers control business assets by approving (or disapproving) quarterly budgets that have to be sent in long before any withdrawal. And even then, getting them to okay a request often has less to do with the soundness of the budget than the size of the accompanying bribe." Other sources of financing—the capital markets—developed in the early United States, as well, and thus the dependence of business on government as a source of funds was minimal.

The Interstate Commerce Clause. For the economy, one of the unique aspects of the U.S. Constitution was the combination of decentralization of authority—the central government was relatively weak—and the limitations it placed on the powers of state authorities through the interstate commerce clause. The result was a considerable limitation on the influence of government economy and a check on the powers of state governments through people and businesses' ability to move to competing jurisdictions.

Taxation. Taxes were low by today's standards, reflecting the low level of government spending. There was no income tax until 1913. Businesses paid no payroll taxes. The federal government collected only customs duties and excise taxes on tobacco and alcoholic beverages (Webber and Wildavsky 1986). The low level of taxation for much of the nation's history may be responsible for the tradition of voluntary compliance and for the low level of corruption of tax authorities.

In addition, the nineteenth-century United States was a country with a low median age, a minimum bureaucracy, few regulations, virtually no welfare state, a weak central government, capital inflows rather than capital flight, and courts that could draw on the common law to deal with economic change.

Criminals, Not Capitalists

In sum, there is little support for the view that the fraud, violence, and development of mafias in Russia are simply an early stage of capitalism. They have no counterpart in the early history of the United States and have arisen instead from the legacy of the communist era: excessive bureaucratic regulation, massive illegal markets, and, with the demise of the Communist Party, a vacuum of power engendered by confusion in the legal code and unsureness about what should and should not be legal.

These conditions are not an early stage of capitalism but an early stage of organized crime, when gangs abound, compete for territories and markets, and are especially violent. As some competitors are eliminated (often with the complicity of law enforcement), spheres of influence are established, and future gang wars arise primarily when there are new markets to contest.

An appealing feature of the early stage of capitalism argument is that time and the normal course of development will provide the cure. Unfortunately this is not the case. Mafias tend to be extraordinarily persistent, probably because the governments that control law enforcement are themselves beneficiaries of the underworld through corruption or other benefits provided by the mafia organizations. . . .

The greatest risk of the mafia phenomenon in Russia is that an entrenched alliance between central or local officials and mafia groups will prevent competition in many markets and reduce the benefits of the fledgling market economy. Theft from state-owned enterprises and export for personal gain will continue and perhaps accelerate. More serious is control over market entry in legitimate businesses to create competition with state-owned enterprises or other private enterprises. The means to limit entry is extensive, ranging from demands for excessive bribes to control of permits and licenses, enforcement of detailed regulations, and violence. Significant in this mix is control of the banking system and thus enterprises through the banking system. The primary objective of law enforcement in the economic arena should therefore be the encouragement and protection of genuine competition.

References

Brown, Richard Maxwell. "Historical Patterns of Violence in America." In Hugh Davis Graham and Ted Robert Curr, eds. *Violence in America: Historical and Comparative Perspectives: A Report to the National Commission on the Causes and Prevention of Violence*. New York: New American Library, 1969, pp. 43–80.

Handelman, Stephen. "Why Capitalism and the Mafiya Mean Business." *New York Times Magazine*, January 24, 1993, pp. 12–50.

Maier, Pauline. "Popular Uprisings and Civil Authority in Eighteenth-Century America." In Lawrence M. Friedman and Harry N. Scheiber, eds., *American Law and the Constitution Order: Historical Perspectives*. Cambridge, Mass.: Harvard University Press, 1978, pp. 69–84.

McGrath, Roger D. "Violence and Lawlessness on the Western Frontier." In Ted Robert Curr, ed., *Violence in America*, vol. 1, The History of Crime. Newbury Park, Calif.: Sage Publications, 1989, pp. 122–45.

Melloan, George. "Steering Clear of Russia's Mafias." *Wall Street Journal*, March 16, 1992, p. A9.

Nelson, William E. *Americanization of the Common Law: The Impact of Legal Change on Massachusetts Society, 1760–1830*. Cambridge, Mass.: Harvard University Press, 1975.

Noonan, John T., Jr. *Bribes*. New York: Macmillan Publishing Company, 1984.

Scammell, Michael. "What's Good for the Mafia Is Good for Russia." *New York Times*, December 26, 1993, p. IIE.

Thomas, Bill, and Charles Sutherland. *Red Rape: Adventure Capitalism in the New Russia*. New York: Dutton, 1992.

Webber, Carolyn, and Aaron Wildavsky. *A History of Taxation and Expenditure in the Western World*. New York: Simon and Schuster, 1986.

THE NUCLEAR THREAT

Seymour M. Hersh

One of the most frightening aspects of Russia's organized crime problem is the possibility that criminal groups might gain access to the former Soviet Union's stockpile of nuclear materials and weapons. Potentially enormous profits provide an incentive for the Russian Mafia to become involved in nuclear trafficking, says Pulitzer Prize–winning investigative reporter Seymour M. Hersh. Hersh maintains that safeguards in Russia are dangerously lax: Corruption in the army has resulted in the sale of guns and other weapons to militants and criminal groups. American law enforcement has dangerously underestimated the risk of similar trafficking occurring in nuclear weapons, he warns.

A myriad of official statistics and publications describe the extent of criminal penetration of Russia. But among them there is special significance to one recent and until now unpublicized U.S. study: an analysis of "the Russian mafia" compiled in 1993 by the Department of Energy's Office of Threat Assessment. The office provides the U.S. intelligence community with specific analyses of the engineering equipment and high-tech data available to those nations around the world suspected of building—or wanting to build—nuclear-weapons arsenals. It has also begun a study of Russian control over nuclear warheads and fissionable materials—clear evidence that at least some in Washington are worried that organized crime is threatening Russian nuclear security.

Collecting Intelligence

The DOE's mafia study, officials at the department say, was the first step in what has become a large effort to collect intelligence on the potential nuclear threat from organized crime in Russia and the former Soviet republics. "Discussion of nuclear proliferation today," the report said, "must cover the risk of criminal proliferation." The report cited evidence showing that in 1991 about 4,000 organized-crime groups or gangs were operating inside Russia. The study included other findings:

- One quarter of the organized-crime groups are believed to have

Excerpted from "The Wild East," by Seymour M. Hersh, *The Atlantic Monthly*, June 1994, by permission of the author.

ties to similar criminal groups abroad or in the former Soviet republics. A significant number of the groups have merged some or all activities with corrupt government and police officials.

- Forty percent of private businesses and 60 percent of state-owned companies have been corrupted by organized crime.
- The Russian mafia may own half the nation's commercial banks and 50 to 80 percent of the shops, hotels, warehouses, depots, and service industries in Moscow. A substantial portion of the commercial district in St. Petersburg is similarly in the control of criminal elements, with businessmen being forced to pay 15 percent of their income for protection.
- Corruption in the Russian army is widespread. In February 1993 Russian defense officials announced that they planned to discipline 3,000 officers for questionable business practices and that forty-six general officers faced court-martial proceedings on corruption charges. The illicit "movement of military materiel through organized crime channels has resulted in the spread of former Soviet guns and weapons throughout the FSU [former Soviet Union] arming militants, nationalists, and criminals—and the world at large." Russian armories are physically deteriorating and are guarded by soldiers whose indifference makes them vulnerable to criminal elements.
- Organized crime now uses high-tech communications equipment, including fax machines, shortwave radios, and cellular phones, far more sophisticated than anything used by Russian law-enforcement officials.

So far there has been no documented case of the successful theft or illicit sale of a nuclear warhead or enriched materials from a Russian or former-republic stockpile. Despite many press reports of illicit sales and attempted smuggling of nuclear materials, some of the men now responsible for the Clinton Administration's policies have insisted in interviews with me that since there is no clear-cut evidence, there is no crisis. "Worry isn't a policy," says a senior State Department official. "It's a judgment call. Anybody who says we are not engaged in a risk is crazy. As a statesman, all you can do is try to make it come out right." Another official, who feels the burden of the economic chaos in Russia, told me resignedly, "Unless you are able to come up with a credible story that a warhead has made it out of Russia, it's not particularly important."

Nonetheless there is powerful evidence that organized crime in the former Soviet Union has been systematically seeking access to the nuclear stockpiles, with their potential for huge profit. There is also evidence that the Russian government is unable to account for all its bombs and all its weapons-grade uranium and plutonium. The nuclear weapons most at risk are Russia's tactical nuclear warheads, many of which are believed to carry an explosive force far greater than that of the atomic bomb dropped on Hiroshima in 1945. These warheads, designed for use in artillery shells, aircraft bombs, land mines, and torpedoes, are stored under less-than-secure conditions on many military bases.

Dr. Thomas B. Cochran, a senior scientist at the nonprofit Natural Resources Defense Council (NRDC) and one of the leading U.S. experts on Soviet nuclear issues, explained in an interview that Washington has been preoccupied with negotiating a reduction in the former Soviet Union's strategic forces—the huge intercontinental ballistic missiles capable of hitting targets in the United States. The destruction of most of the launchers for those missiles, which are placed in Russia and three former Soviet republics—Ukraine, Belarus, and Kazakstan—will be verified under current U.S.-Russian strategic-disarmament agreements. But, Cochran said, there is no U.S.-Russian mechanism in place for independently verifying the destruction of the warheads for the strategic delivery systems.

Counting Bombs

In mid-1992 the Central Intelligence Agency, telling Congress that it had only a "highly uncertain estimate" of the size of the Russian tactical nuclear arsenal, estimated Russia's warhead count at 30,000 for both strategic and tactical weapons, with a margin of error of 5,000 warheads. "We don't know how many warheads they've destroyed," Cochran told me. "In fact, we don't know within thousands how many warheads they had. And we don't know within hundreds how many they're destroying in any given year. We also don't know how much fissile material"—weapons-grade uranium or plutonium—"the Russians have within hundreds of tons." In mid-1992 the Bush Administration agreed to buy 500 tons of highly enriched uranium from the Russian stockpile "without knowing whether they have seven hundred or twelve hundred tons," Cochran said. The major piece of legislation that Congress has passed on the Russian nuclear issue is aimed at ensuring the safe transport, storage, and destruction of nuclear weapons. The law, signed into effect by President Bush in 1991, provides funds for secure containers and improved safety conditions on the Russian railway cars that ferry the weapons. "The legislation is a joke," Cochran said, referring to its implementation. "For example, it gives them training on how to respond to a nuclear accident but provides nothing for cleanup afterwards. They've already had two horrible nuclear accidents"—one in 1957, at a plutonium-production plant in the Urals, and the other at Chernobyl, in 1986—"and instead of helping clean them up, we're giving them training on how to handle the next one."

Cochran said that his frustration over the lack of nuclear intelligence is heightened by the fact that he and his colleagues in the NRDC were rebuffed by the Bush Administration in 1991 when they proposed a joint program to find, identify, and tag all nuclear weapons in Russian and American stockpiles. The White House rejected the idea because Russian military leaders, in offering full access to their tactical and strategic nuclear storage areas, were insisting on reciprocity inside the United States. "My belief is that many people in the Defense Department and White House thought, 'We won the Cold War and we don't want any Russian oversight over our arsenal,'" Cochran said. "As a consequence, we don't have any oversight over their arsenal."

The NRDC's proposed joint operation had the added advantage, Cochran pointed out, of giving out-of-work and out-of-money Russian nuclear scientists and technicians something to do in lieu of selling their expertise to the highest foreign bidder. Clinton's election did not solve the problem, Cochran added angrily: the U.S. government still has not advanced a coherent program for verifying the elimination of Russian nuclear warheads and tracking the ultimate disposition of tons of surplus weapons-grade materials. "And [in 1994], three years after the Russians agreed to do joint research on the destruction of nuclear warheads," Cochran told me, "we have nothing. I think control of warheads and fissile material in Russia should be the number-one national-security issue for America."

Keeping Quiet

In subsequent interviews many well-informed national-security officials said privately that they agreed with Cochran but questioned the value of raising the issue in public. A top administrator of one agency involved with nuclear matters told me that there is "a lot of legitimate and deep concern" inside the Clinton Administration about organized crime in Russia and the vulnerability of the Soviet tactical nuclear arsenal. "Could a Russian weapons storage area be raided?" the official asked rhetorically. "Yes. By Western standards they are minimally defended."

At this point the official, who has discussed many other sensitive issues with me in the past, suggested that I not publish my information on the link between organized crime and Russian nuclear-weapons security. "I'm a very strong supporter of freedom of the press," the official said. "But even an investigative reporter would support the notion that you don't yell 'Fire' in a theater."

"Let me put it this way," another well-informed national-security analyst told me. "We're gambling that Yeltsin can somehow keep control of the most important things most of the time. It's a gamble imposed on us not by our own policy but by a course of events beyond our control. Yes, our public posture is Pollyannaish, but there is some value in not panicking the whole world. The question is whether we're in the process of fooling ourselves—whether we're screwing things up. After all, a government that can't figure out how to deal with safety on the streets in Washington should not try to deal in Russia. On the other hand, by turning a blind eye to this I hope we're not encouraging someone to think he's sitting on a pot of gold." This official said that he, too, could see an argument for not writing about the nuclear-theft risk posed by organized crime: "The very last thing we should do is provide free advertising to people who are thinking about it."

Ineffective Russian Security

Despite his doubts, the official went on to summarize some immediate security problems. The essential concern is that the new Russian government, weakened as it is, no longer controls its territory and its people. "It's not even close to what the old Soviet Union had," the official said. Because of rigid internal controls, the Soviet nuclear establishment had no need for extensive physical barriers at the weapons-storage sites. "Back in the old days," the official explained, "the lack of physical safeguards didn't matter. Even if someone had shot off a lock [and seized military goods], the government would send the KGB after them. The basic assumption was that physical security was backed up by overall control.

"If you go to a typical U.S. installation with sensitive stuff, it's hard to get on and off the base—lots of guards—but you don't have locks on every door. The assumption is that no one is going to get on the base. In the old Soviet Union the really tough perimeter fence was the one around the border. What mattered was that the KGB had two divisions, with helicopters and all that. And now that's gone away and the Russians don't have the resources to retrofit the installations with the kind of protection you'd want. None of this is a secret to us, but I don't think there's any advantage in talking about it."

"Would they let us help them?" The official answered his rhetorical question with a noncommittal shrug. "If they asked for help, would we give it? Of course. The fact is that our options are limited."

Paul A. Goble, who resigned from the State Department in 1991 as the special adviser on Soviet nationality issues, explained to me that the notion of limited options is heightened by the American "assumption that in any given territory the strongest force is the government." He said, "It's reassuring for our leaders to think other leaders have more power than they actually do." In Russia, he added, "we're watching the death of a state." Goble, now a senior associate at the Carnegie Endowment for International Peace, was willing to say what no one in the Clinton Administration wants said: "I'm convinced that if I had twenty-five million dollars, I could buy a warhead and the launch codes.". . .

Underestimating the Criminals

Questions about the extent of organized crime in Russia are being raised these days. . . . "I think in many areas of the former Soviet

Union—not in Russia yet—the state is so weak that organized crime is capable of control," says Paul Goble, who served as a CIA analyst before joining the State Department. . . .

Russia's strong central government and its internal police force, the KGB, have simply disappeared, and no other state institution has replaced them. . . .

"Organized crime," one fully informed Treasury Department economist told me, "is now much more powerful than the state and gaining power. It's not even close. An economist would argue that the mafia exists where there are inefficiencies. You cannot fight it just with law enforcement, but you've got to change the inefficiencies" of the economic system. This was one of the goals, he said, of the Bush and Clinton Administrations in their endorsement of economic "shock therapy"—the attempt to force the state-controlled economies of Russia and the former republics into free-market systems. . . .

In retrospect, the Treasury official said, one of the most significant mistakes made by the American shock-therapy proponents was their failure to anticipate fully the viciousness and rapaciousness of the criminal element. "We had a belief that the first generation of Russian capitalists would be nice guys, but they are ruthless motherfuckers," the official said. "Much worse than the American robber barons. These guys take the fillings out of teeth after murder. It's a nightmare. Production has ceased. The only institution that's growing is the mafia."

"The Wild West, Alaska frontier, and Chicago in the twenties" is the way a senior State Department official involved in day-to-day Soviet economic strategy describes Russia today. "Anyone who says there isn't a crisis of governance would be crazy." A former national-security official, who worked in the Reagan and Bush Administrations, says, "The chaos scares me. Here we have a 1930s situation in Chicago, except that Al Capone has access to nuclear weapons."

CHAPTER 4

TRANSNATIONAL
ORGANIZED CRIME

INTERNATIONAL CRIMINAL ORGANIZATIONS

Roy Godson and William J. Olson

During the 1980s and 1990s, organized crime groups have become increasingly sophisticated, with operations that are not constrained by national boundaries, write Roy Godson and William J. Olson. The authors describe the defining characteristics of these international criminal organizations (ICOs) and warn of the particular dangers these groups pose to national governments and economies. The threat of groups such as the Colombian drug cartels, the Chinese Triads, and the Sicilian Mafia, the authors contend, is not limited to the usual problems of "underground" criminal activity and internal violence: ICOs may sometimes be powerful enough to openly challenge a country's government, they maintain. Godson is a professor of government at Georgetown University and director of the National Strategy Information Center in Washington, D.C. Olson is a senior fellow at the center; he formerly served as deputy assistant secretary of state at the U.S. State Department's Bureau of International Narcotics Matters.

On August 18, 1989, in the middle of an adoring crowd, a gunman murdered Luis Carlos Galan, the leading candidate for the presidency of Colombia. The act shocked the nation. Political murder was not a new phenomenon in Colombia. What was new were the perpetrators. The assassin was not an individual acting alone, nor was he a member of a guerrilla group, of which Colombia has several violent examples. Instead, the assassin was a hireling, a *sicario*, acting on the orders of the Medellín Cartel, one of the world's major international criminal organizations. The murder was only the beginning. The Medellín Cartel launched a full-scale terrorist assault on the country. Public facilities and newspaper offices were bombed. Members of leading families were kidnapped. Hundreds of policemen were murdered. A national airline flight was blown up in mid-flight. The cartel waged war against the Colombian state. Its aim was to force the government to come to terms with the cartels, in effect, to share power with the drug traffickers.

The Colombian government, which had been trying to control not only Medellín groups but also the [then] less prominent Cali group, now faced a far more violent and direct threat to its institutions. It called for help. The United States, which was already trying to support Colombian efforts, came forward with an emergency aid package and promises of more aid to follow. The United States provided upwards of $400 million in police, military, and advisory assistance over five years. These funds were intended to eliminate the major drug trafficking organizations in Colombia, and many millions more were spent to help attack the overseas operations responsible for producing and transshipping almost all the cocaine in the world.

Undermining National Authority

The level of support and cooperation was unprecedented. And the threat? A drug-trafficking organization with the wealth and power to challenge the internal stability of one country while it defied the power and authority of the world's remaining superpower. Hubris? Perhaps, but the nature of the confrontation . . . says something fundamental about the modern world, about the nature of state power, international relations, and the stability of governments. And the situation in Colombia is far from the whole picture.

In 1991 and 1992 the disruptive influence of organized criminal activity rocked the foundations of political stability in Italy. Since World War II organized crime has carried out a wide range of domestic activities, using violence, extortion, bribery, and murder to advance its interests. More recently the Sicilian Mafia specifically has been locked in a murderous struggle with the government, assassinating judges, policemen, and those seen as interfering in its operations, and, more ominously, using its economic power to try to corrupt the political process itself. The scandals surrounding official corruption linked to the Sicilian, Neapolitan, and Calabrian Mafias have touched the very heart of the Italian government, undermining its credibility and effectiveness.

In Burma, large parts of the country are under the control of separatist movements who finance their activities by selling opium on the international market. The government itself engages in or countenances the production and trafficking of opium to help finance its operations. All over Asia, organized criminal groups, Pakistani, Thai, Chinese, or Japanese, operate vast international organizations trafficking in drugs or engaging in a wide variety of other criminal activities, in many cases with the complicity of local government and military officials.

In the former Soviet Union and in the struggling states of Eastern Europe, criminal organizations, long held in check, are beginning to grow. They have developed international links to improve their own organizational abilities and marketing contacts. Of more concern, these criminal groups are penetrating local governments (which are often struggling for cohesion and lacking resources) by using bribery and violence to win protection for their expanding operations. Governmental resources, strained to cope with a wide range of social and economic problems, are completely inadequate to respond; in fact governments are unable to assess the extent of the problem accurately. Political paralysis and economic hardship have combined to give various criminal organizations considerable freedom to operate, even when local governments are not cooperating with criminal elements. Governments, however, are not the only institutions vulnerable to criminal penetration.

In a New York courtroom in 1992, Clark Clifford, an adviser to presidents and one of the most respected men in the United States, was called as a defendant in a case involving a vast illegal international financial enterprise, the Bank of Credit and Commerce International (BCCI). So far, BCCI is the biggest such case, but it illustrates only too graphically the extent to which banking and financial systems are vulnerable to penetration, manipulation, and fraud by criminal groups. The mechanisms whereby incredible sums of illegal proceeds—perhaps $300 billion in drug money alone—are laundered and massive frauds are perpetrated through the world's financial markets are still only dimly understood, but the realities of the process underscore the permeability of the system. This permeability of governments and private business and the growth of major international organized crime raise concerns for the future.

A Threat to International Stability

Whether in the developed or in the developing world, criminal organizations' scope of action and range of capabilities are undergoing a profound change. Decline in political order, deteriorating economic circumstances, a growing underground economy that habituates people to working outside the legal framework, easy access to arms, the massive flow of emigrants and refugees, and the normal difficulties involved in engendering meaningful state-to-state cooperation are working to the advantage of criminal organizations. The rise of better-organized, internationally based criminal groups with vast financial resources is creating a new threat to the stability and security of the international system. As Senator John Kerry noted, "this is new. This is something that none of us has ever experienced before. It is not ideological. It has nothing to do with right or left, but it is money-oriented, greed-based criminal enterprise that has decided to take on the lawful institutions and civilized society." The growth of these organizations presents a major challenge to the quality of life in the United States and to U.S. interests. . . .

Characteristically, organized crime is defined by a more or less formal structure that endures over time, is directed toward a common purpose by a recognizable leadership operating outside the law, is quite often based on family or ethnic identity, and is prepared to use violence or other means to promote and protect common interests and objectives. There is nothing particularly new about such organizations; they have existed for centuries. A number of factors are now at work that argue that the nature and role of these organizations are raising to a new level the threat that they pose to social order and the stability of nations.

Identifying International Criminal Organizations

There are three major new characteristics of organized crime at the end of the twentieth century. First is the broader, global canvas of the traditional criminal activity. Second is the growth of transnational links between criminal organizations and between criminal organizations and other groups. Third is the growing ability and power of international criminal organizations (ICOs) to threaten the stability of states, to undermine democratic institutions, to hinder economic development, to undermine alliance relationships, and to challenge even a superpower.

There are a number of factors that aid the ICOs' growing ability to challenge individual states. These factors are not so much characteristics of ICOs as of the environment in which they exist. They benefit, for example, from weak governments without the will or the resources to cope with rich and powerful ICOs. They enjoy fantastic sums of money generated by illegal activities, especially drug production, which gives them maximum flexibility to employ bribery or violence to achieve their ends. They are able to take advantage of the movement of large numbers of people internationally, which gives various organizations a recruitment base around the world. They are also able to capitalize on a decline in economic and political order, especially thriving on the growth of parallel or informal economies that subvert loyalty from the nation-state and government and habituate people to operating outside the legal framework. The ready availability of sophisticated arms and other technologies gives ICOs better means to protect and promote their interests. And systemic limits on the ability of individual states and international organizations to coordinate effective transnational anticriminal programs provide ICOs with maneuvering room to adjust to enforcement threats.

These features, taken separately or together, mean that today's international criminal syndicates are powerful enough to challenge, sometimes to destabilize, and so far, rarely, to control small, weak states. As a recent U.S. Senate report noted, these "new international criminals" represent a threat to international security that no single state can control alone. . . .

The major ICOs have all the same characteristics and features of more traditional, nationally based criminal organizations. What distinguishes their ability to conduct global operations on the order of a major multinational corporation is their transnational scale and their ability to challenge national and international authority. Disposing of large quantities of ready cash, diversified into a wide range of activities, and employing a workforce spread around the globe, the ICOs represent a different order of magnitude in criminal operations.

Crossing National Boundaries

The ICOs differ from traditional criminal organizations in the *global scope of their operations*. Traditional organized crime groups have their roots within individual countries, and although they may have overseas connections they do not operate on an international scale. Their organizations and operations are confined to nations or regions, and cities within nations. The America Mafia, also commonly known as La Cosa Nostra (LCN), is a well-known example of this older type. LCN emerged in the 1930s from conflict among gangs of Sicilian immigrants in U.S. cities. Although its members drew on the traditions of their Sicilian origins, LCN was never a subsidiary or arm of the Sicilian Mafia; it is a distinctly American organization. While LCN has had international connections, these have been largely related to being buyers of alcohol and heroin from foreign groups, not as being part of those groups. LCN's organization and operations are essentially domestic and regional.

Many other organized crime groups operating in the United States are primarily of this type. Black and Hispanic groups, for example, are generally localized gangs. They often dominate criminal activity in their respective ethnic neighborhoods. Typically, they control much street-level drug dealing and some distribution activity above the street level. They often interface with international traffickers who control wholesaling and regional distribution. Motorcycle gangs, such as the Hell's Angels, have also become well organized and engage in a wide variety of criminal activity, sometimes developing international suppliers.

The new international criminal groups differ sharply from these domestic groups. They are organized for and engage in large-scale criminal activity across international boundaries. Perhaps the greatest such organizations are Colombian. The Colombian cartels are vertically integrated global businesses. They have tens of thousands of specialized employees and associated individuals or businesses worldwide. Similarly, the Chinese Triads, although more loosely structured, have also developed extensive overseas operations, often in the wake of Chinese emigration. Such global networks provide mobility, an effective communications infrastructure, and international connections for criminal enterprise and sometimes for noncriminal groups who want to use their services. These structures also enhance the criminal groups' ability to create whole new markets for goods and services. This can be done either by creating new products, like "crack," which revolutionized the U.S. cocaine market in the mid-1980s, or by opening up new market areas, as the cocaine cartels have attempted to do in Europe, establishing links to the Mafia or other European criminal organizations.

International networks also provide flexibility to adapt quickly and creatively to enforcement efforts. For example, after U.S. enforcement efforts shut off the flow of heroin originating from Turkey, new sources developed in Southeast and Southwest Asia and Mexico. U.S. law enforcement agencies noted in 1991 the "inherent flexibility" of traffickers in shifting routes and modes of transport in response to enforcement efforts. When enforcement was stepped up in Florida and the Caribbean, cocaine was routed increasingly through Central America and Mexico. There is another aspect to this flexibility: by operating in the international arena, crossing national boundaries at will, the ICOs are often able to thwart localized law enforcement efforts. Diversification of operations and locale and diffusion of risk greatly enhance the ICOs' ability to recover from losses. They are also better able to adjust to changing situations in one country and exploit gaps in international law enforcement cooperation.

ICOs Dwarf Traditional Crime Groups

The new international organized crime groups are also bigger and much more profitable than traditional groups. The FBI estimated in 1988 that LCN consisted of twenty-five independent families with a total of 2,000 members. Conversely, in 1989, Senate investigators reported estimates of as many as 100,000 members of the Colombian cocaine industry, not counting Peruvian and Bolivian groups. While it is difficult to be certain about such numbers in basically secretive organizations, the Drug Enforcement Administration computers listed the names of 24,000 persons and businesses known to be working with Colombian drug cartels in 1989. Similarly, in 1992 "conservative" estimates placed the membership of the Sun Yee On, the largest Hong Kong Triad, at 25,000, not counting its overseas members. Although not all of these were necessarily engaged in crime, the size of this one Triad indicates the potential scope of the networks available to those who are.

The scale of monetary returns on these activities also dwarf those of traditional groups. The main driver for this is the large-scale profits generated by illegal drug trafficking. The Colombian cartels alone probably make more in a week than the American Mafia does in a year. The Colombian cartels now outperform most Fortune 500 companies. A conservative estimate of illegal drug sales at the retail, or user, level in the United States alone is $50 billion. Colombian cartels are estimated to make a profit of about $20 billion annually from these revenues. By comparison, the gross domestic product (GDP) of Colombia is only around $45 billion. The combined budgets of the governments of Colombia, Bolivia, and Peru is only about $9 billion annually. The Chinese Triads and the top manipulators of international frauds may not be making as much as the Colombians, but their profits also dwarf those of most traditional organized crime groups.

One of the emerging characteristics of the major ICOs is the extent of their *transnational links:* their growing interconnectivity with other transnational, nonstate actors. Although traditional criminal organizations have links to similar groups outside their own countries, they generally do not conduct extensive overseas operations and have only limited contact with other criminal groups. The major ICOs, however, have an international focus and operate vast transnational business empires. Their activities go beyond establishing subsidiaries. In addition to operating across international boundaries, the new ICOs have also begun to establish links to other nonstate groups, such as insurgents and terrorists, and similar criminal organizations. These linkages are diverse and in some cases tenuous and tense, but the trend that is emerging is toward closer cooperative relationships. The nature of the relationship can be quite complex. . . .

The Global Drug Network

In the Andes, for example, the drug organizations in Bolivia and Peru typically act as regional subsidiaries of the Colombian cartels. The Bolivians and Peruvians deal directly with the growers, initiating the first stages of refining raw coca into cocaine paste or base, precursors to cocaine hydrochloride (HCL). The Colombians provide the transportation network to move these products to labs in Colombia for final processing, and, of course, they bring in vast quantities of cash to pay for the raw product. Until recently the Colombians generally did not involve themselves directly in these regional efforts, but with increased law enforcement successes, particularly in Bolivia, that have rolled up whole local organizations, the Colombians have begun to take more direct control.

For the development of the transportation system to move cocaine north, the Colombians established links to Mexican organized crime. These ties are arrangements of convenience. The Colombians often complain of Mexican incompetence and dishonesty, but they need the Mexicans to run the network of local landing strips, safe houses, and logistical-support systems—including the network of corrupt officials that the Mexican organizations had developed over the years—necessary to sustain huge long-range drug-trafficking operations. Similar arrangements were made in Guatemala and throughout the Caribbean. As the Colombians have sought to develop a European market they have explored similar contacts with the Sicilian Mafia and other organized groups in Europe. They are also establishing links, especially potential money laundering channels, to Eastern Europe and Commonwealth of Independent States criminal organizations.

The Colombians are also trying to expand their markets into Asia. They are establishing links to major Asian heroin traffickers, sometimes exchanging cocaine for heroin. Moreover, the Colombian cartels are exploring, on a large scale in the Andes, the potential of growing opium in marketable quantities. This gambit has relied on importing lab technicians and experts from Southwest Asia. As this example shows, links among ICOs permit considerable diversification and division of labor.

The major Asian heroin-trafficking networks have established ties to Nigerian criminal groups and have basically contracted with them to help in their international distribution system. Today, one of the principal means Asian heroin is smuggled into the United States is in the stomachs and intestines of Nigerian "mules," individual carriers who have swallowed heroin sheathed in condoms. These mules are recruited and trained by Nigerian agents. There is a three-cornered network: Mules travel from Nigeria to Thailand with money, pick up the drugs, and arrangements are made for them to enter the United States and Europe with the drugs in their body cavities. Enforcement efforts have led to variations, with Nigerians traveling from many different places, often on forged or stolen travel documents; in some cases it appears that the Nigerians are now recruiting non-Nigerians, including Europeans.

These types of contacts extend the operational range and capabilities of the cartels and other ICOs, and, more important, they allow for an exchange of information on international law enforcement efforts and on techniques for protecting operations. All the major criminal organizations have the advantage of any institutional arrangement: Since they endure over time and exist for a purpose, they are capable of learning from experience and using that knowledge to adjust to changing circumstances. . . .

Challenging Authority

Traditional, nationally based criminal organizations pose a variety of threats to public order and legitimate business. The U.S. experience with LCN is typical: corruption of officials, penetration of unions, money laundering, prostitution, street crime, gambling, violent internecine power struggles, drug trafficking; in short, the whole range of criminal activity that can be organized for profit. As rich and powerful as these organizations have been, however, they are generally in no position to challenge political order directly. Indeed, in the case of the LCN, recent law enforcement successes have decimated its ranks and may have dealt it a crippling blow. The major ICOs, however, pose a more dangerous threat, one that is again defined by its scope and sheer audacity: a *challenge to authority*.

The Medellín Cartel felt powerful enough to challenge the sovereignty and integrity of the Colombian state, and along with it the United States. Years of struggle have damaged the Medellín Cartel, at considerable loss of life and capital, but the Colombian cocaine entrepreneurs remain in business, not only evading annihilation but continuing to prosper and diversify their operations. Alone or in conjunction with various guerrilla groups in Colombia and Peru, they are able to control large areas of the Andes in defiance of government authority. They are also able to transship immense quantities of drugs through the Caribbean, Central America, and Mexico to the United States. In many cases, even in totalitarian Cuba, the Medellín Cartel has been able to corrupt officials throughout the hierarchy, including ranking military officers and ministers of state. Their ability to penetrate governments has even led to major disruptions in the relations between nations, as the Enrique Camarena case in Mexico showed only too clearly. [In 1985 U.S. Drug Enforcement Administration agent Camarena was tortured to death by drug traffickers and corrupt police.] . . .

The major ICOs enjoy a number of advantages denied to smaller groups. The scale of their operations, their growing international connectivity, and the power and influence that they have garnered at the expense of governments make them a formidable challenge. They enjoy the advantages of economy of scale in their operations. Their enormous financial resources and diversification operations give them maneuvering room in responding to law enforcement encroachments. Their ability to operate across many legal jurisdictions reinforces this inherent flexibility. Moreover, their contacts with other nonstate actors, such as insurgent groups and terrorists, means that they can call increasingly upon allies to help distract the government or even challenge its authority. The cumulative effect of these advantages puts them in a position of great strength. . . .

ICOs Will Expand

International criminal groups in the United States and worldwide are likely to expand. A number of factors are likely to aid their growth. . . .

International ungovernability. The growth of international crime parallels a global trend toward ungovernability, that is, the declining ability of governments to govern, to manage a modern state, and to provide adequate or effective services. In some cases criminal organizations have been able to capitalize on the fact that large areas, such as the Andes and the Amazon regions of Latin America, were never under much central government control. They have moved into these remote regions and have begun to provide the major form of authority in much of the region. In other cases, they have begun to contest local control of areas with the government, as have groups in Burma. There are dozens of places, such as Peru and Burma, where state authority has lapsed in whole or in part. It is not limited to small states, either. There are indications that areas of some of the Central Asian Republics have been given over to drug cultivation. Similarly, areas in Mexico, Pakistan, and southern China appear to be largely beyond government control. This situation provides favorable conditions for criminal groups and bases of operations and safe havens in areas key to drug trafficking and alien smuggling. Experts in political geography predict continuing global fragmentation. Criminal organizations thrive where governments are weak. . . .

Border porosity. The United States' long open borders with Mexico and Canada provide ready access for criminals and illegal goods, and tens of thousands of miles of U.S. coastline are virtually uncontrollable. The opening of free-trade areas, such as the North American Free Trade Agreement and the European Community, will lower many existing safeguards and customs inspections as well.

Trends in technology. Continued advances in technology and international transportation will facilitate growth in international organized crime. The ease of modern communications makes contact among international criminal organizations easy, fast, and more secure. For example, new digital technologies make it more difficult for law enforcement bodies to intercept their communications. The movement of trillions of dollars in wire transfers each day makes it possible for many actors to evade state monitoring.

Relative disorganization of law enforcement. Preventing, disrupting, and successfully prosecuting organized crime in most parts of the world is difficult enough in the best of times. Many traditional organized criminal organizations have survived the onslaught of law enforcement organizations for decades.

Now, however, the U.S. and other states are faced with international criminal groups. As was described earlier, they are bigger and more powerful than most of their predecessors. They operate globally, making it impossible for law enforcement in any one jurisdiction to neutralize major parts of their activities. While some degree of cooperation exists among law enforcement agencies, and new initiatives are getting under way, many observers believe that it is inadequate to the task. In 1992, for example, a U.S. Senate report noted that there is little evidence to suggest that either U.S. or foreign law enforcement entities are currently equipped to meet the challenge of this new breed of international criminal.

THE FIGHT AGAINST TRANSNATIONAL ORGANIZED CRIME

Louis J. Freeh

In the following selection, excerpted from his 1997 statement before the U.S. House of Representatives International Relations Committee, FBI director Louis J. Freeh describes the growth of transnational organized crime and the problem it poses for law enforcement, both in the United States and throughout the world. He explains the need for international cooperation among law enforcement agencies and details the FBI's efforts to foster such cooperation. Through the Legal Attache program, international training programs, and the International Law Enforcement Academy, says Freeh, the FBI hopes to provide other countries with the training and resources they need to successfully combat organized crime, as well as to help build stronger relationships with those countries' law enforcement agencies.

The FBI serves as the principal investigative agency of the federal government, and is responsible for detecting and investigating crimes against the United States and performing other duties connected with national security. Unlike other federal law enforcement agencies that have more specialized missions, the FBI's mission extends across the full spectrum of federal offenses.

In recent years that spectrum and the FBI's domestic law enforcement and national security missions have expanded. In the first half of the twentieth century, the FBI earned its reputation as the preeminent law enforcement agency because of our response to the advent of interstate crime. We now stand witness to an unprecedented growth in transnational crime. Contributing to this growth is the end of the cold war, the emergence of truly global economies and the explosion of new computer and telecommunications technologies. Acts of terrorism, the theft of nuclear materials in Europe, organized crime, computer crime and drug trafficking no longer are constrained by boundaries or inhibited by global distances.

Inevitably, in the global economy I referred to, the United States also has become a major importer of crime. We are the center of the

Excerpted from "The Threat of International Organized Crime and Global Terrorism and the International Law Enforcement Programs of the Federal Bureau of Investigation," statement made by Louis J. Freeh before the House International Committee, October 1, 1997.

financial universe and the leader of the free world. As a consequence, everything from telemarketing fraud and other facets of financial institution fraud to the more traditional drug and organized crime comes regularly to our shores. Sadly, terrorism has come as well. The international exporters of crime and terrorism who capitalize on the vulnerable free society include South American drug cartels, terrorists from the Middle East, and an array of organized crime groups from Europe, the former Soviet Republics and Asia. Regardless of origin, these and other international crimes daily impact directly on our citizens and our economy.

Regrettably, amazing modern technology and transportation have, with all of their enormous benefits, also given us a world where terrorists bomb targets in New York City and conspire to blow up tunnels and federal buildings. Where American soldiers stationed in Saudi Arabia are killed in a terrorist bomb attack, where a criminal in St. Petersburg, Russia, can steal over ten million dollars from Citibank in New York using only his computer, where U.S. citizens are kidnaped by narco guerillas in Colombia, South America, where terrorists plot to place bombs aboard American passenger aircraft in Asia, and where the threat of proliferation of nuclear, chemical and biological weapons of mass destruction that remain under the control of the former states of the Soviet Union still exist. These are not the crimes of tomorrow.

Because a substantial portion of FBI cases have some foreign connection, international crime has rapidly become one of the most important challenges to face the United States and the law enforcement community. We must act to develop the strategies necessary to address these challenges now and to minimize the impact of international crime on the citizens, economy, and national security of the United States. Our success is going to be measured by how thoroughly we prepare for what is upon us and how quickly we respond to the emergence of international crime. . . .

Further, we are at a unique position in modern history where we can help contribute to the development of professional law enforcement agencies in foreign countries. We can do this by promoting the rule of law in the former Soviet Union's newly independent states, and by building cop-to-cop relationships with our overseas counterparts. Without these relationships, we will not have the commonality of purpose and open communication required for effectively combating international crime. Commonality of purpose is not about a transitional liaison relationship. It is about a long-term commitment and should be read in the broadest context. It means dedication to mission and the rule of law.

International Law Enforcement Programs

There are three key elements to the FBI's international law enforcement initiative. First, the FBI must have an active overseas presence that fosters the establishment of effective working relationships with foreign law enforcement agencies. There is already a well-documented history of our Legal Attaches who have drawn upon their investigative experiences and backgrounds and enlisted the cooperation of foreign law enforcement on innumerable cases enabling the arrest of many U.S. fugitives and solving serious U.S. crimes.

Second, training foreign law enforcement officers in both basic and advanced investigative techniques and principles is a powerful tool for promoting cooperation. We use the FBI's National Academy program as our model. For decades it has fostered comity with state and local law enforcement agencies.

Finally, institution building is necessary to help establish and foster the rule of law in newly democratic republics. Establishing rule of law will promote greater confidence and stability in these new governments by their citizens. This is a foreign policy and national security consideration for the United States. Stability will also provide an environment more conducive to protecting United States' interests and citizens in those countries. . . .

I firmly believe the FBI's initiatives in response to the problem of international crime are based upon sound and proven approaches that have been successfully used here and abroad. This approach must now be extended to other partners in the international arena.

The Legal Attache Program

The first element of the FBI's international law enforcement initiative is the Legal Attache [Legat] program. The FBI has long recognized the need for assigning personnel to American embassies abroad. The FBI first began assigning personnel abroad during World War II. Agents who serve as Legal Attaches are among our most experienced investigators. They possess appropriate security clearances, and, with very few exceptions, are fluent in the language of the country to which they are posted.

FBI Legal Attaches are truly our first line of defense in keeping foreign-based crime as far away from American shores as possible and combating more effectively those criminal enterprises that do reach our borders. By stationing agents abroad and establishing operational links with foreign law enforcement and security agencies, the FBI substantially expands the nation's perimeter of law enforcement protection.

The FBI operates 32 Legal Attache offices around the world, staffed by 82 agents and 62 support employees. During 1995, these employees handled over 11,200 matters, ranging from kidnaping to drug trafficking, from terrorism to money laundering, from financial fraud to extortion. These agents and support staff serve as the conduit through which law enforcement information and cooperation flow between the United States and its foreign partners.

All FBI field offices have sought Legat assistance in covering leads, with the largest portion coming from major metropolitan offices. More than 80% of the current caseload handled by Legat offices is in direct support of domestic FBI investigation, not only covering leads, but organizing the arrest and extradition to the U.S. of wanted criminals.

I would like to mention the close working relationship our Legat office in Rome has with the Italian National Police. FBI agents and the Italian National Police have worked side-by-side on investigations into the assassinations of judges Giovanni Falcone and Paolo Borsellino by the Sicilian mafia.

The Legat office in Moscow—opened in July 1994 as part of our expansion plan—provides another excellent example. It opened with a caseload of approximately 35 cases; three years later, Moscow's caseload totals 284, covering some 150 leads from U.S. FBI investigations. We opened the Moscow office because Russian-related crimes were increasing in certain U.S. cities. We quickly learned, as a result of increased inquiries from FBI field offices and growing cooperation with Russian authorities, that the problem was more extensive than we had thought.

Interagency and International Cooperation

News reports of international terrorism, drug trafficking and transnational economic crime remind us daily of the increasingly global nature of crime. Recall the headline story of January 25, 1993. Five Americans on the way to work are shot by a terrorist outside of CIA Headquarters in McLean, Virginia—two die. On June 17, 1997, Mir Aimal Kansi was arrested for the crime and brought to the United States for trial. The capture of a criminal many believed was out of our reach was a direct result of unprecedented cooperation between the FBI, CIA, State Department and foreign law enforcement officials working together.

In 1997, an employee of a Jacksonville, Florida, armored car company perpetrated a robbery of almost 19 million dollars in cash. He was arrested crossing the Mexican border into the United States. An investigation conducted by our Legat office in Mexico City identified the hiding place for the stolen money in North Carolina. As a direct result of Legat Mexico's efforts, 99.4% of the money was recovered.

These case examples represent a very early return on Congress' confidence and investment in our Legat Expansion Program. We need them in key locations around the world.

Until fiscal year (FY) 1995, agents served in only 23 countries. This group included Mexico, Colombia, Russia, and Hong Kong. Without these Legat offices, we would not have been prepared to deal with the threats of drug cartels, Russian gangs or the Yakuza.

The threat of international crime and terrorism continues to expand and grow exponentially. In my early career as an agent, organized crime was focused on the traditional La Cosa Nostra. Today, it includes groups from Asia and Eastern Europe. Early in my tenure as Director, I tasked our criminal and national security experts to develop a plan to address the emerging organized crime threats. A major facet of their recommendation was an expansion of the Legat program. We need to be on the ground where the crimes and conspiracies originate. We need to have agents in the Middle East, Africa, and elsewhere.

There's an old agent's expression—we are only as good as our information. We need Agent-Legats to be stationed where they can have access to information in a timely fashion, where other foreign law enforcement colleagues can provide this information in an arms-length fashion. Even if we cannot prevent a Khobar Towers bombing [which occurred at King Abdul Aziz Air Base in Saudi Arabia on June 25, 1996, killing 19 U.S. airmen], we need the capability to respond without delay. If international crime victimizes our citizens in New York or Moscow, the American public must be confident in our capability to respond.

Legats are the FBI's first line of defense beyond our borders. They are part of a sensible permanent presence that is alert to the potential perils around the world on a 24-hour-a-day basis. Their goals are simple—to keep foreign crime as far from American shores as possible and to help solve those international crimes that have preyed upon us, as rapidly as possible.

Finally, it is important to note that FBI agents stationed overseas are not intelligence officers or shadow intelligence officers. They do not engage in espionage. The FBI's Legats are in place to facilitate the international battle against crime and terrorism.

International Training Programs

The second element of the FBI's international law enforcement initiative is training. The FBI considers training of foreign law enforcement officers to be particularly critical to combating international crime. This training is especially needed by the countries of the former Soviet Union. These newly independent states realize that success in earning the confidence of their citizens in law enforcement agencies depends upon the development of professional law enforcement officers who understand and operate under the rule of law. In return for this investment in training programs, the FBI is able to work cooperatively with foreign law enforcement agencies that share a common perspective and understanding of investigative procedures. Between 1994 and 1997, the FBI has provided training for over 6,746 foreign law enforcement personnel from over 40 countries.

Through a program of in-country training, the FBI conducts one- and two-week schools in foreign nations which are designed to meet a country's particular training needs. The schools concentrate on subjects such as basic and advanced police operations, technical skills, ethics, and internal police controls. Senior FBI agents serve as instructors, bringing their knowledge and expertise to these programs. Their credibility is not only essential for effective instruction, but also very effective for building the cop-to-cop bridges that we so critically need. During fiscal year 1996, 52 in-country training courses were conducted for 2,078 students from 21 countries.

Practical Case Training (PCT) is also an important part of the FBI's international training program. Practical Case Training is an on-the-job training program that enables foreign police entities and FBI agents to work together on actual investigations of mutual interest. This initiative has resulted in a number of successful investigations. Under this program, Russian Federation Ministry of the Interior (MVD) officers traveled to the FBI's New York field office to participate in an unprecedented cooperative investigation targeting Russian organized crime figure Yvacheslov Kirillovich Ivankov. Ivankov led an international criminal organization with operations in the U.S., Europe and Canada. Russian MVD officers worked side-by-side with FBI agents on this investigation and were able to recognize and decipher codes used by the Ivankov organized crime group. This immeasurably aided the investigation and directly led to the conviction of Ivankov and five of his associates.

The International Law Enforcement Academy

The third element of the FBI's international law enforcement initiative is the International Law Enforcement Academy, or ILEA, in Budapest, Hungary. The Academy serves as a law enforcement training center for officers from many Eastern European and Eurasian nations and Russia. Instructors at the Academy represent a true cross-section of federal law enforcement agencies, including subject experts from the FBI, Drug Enforcement Administration, Bureau of Alcohol, Tobacco, and Firearms, United States Customs Service, and the Federal Law Enforcement Training Center. We have also used law enforcement instructors from other countries and the European Law Enforcement College.

All participants agree that ILEA is a tremendous success. . . . As of October 1997, there have been 497 students trained in the eight-week program at ILEA. A total of 20 countries have participated in this training.

Training at the Academy is designed to meet the needs of participating countries. For example, the FBI and the Department of Defense recently provided counter proliferation training to law enforcement officers from the nations of Kazakhstan and Kyrgystan. This training is of international importance in preventing hostile nations from obtaining nuclear weapons capabilities. More importantly, we are building cop-to-cop relationships not only between law enforcement from the United States and participating countries, but also between officers from participating countries themselves.

The Academy has also fostered cooperation between nations. Hungarians and Romanians have executed various memorandums of understanding (MOUs) because of their introduction to various officials while attending ILEA. These law enforcement MOUs were the foundation for national treaties between the countries regarding human rights and minority issues.

Ukraine and Hungary have established a close working relationship on their border as a result of their students attending the Academy. Together, they have apprehended organized crime members that have ties to U.S. cells.

Baltic countries have sought FBI assistance on organized crime matters that directly affect U.S. national security. It was former ILEA graduates who spearheaded the contacts with U.S. law enforcement. Polish students used techniques learned at the Academy to detect and subsequently dismantle a clandestine drug laboratory. Some of these drugs were destined for the U.S. These are just a few examples of the success stories coming out of the Academy.

A Continuing Struggle

We are confronted on a daily basis with the reality that the safety and security of American citizens is increasingly threatened here and abroad by criminals who know no boundaries. . . . The only way to reduce that threat is to create and develop substantive international links—personal networks of law enforcement professionals dedicated to bringing these criminals to justice. I feel strongly that the FBI is addressing the threat of international organized crime and terrorism through the international law enforcement initiatives that I have just described. However, we must continually reexamine and assess international crime problems. Currently this assessment calls for an expansion of the Legat program. The above cited examples clearly illustrate that the expansion our Legat program experienced in FY 96 and FY 97 has been invaluable to the FBI. We now have solid relationships with police and security agencies in countries which are crucial to addressing crime in the U.S.

The overseas program of the FBI is the most effective tool available in protecting our nation from the threat of international organized crime and global terrorism. Increasingly, crime in the United States is influenced from outside our borders. It is essential that we have experienced FBI personnel posted in foreign countries to enable us to get the information we need to accomplish our domestic mission.

INTERNATIONAL MONEY LAUNDERING

Financial Crimes Enforcement Network

Money laundering is the process of disguising illegally gotten funds so that they can be used without detection—making "dirty" money "clean." But not all countries recognize money laundering as a crime. For example, some Caribbean islands are home to so-called offshore banks, banking havens that protect their clients' anonymity and in so doing frustrate law enforcement efforts to trace criminals' illicit profits. The Financial Crimes Enforcement Network (FinCEN), a bureau of the U.S. Treasury Department, is the U.S. agency charged with providing leadership in counter–money laundering efforts. In the following selection, taken from its publication "The Global Fight Against Organized Crime," FinCEN defines money laundering and explains how this practice allows organized crime groups to prosper. The authors detail FinCEN's plan to coordinate international anti–money laundering efforts, including the establishment of anti–money laundering laws in countries that lack them.

In recent years, crime has become increasingly international in scope and the financial aspects of crime are complex due to the rapidly changing advances in technology. International organized crime is an enormous and multifaceted problem. It is not only a law enforcement problem but a national and international security threat as well.

Many countries around the world already engage in a concerted effort to combat international organized crime. Through the enactment of counter–money laundering laws, bilateral and multilateral agreements, and other cooperative efforts, nations have joined together to foster an international awareness of the seriousness and threat of organized crime and to acknowledge this problem directly. An increasing number of countries have moved to deny criminal enterprises unfettered access to their financial systems. While much progress has been made, and despite all these efforts, there are still nations that have not yet adequately addressed this problem. And the international criminal is taking full advantage, moving vast sums of illicit money through the world's financial systems. International criminals know no

Excerpted from "The Global Fight Against Money Laundering," a publication of the Financial Crimes Enforcement Network, U.S. Treasury Department, April 1996.

geographic boundaries and can still find safe havens in which to hide.

If the United States, along with its international partners and allies, is ultimately going to be successful in this fight, then we must make it even more difficult for criminals. Efforts must focus upon those areas where the criminals are now going and foster cooperation, one way or another, with those nations that, heretofore, have allowed criminal enterprise to flourish unchecked.

The President of the United States, during his address to the United Nations on October 22, 1995, authorized a number of actions which provide an even more aggressive approach to dealing with international criminal organizations. Those countries in which these organizations are now allowed to operate and prosper, unrestricted by counter–money laundering efforts, will be compelled to conform to the international goals established to deal with the issue of international crime. These countries will be held publicly accountable for their role in the common effort to deter international criminal activities. In order to implement his goals, the President is assigning a very high priority to negotiating agreements that ensure governments' compliance with internationally accepted anti–money laundering standards. The Department of the Treasury is coordinating this initiative and working with the Departments of State and Justice, the bank regulators, and the intelligence community to expedite this process.

What Is Money Laundering?

With few exceptions, criminals are motivated by one thing—profit. Greed drives the criminal, and the end result is that illegally gained money must be introduced into a nation's legitimate financial system. Money laundering involves disguising assets so they can be used without detection of the illegal activity that produced them.

The success of organized crime is based upon its ability to launder money. Through money laundering, the criminal transforms the monetary proceeds derived from criminal activity into funds with a seemingly legal source.

This process has devastating social consequences. For one thing, money laundering provides the fuel for drug dealers, terrorists, arms dealers, and other criminals to operate and expand their operations. Criminals manipulate financial systems in the United States and abroad to further a wide range of illicit activities. Left unchecked, money laundering can erode the integrity of our nation's and the world's financial institutions.

The profits of crime that creep into the financial systems of the United States and other nations are staggering. In just the United States alone, estimates of the amount of drug profits moving through the financial system have been as high as $100 billion.

Consider the fact that money laundering extends far beyond hiding narcotics profits to include monies tied to crimes ranging from tax fraud to terrorism and arms smuggling, adding many additional billions of dollars to the criminals' profits. Criminal activities, without restraint, fundamentally destabilize political and economic reform. As history demonstrates again and again, political stability, democracy and free markets depend on solvent, stable, and honest financial, commercial, and trade systems.

There is now worldwide recognition that we must deal firmly and effectively with increasingly elusive, well financed, and technologically adept criminal organizations. These organizations are determined to use every means available to subvert the financial systems that are the cornerstone of legitimate international commerce. As organized crime develops economic power, it corrupts democratic institutions and undermines free enterprise. Money laundering is now being viewed as the central dilemma in dealing with all forms of international organized crime because financial gain means power. Organized crime is assuming an increasingly significant role that threatens the safety and security of peoples, states and democratic institutions.

The Department of the Treasury's Role

The Treasury Department plays a major role in implementing and directing efforts devoted to combating international organized crime. It strives to advance counter–money laundering measures through prevention, detection and enforcement of financial crime, as well as other international criminal activity.

The Financial Crimes Enforcement Network (FinCEN) is a key component of the U.S. international strategy to combat organized crime. The Department of the Treasury has designated FinCEN as one of the primary agencies to formulate, oversee and implement policies to prevent and detect money laundering, serving as the link between the law enforcement, financial and regulatory communities. Its mission: to provide world leadership in the prevention and detection of the movement of illegally derived money and to empower others by providing them with the tools and the expertise needed to combat financial crime.

FinCEN accomplishes this in several ways. It uses counter–money laundering laws and provides intelligence and analytical case support to its customers: federal, state, local and international investigators and regulators.

As the U.S. continues to implement policies to counter global money laundering efforts, FinCEN has become an international leader in the fight against financial crimes and the corresponding corruption of international economies. FinCEN's unique staffing both reflects and sustains its mission. The majority of its 200 employees are permanent FinCEN personnel, including intelligence analysts and criminal investigators as well as specialists in the financial industry and computer field. In addition, approximately 40 long-term detailees are assigned to FinCEN from 21 different regulatory and law enforcement agencies.

An integral part of FinCEN's role in the international community focuses upon its work and support of the following global initiatives.

Efforts to Combat Money Laundering

FATF. The Financial Action Task Force (FATF) is one of the key organizations that addresses the global problem of money laundering. Formed by the G-7 Economic Summit in 1989, the FATF is comprised of 26 countries, the European Commission and the Gulf Cooperation Council. It is dedicated to promoting the development of effective anti–money laundering controls and enhanced cooperation in counter–money laundering efforts among its membership and around the world.

The cornerstone of the Task Force's work is the promotion of 40 recommendations designed to provide countries with a blueprint for the establishment and implementation of anti–money laundering laws and programs. On July 1, 1995, then Treasury Under Secretary for Enforcement Ronald K. Noble assumed the presidency of the FATF, which rotates annually. FinCEN is serving as the lead agency for coordinating the U.S. role within the FATF.

Under Mr. Noble's leadership, the FATF is focusing on a thorough review or stocktaking of the 40 recommendations to ensure their continued applicability in light of constantly changing money laundering methods and the emergence of new technologies and services within the financial services sector. Some of the key proposed modifications to the recommendations are: to encourage members to extend the offense of money laundering beyond drug related crime to include all serious crime; to encourage mandatory suspicious transaction reporting; and to urge the establishment of effective Know Your Customer programs within the financial services community. . . .

FIUs. The FATF efforts, in part, have resulted in the establishment of Financial Intelligence Units (FIUs) in various countries around the world to protect the banking community, to detect criminal abuse of its financial system and to ensure adherence to its laws against financial crime. FinCEN is one model of an FIU, and others exist in such countries as Great Britain, France, Belgium, the Netherlands, Argentina and Australia. As world policy efforts intensify in addressing international crime, the Treasury, State and Justice Departments are assisting with the establishment of FIUs in countries such as Poland, Panama and Ecuador.

Perhaps one of the most significant qualities of the FIUs is that many operate separately from the Justice Ministries in their respective countries. The FIUs have independent and unique relationships with banks, central banks and law enforcement. These relationships allow FIUs to foster the partnerships that are essential to combating money laundering and financial crime. They bridge the private and governmental sectors in an effort to force attention to this problem outside of the narrow bureaucratic thinking of the past. . . .

Interpol. Interpol is an international organization established to facilitate information sharing and coordination among nations in worldwide criminal investigative matters. At the 64th session of Interpol's General Assembly held in October 1995, a resolution was unanimously adopted establishing the first major anti–money laundering declaration in the organization's history. This resolution consolidates the ten previous actions of Interpol since 1960 and calls for major legislative reforms by the 170 Interpol member nations.

The adoption of this major money laundering resolution by the member countries illustrates Interpol's commitment to thwarting international financial crimes and their desire to strengthen international cooperation. The resolution recommends that Interpol member countries consider adopting national legislation that would:

- provide for the criminal prosecution of persons who knowingly participate in the laundering of proceeds derived from serious criminal activity;
- allow for the seizure of property, with sufficient legal investigative authority for law enforcement officials to identify, trace and freeze assets derived from illicit activities;
- allow for reporting of unusual or suspect currency or other transactions by banks and other financial institutions to appropriate officials who would have authority to conduct further investigative inquiries;
- require financial institutions to maintain, at least for five years after the conclusion of the transaction, all necessary records on transactions, both domestic and international, in order to enable member countries to properly investigate money laundering, and to enhance international cooperation by enabling member countries to respond to requests from authorities in other countries for such records;
- allow for the expeditious extradition of individuals charged with money laundering offenses.

THE THREAT TO WORLD ORDER

Louise I. Shelley

Louise I. Shelley is a professor at American University's School of International Service and director of its Center for Transnational Organized Crime and Corruption in Washington, D.C. In the following selection, Shelley details the consequences of international criminal activity and the destabilizing effect that corruption can have on national governments. She warns that, because of international criminals' versatility and mobility, no single nation can control the most powerful criminal groups. Therefore, she concludes, an international effort to combat organized crime must be developed before more national governments are infiltrated by transnational criminal organizations.

Transnational organized crime has been a serious problem for most of the 20th century, but it has only recently been recognized as a threat to the world order. This criminality undermines the integrity of individual countries, but it is not yet a threat to the nation-state. Failure to develop viable, coordinated international policies in the face of ever-growing transnational criminality, however, may undermine the nation-state in the 21st century.

The "global mafia" has been sensationalized by an international press eager for exciting copy, and intelligence organizations are assessing the dimensions of international drug trafficking. Furthermore, in November 1994 the United Nations sponsored an international conference to develop strategies to combat organized crime. The European Union is also taking numerous initiatives in this area. Attention to such a serious international problem is long overdue.

The seriousness of the problem lies in the complexity of these organizations and their activities, their global penetration and the threat they pose to democracy and legitimate economic development—these organizations clearly undermine the concept of the nation-state. For the purposes of this article transnational criminal organizations will be considered as organized crime groups that 1) are based in one state; 2) commit their crimes in one but usually several host countries, whose market conditions are favorable; and 3) conduct illicit activities affording low risk of apprehension.

Excerpted from "Transnational Organized Crime," by Louise I. Shelley, *Journal of International Affairs*, vol. 48, no. 2 (Winter 1995). Reprinted by permission of the *Journal of International Affairs* and the Trustees of Columbia University in the City of New York.

The complexity of transnational organized crime does not permit the construction of simple generalizations; there is no prototypical crime cartel. Organized crime groups engage in such widely publicized activities as drugs and arms trafficking, smuggling of automobiles and people and trafficking in stolen art. They also engage in such insidious activities as smuggling of embargoed commodities, industrial and technological espionage, financial market manipulation and the corruption and control of groups within and outside of the legal state system. Money laundering through multiple investments in banks, financial institutions and businesses around the globe has become a central and transnational feature of these groups' activities, as they need to hide ever-larger revenues.

The Post–Cold War Response

Given this level of complexity and the political dynamics of the post–Second World War period, it is hardly surprising that no comprehensive international effort against organized crime has been initiated until recently. Transnational organized crime has been problematic for the last couple of decades, but it is only since the end of the Cold War that it has been addressed by so many countries and international bodies. The recently mounted attack on transnational organized crime is, indeed, partly a consequence of the need for security bodies (such as the CIA, KGB and the Mossad) and international organizations (such as the U.N. and the Council of Europe) to develop new missions in the post–Cold War era. While the world focused on such highly visible problems as the superpower conflict or regional hostilities, the increasingly pernicious and pervasive transnational crime that now threatens the economic and political stability of many nations was ignored. Long-term neglect of this problem means that the world now faces highly developed criminal organizations that undermine the rule of law, international security and the world economy and which, if they are allowed to continue unimpeded, could threaten the concept of the nation-state. . . .

Pernicious Consequences of Organized Crime

The costs of transnational organized crime are not exclusively monetary. Transnational organized crime undermines political structures, the world economy and the social order of the countries in which the international crime groups are based and operate. The resulting instability invites more crime, and may preclude the institutionalization of democratic institutions, the rule of law and legitimate markets.

Transnational organized crime undermines civil society and human rights. Through intimidation and assassination of journalists in different countries, it limits freedom of the press and individual expression. Transnational organized crime also undermines the creation of civil society by dominating independent philanthropic organizations and by intimidating citizens in movements that challenge organized crime. The infiltration of these groups into labor unions violates citizen labor rights. International trafficking in prostitution and pornography demeans both women and children, and the illegal smuggling of individuals to work in situations where they are often exploited raises serious human rights concerns.

Transnational Crime, the State, and World Order

The world political order becomes increasingly stable when more nations establish democratic forms of government based on respect for the rule of law and government through consensus. International organized crime is detrimental to existing democracies and to societies in transition to democracy. Transnational crime undermines the rule of law and the legitimacy of democratic government through its corruption of individuals and the judicial process. Organized crime groups often supplant the state in societies undergoing a transition to democracy, as their representatives assume key positions in the incipient legislatures, which are responsible for crafting the new legal framework for the society. Their presence within legitimate state institutions undermines political stability because their goals are to further their own criminal interests (illicit profits), not the interests of the populace at large.

Transnational organized crime groups in both developed and developing democracies seek to corrupt high-level government officials both on the groups' home turf and in the countries where they operate. But these groups are often more successful when their efforts are conducted in nation-states that are in political transition, because the controls over the legal process do not yet function as they do in a stable democracy.

Transnational organized crime groups also threaten states through their trafficking in nuclear materials. Now the world no longer worries about nuclear conflict between the world's superpowers. Instead, today the nuclear threat comes largely from the arms trafficking of organized crime, a new and highly pernicious form of illicit activity. The smuggling of nuclear materials may enable some country or crime group to independently produce a nuclear weapon, therefore raising the potential for nuclear blackmail.

Traditional scholarship applies the concept of the criminalized state to Nazi Germany. Yet it is equally valid to apply the term to a state apparatus used to further the goals of *organized crime groups*. This is evident in Italy where, for more than a century, a symbiotic relationship has existed between crime and politics. The seven-time prime minister, Giulio Andreotti—the stalwart of the preeminent post-war Social Democratic Party—has twice been deprived of his parliamentary immunity for charges of collaboration with the mafia. Another former prime minister, Bettino Craxi of the Socialist Party, has been officially charged with corruption. The consequences of the criminalization of the state in this way have deprived Italy of influence commensurate with its role as a major economic power. . . . As a noted mafia commentator has remarked, "Italy is distinguished in Europe today by the penetration of organized crime into the state."

In Colombia, the relationship between the government and the drug cartels is not as long-standing as in Italy, but its impact on the state and its democratic institutions has been devastating. The democratic process and the rule of law have been severely undermined in both the legislative process and the administration of justice. In the former Soviet Union, the infiltration of organized crime into the political process may lead to political clientelism and controlled markets, a variation on the old ways of Soviet government, only without the official state ideology. As political campaigns are financed by organized crime groups and their representatives or emissaries are elected to parliament, the possibilities of producing the legal structure needed to move a society from authoritarian to democratic rule are diminished.

Both Italy and Colombia have discovered that once organized crime penetrates the state, the latter will not be able to disassociate itself from the former—even with the investment of significant human and economic resources, the application of intense repression and the sacrifice of many well-meaning individuals. The states of the former Soviet Union that lack both the resources and the will to combat organized crime as well as a history of uncorrupted government will be even more susceptible to penetration than Italy or Colombia. While it is premature to classify any of the successor states to the Soviet Union as mafia-run governments, some regions of Russia as well as other newly independent states have already fallen under the influence of criminal organizations. The consequences of penetration by organized crime into the state sector are devastating because the penetration effectively prohibits the state from combatting these groups in their home territories, thereby undermining legitimate democracy.

Transnational Organized Crime and the World Economy

The impact of international organized crime groups on the world economic order is equally disturbing. Much has been written about the pernicious effects of multinational corporations that transfer operations outside their domestic base, often in order to elude domestic legal controls. Author William Greider provides a typical critique, concluding that their "exploitative effects on rich and poor nations remain unchecked." International law lacks the legal enforcement power necessary to control the behavior of such international corporations. The innate obstacles to regulating the abuses of multinationals (i.e., the diversity of laws among nations, the lack of extradition treaties and the desire of developing nations to attract foreign capital at any cost) are only amplified when replaced by illicit multinationals—transnational organized crime.

The practice by transnational criminal organizations of large-scale money laundering, of corrupting of key officials in economic and customs positions and of utilizing banks, stock exchanges, venture capital opportunities and commodities markets, all undermine the financial security of world markets. The pensions and savings of ordinary citizens are also jeopardized when banks and stock funds collapse because of illegal manipulation of the financial sectors by international organized crime groups. . . .

Social Consequences of Transnational Crime

The social consequences of transnational organized crime are often understated. The most visible manifestations—violence, drug trafficking, gambling, prostitution and the spread of AIDS—all have a very direct effect on quality of life. Not only do international crime groups run these illicit markets, but they coerce women and children into prostitution and develop drug dependencies among millions of individuals in order to create a market for their narcotics.

Furthermore, the control of illegal markets by international organized crime has a ripple effect throughout the economy, thereby affecting the quality of life of even those who do not participate in the market of illicit goods and services. Extortion activities and the monopoly of markets increase the costs of consumer goods. As a consequence, citizens pay more for food, housing and medical services.

Because organized crime groups are oriented toward immediate profits, their activities (cultivating drugs on unsuitable soil, harvesting and selling of protected species and illegally overfishing sturgeon for the lucrative caviar trade) often lead to serious environmental damage.

The Complexity of Organized Crime

Transnational organized crime groups thrive in different political environments, functioning with diverse internal structures and in various areas of activity. . . . International organized crime groups are based on every continent, and their activities, while probably most pronounced in the regions closest to their home country, are increasingly conducted across continents, often in conjunction with organized criminals from other parts of the world. Divergent legislative and enforcement policies among nations permit these transnational crime groups to more easily elude authorities by exploiting a particular environment. For example, the favorable banking laws and the lack of enforcement have made several Caribbean islands havens for money laundering.

The complexity and transnational nature of organized crime is probably most apparent in the area of drug trafficking. But this activity is not confined only to the distribution of narcotics, as these same networks can be (and have been) used to smuggle weapons and may be used to smuggle nuclear materials with equal facility. Indeed, the trading and sale of drugs and weapons are often interrelated when drugs become the most easily obtainable currency.

The multinational character of the drug trade is revealed in major cases detected by law enforcement. For instance, one unmasked network involved criminals from Pakistan, Africa, Israel, Eastern Europe and Latin America. The drugs (hashish) originated in Pakistan and were delivered to the port of Mombasa (Kenya), where they were added to a cargo of tea and reshipped to Haifa (Israel) by way of Durban (South Africa). At Haifa, the cargo was put onto a ship of a company that ships to Constanza (Romania) every 15 days. From there, it was to have been shipped by an Israeli-Romanian company to Italy, via Bratislava (Slovakia). The head of the network was a German citizen of Ugandan origin who worked for a Romanian company. This complex network was only disclosed because the perpetrators were apprehended in Constanza.

In contrast, another large drug seizure of 517 kilos of cocaine at a Polish port linked Poles with Ecuadorians, members of the Cali cartel of Colombia and members of Italian organized crime. This drug network illustrates the collaboration of three of the most important transnational organized crime groups—the Colombian, Italian and the recently emergent Eastern and Central European (unlike the previous case, which involved only a limited number of participants from these major crime groups).

Apart from these three major transnational organized crime groups, the Chinese Triads, Japanese Yakuza and various Nigerian groups are also significant players in transnational organized crime. Indeed, after the collapse of its oil boom, Nigeria became one of the largest drug-trafficking nations in the world, strategically placed as it is along ancient trade routes that link Asia and Europe as well as the Americas. At present there is not one region in the world without an indigenous transnational organized crime group or that is not plagued by the activities of an international organized crime group. . . .

Combatting Transnational Organized Crime

The very nature of transnational organized crime precludes any one country from launching an effective campaign against transnational organized crime groups. The extensive penetration of such groups into the state sector has immunized most transnational groups from the law enforcement controls of their home countries. These groups seek to corrupt the legal institutions in their host country or render them impotent through targeted attacks on judicial personnel. A criminal organization that evolves into a transnational organized crime group has typically been successful in controlling local law enforcement efforts against it. Once it *does*, indeed, become international, the likelihood of enforcement diminishes radically.

Transnational organized crime groups are now so multinational that no state can be fully responsible for their control. Moreover, even if one state cracks down on members of a particular group, these members can frequently find refuge in another country. The enforcement net, therefore, has too many holes. A successful policy must seek international harmonization in legislation combatting crimes in the areas of banking, securities law, customs and extradition in order to reduce the opportunities for criminal activity and minimize the infiltration of transnational organized crime groups into legitimate business. Extradition treaties and mutual, legal assistance agreements among the broadest number of signatories would best protect against the ability of transnational criminals to elude detection. All nations must engage in a coordinated law enforcement campaign to ensure that criminals do not exploit differentiated enforcement strategies. . . .

Law enforcement coordination must also include the sharing of intelligence concerning the activities of transnational organized groups. . . .

But limits to such efforts exist both at the national and international levels. The United States, for example, is currently vulnerable to the activities of transnational crime groups because federal law prohibits the CIA from sharing with the FBI intelligence that it collects abroad. Many legal protections of the American citizenry, particularly relating to rights of the accused, are exploited by the sophisticated transnational criminals. Other gaps between intelligence gathering and law enforcement are similarly exploited by transnational groups throughout the world and need to be addressed by legal reforms.

In its policy proposals for the 1994 Ministerial Conference on Organized Transnational Crime, the United Nations suggested that the fight against these groups could be enhanced if more nations adopted legislation on the criminalization of participation in a criminal organization (which does not exist in many criminal codes), the criminalization of conspiracy, the prohibition of laundering of criminal profits and the implementation of asset forfeiture laws. The U.N. proposals also advocated the adoption of a convention specifically targeting transnational organized crime. While an increasing number of countries is likely to participate in such international efforts, there will always be countries whose governments are too corrupted, or whose legal infrastructures are too primitive, to allow them to actively participate in such arrangements. Gaps will invariably remain in the international legislative framework and, consequently, in the enforcement capacities of different states.

The Threat to Nation-States

Transnational crime is growing rapidly and represents a global phenomenon that is penetrating political institutions, undermining legitimate economic growth, threatening democracy and the rule of law and contributing to the post-Soviet problem of the eruption of small, regionally contained, ethnic violence. The disintegrative effect on the world political, economic and social order transcends the enforcement ability of the nation-state. Indeed, the post-Soviet proliferation of nations, each with its own legal system, and the lack of adequate border controls in a vast geographical area (that now stretches from Western Europe to the Pacific borders of the former Soviet Union) alter profoundly the previous world order, based on relatively stable, unified nation-states.

Another example of this geopolitical change is the European Union, which seeks the free movement of people and goods on a regional, transnational basis. In addition, the weakness of many states in Africa, parts of Latin America and Asia that are unable to control their existing boundaries or establish proper internal legal institutions, creates vast areas in which boundaries are no longer delineated by walls—these borders have become webs of netting through whose holes passes the business of organized crime.

The threat to nation-states is not that of a single monolithic international organized crime network. Rather, the multiplicity of politically and economically powerful crime groups operating both regionally and globally is what truly threatens to undermine political and economic security as well as social well-being. In many countries, the infiltration of organized crime into political structures has paralyzed law enforcement from within. Moreover, in many parts of the world where organized crime groups have supplanted the functions of the state, they impede economic development and the transition to democracy.

There is no economic incentive for transnational organized crime to diminish, and thus it will continue to threaten the world order into the 21st century. The international community must act now to abate the pernicious social, political and economic consequences of transnational crime, but with the understanding that it will never be able to achieve fully consistent policies and enforcement that will eradicate transnational organized crime, though such efforts can constantly thwart it. Internationally coordinated legislative and law enforcement efforts must be supported, because in their absence transnational crime threatens to penetrate to the core of democratic states. The corrupting influences of organized crime on the democratic governments of Colombia and Italy make this all too clear. Unless countries are willing to make a concerted effort against organized crime, they threaten their own institutions and the stability and longevity of their governments.

GLOSSARY

borgata   A "crew" or "team" within a **La Cosa Nostra** crime family.

Cali group   The dominant cocaine cartel in Colombia.

capo   "Captain" or "boss" of a **borgata**; a capodecina is a "boss of ten"; capo di tutti capi means "boss of all bosses" and is a supposedly obsolete title gangsters vied for during Prohibition.

Commission, The   An underworld board of directors made up of leaders of **La Cosa Nostra's** major crime families; because of its secretive nature, experts disagree on how much influence the Commission has over individual families, exactly which family leaders make up the Commission, and whether the Commission is a national organization or is limited to New York and New Jersey.

Commission case   *United States v. Salerno* (1986); major mob trial in which three of the bosses of New York's five families were convicted on **racketeering** charges; significant because surveillance tapes and detailed testimony of **La Cosa Nostra** turncoats proved the existence of a New York **commission** of organized crime leaders and suggested the possibility that a national commission also existed.

consigliere   Adviser to the boss of a **La Cosa Nostra** crime family.

gumbah   "Companion in crime"; term used by **La Cosa Nostra** to denote nonmembers who are friendly to the family.

La Cosa Nostra   "Our thing"; most often used to refer to the American Mafia, this term, like the generic "Mafia," is also sometimes used in reference to the Sicilian Mafia or to encompass both groups.

Medellin group   Major drug cartel based in Colombia; was dominant until the mid-1980s, when it was succeeded by the **Cali group**.

omerta   The Sicilian and American Mafias' "code of silence."

Organizatsiya   "The organization"; collective term, like "Russian Mafia," used to encompass the many Russian organized crime groups.

Pizza Connection case   *United States v. Badalamenti* (1987); one of the largest and most complex investigations or prosecutions brought against **La Cosa Nostra**; dubbed the "Pizza Connection case" because several defendants used pizzerias as fronts for heroin trafficking operations; this case exposed many of **La Cosa Nostra's** ties to the Sicilian Mafia.

racketeering   Engaging in organized illegal activity; as defined by **RICO**, racketeering includes virtually all federal and most state felonies.

RICO   Racketeer Influenced Corrupt Organizations Act; part of the Organized Crime Control Act of 1970. Allows the government to prosecute "enterprise criminality" rather than just individuals: Almost every major case brought against organized crime since 1980 has been a RICO prosecution.

tongs   Originally Chinese-American merchant organizations formed in the nineteenth century, tongs continue to be legitimate civic organizations in many cities and include members who are often community leaders; however, some of these societies are corrupt and act as fronts for criminal activity.

Triads   Centuries-old Chinese criminal organizations that are based in Hong Kong and Taiwan but also active in the United States; most notorious for heroin trafficking and immigrant smuggling.

underboss   The number two man in a **La Cosa Nostra** crime family; may advise a boss, but holds more authority within the family than would a **consigliere**.

vory v zakone   "Thief in law"; an honorific title within the Russian Mafia, similar to **La Cosa Nostra's** "godfather."

yakuza   Common name for the Boryokudan, the dominant organized crime group in Japan.

zip   Derogatory slang word, used by American mafiosi in reference to their Sicilian counterparts.

ORGANIZATIONS TO CONTACT

The editors have compiled the following list of organizations concerned with the issues presented in this book. The descriptions are derived from materials provided by the organizations. All have publications or information available for interested readers. The list was compiled on the date of publication of the present volume; the information provided here may change. Be aware that many organizations take several weeks or longer to respond to inquiries, so allow as much time as possible.

Central Intelligence Agency (CIA)
web address: http://www.odci.gov/cia/

The CIA assists the president, the National Security Council, and all others who make and execute U.S. national security policy. It provides foreign intelligence regarding national security and conducts counterintelligence activities related to foreign intelligence and national security as directed by the president. The CIA assists U.S. efforts to eliminate drug trafficking by providing intelligence information to the Drug Enforcement Administration, the Federal Bureau of Investigation, and the State Department. Its publications include *The World Factbook 1997* and the *1997 Factbook on Intelligence* as well as various maps and reports.

Chicago Crime Commission (CCC)
79 W. Monroe, Suite 605, Chicago, IL 60603
(312) 372-0101 • fax: (312) 372-6286
e-mail: chgocrcm@ix.netcom.com
web address: http://pw1.netcom.com /~chgocrcm/

CCC is a nongovernmental organization that educates the public on current crime issues, implements programs and services that address significant crime problems, reviews and reports on pertinent legislation, and monitors the integrity of law enforcement and criminal justice systems. Its publications include *The New Faces of Organized Crime 1997, Gangs: Public Enemy Number One*, and the biannual newsletter *Action Alert*.

Drug Enforcement Administration (DEA)
Information Services Section
700 Army-Navy Dr., Arlington, VA 22202
web address: http://www.usdoj.gov/dea/

The DEA works to enforce the controlled substances laws and regulations of the United States. Its goal is to bring any organization involved in the illegal growing, manufacture, or distribution of controlled substances to the criminal and civil justice system. The DEA is responsible for the development of overall federal drug enforcement strategy, programs, planning, and evaluation. It publishes congressional testimony, press releases, and intelligence reports, such as *The Supply of Illicit Drugs to the U.S.* and *The South American Cocaine Trade*.

Federal Bureau of Investigation (FBI)
950 Pennsylvania Ave. NW, Washington, DC 20535
web address: http://www.fbi.gov

The FBI is the principal investigative arm of the U.S. Department of Justice charged with investigating specific crimes against the United States. The FBI has investigative jurisdiction over violations of more than two hundred categories of federal crimes. Top priority has been given to five areas: counter-terrorism, organized crime/drugs, foreign intelligence, violent crimes, and financial crimes. Its publications include *Crime in the United States for 1995–1996*, the monthly *FBI Law Enforcement Bulletin*, and various press releases, transcripts of congressional hearings, and information on major investigations.

Financial Crimes Enforcement Network (FinCEN)

Office of Communications
2070 Chain Bridge Rd., Suite 200, Vienna, VA 22182
(703) 905-3770 • fax: (703) 905-3885
e-mail: webmaster@fincen.treas.gov
web address: http://www.treas.gov/fincen/

A bureau of the Treasury Department, FinCEN works to support and strengthen international and domestic anti–money laundering efforts. To foster interagency and global cooperation, FinCEN provides information, analysis, and technological assistance. Its publications include *The Global Fight Against Money Laundering* and *The FinCEN Advisory*, which provides information on approaches to combatting money laundering.

International Association for the Study of Organized Crime (IASOC)

Office of International Criminal Justice
University of Illinois
1333 S. Wabash, Box 53, Chicago, IL 60605
(312) 996-9636
web address: http://www.acsp.uic.edu/iasoc/iasoc.htm

IASOC, a program of the Office of International Criminal Justice, publishes *Criminal Organizations*, a quarterly journal that offers news and research on organized crime worldwide.

International Association of Chiefs of Police (IACP)

515 N. Washington St., Alexandria, VA 22314
(703) 836-6767
e-mail: martinm@theiacp.org (specific to organized crime)
web address: http://www.theiacp.org

The association's goals are to advance the science and art of police services. IACP helped create the FBI Identification Division and the Uniform Crime Records system and also spearheaded the national use of fingerprint identification. It publishes *Police Chief* magazine as well as various reports on law enforcement policies, policing trends, and legislative issues.

National Criminal Justice Reference Service

PO Box 6000, Rockville, MD 20849-6000
(800) 851-3420
e-mail: askncjrs@ncjrs.org • web address: http://www.ncjrs.org

A program of the National Institute of Justice, the National Criminal Justice Reference Service serves as a clearinghouse for the exchange of criminal justice information. The service publishes the electronic newsletter *Justice Information* twice each month.

National Institute of Justice (NIJ)

U.S. Department of Justice
PO Box 6000, Rockville, MD 20849-6000
(800) 851-3420 • (301) 519-5212
e-mail: askncjrs@ncjrs.org • web address: http://www.ojp.usdoj.gov/nij/

NIJ is the primary federal sponsor of research on crime and its control. It sponsors research efforts through grants and contracts that are carried out by universities, private institutions, and state and local agencies. Its publications include the research briefs *Gang Crime and Law Enforcement Recordkeeping* and *Street Gang Crime in Chicago*.

Office of International Criminal Justice (OICJ)
University of Illinois
1033 W. Van Buren St., #500, Chicago, IL 60607-2919
(312) 996-9595 • fax: (312) 413-0458
e-mail: OICJ@uic.edu • web address: http://www.acsp.uic.edu/index.htm

In collaboration with individuals, governments, and private corporations, OICJ seeks to foster better understanding of the world's criminal justice systems, assist agencies seeking to establish more humane, effective, and efficient criminal justice services, and provide opportunities for international cooperation. Its publications include the monthly *Crime and Justice International*.

BIBLIOGRAPHY

Books

Jay S. Albanese

Organized Crime in America. Cincinnati: Anderson, 1996.

William Balsam and George Carpozi Jr.

Under the Clock: The Inside Story of the Mafia's First Hundred Years. Far Hills, NJ: New Horizon Press, 1991.

Howard Blum

Gangland: How the FBI Broke the Mob. New York: Simon & Schuster, 1993.

Jules Bonavolonta and Brian Duffy

The Good Guys: How We Turned the FBI 'Round and Finally Broke the Mob. New York: Simon & Schuster, 1996.

Martin Booth

The Triads: The Chinese Criminal Fraternity. London: Grafton Books, 1990.

Diego Gambetta

The Sicilian Mafia: The Business of Private Protection. Cambridge, MA: Harvard University Press, 1993.

Ronald Goldfarb

Perfect Villains, Imperfect Heroes: Robert F. Kennedy's War Against Organized Crime. New York: Random House, 1995.

Stephen Handelman

Comrade Criminal: Russia's New Mafia. New Haven, CT: Yale University Press, 1995.

John Kerry

The New War: The Web of Crime That Threatens America's Security. New York: Simon & Schuster, 1997.

Peter Maas

Underboss: Sammy the Bull Gravano's Story of Life in the Mafia. New York: HarperCollins, 1997.

Linnea P. Raine and Frank J. Cilluffo, eds.

Global Organized Crime: The New Empire of Evil. Washington, DC: Center for Strategic Studies and International Studies, 1994.

Jeffrey Robinson

The Laundrymen: Inside Money Laundering, the World's Third-Largest Business. New York: Arcade, 1996.

Patrick J. Ryan

Organized Crime: A Reference Handbook. Santa Barbara, CA: ABC-CLIO, 1995.

Paul Stares

Global Habit: The Drug Problem in a Borderless World. Washington, DC: Brookings Institution, 1996.

Periodicals

Arnaud de Borchgrave

"The Bubonic Plague of International Crime," *Insight,* October 23, 1995. Available from 3600 New York Ave. NE, Washington, DC 20002.

Christian Caryl

"The Very Long Arm of the American Law," *U.S. News & World Report,* July 7, 1997.

Fredric Dannen

"The G-Man and the Hit Man," *New Yorker,* December 16, 1996.

Fredric Dannen

"Partners in Crime: China Bonds with Hong Kong's

Underworld," *New Republic*, July 14, 1997.

Economist — "Money Laundering: The Infernal Washing Machine," July 26, 1997.

Gayle M.B. Hanson — "Triads and Tongs Team Up to Prey on Asian Populace," *Insight*, March 27, 1997.

Michael Hirsh and Hideko Takayama — "Big Bang or Bust: Mobsters Slow Tokyo's Plan to Join World Markets," *Newsweek*, September 1, 1997.

Dick Hobbs — "Professional Crime: Change, Continuity, and the Enduring Myth of the Underworld," *Sociology*, February 1997.

Anatol Lievan — "Disarmed and Dangerous: The Crumbling, Scary Russian Army," *New Republic*, December 22, 1997.

Anatol Lievan — "The Future of Russia: Will It Be Freedom or Anarchy?" *Current*, March/April 1997. Available from Heldref Publications, 1319 18th St. NW, Washington, DC 20036-1802.

Wayne Lutton — "Russian Mafia Invades California," *Social Contract*, Summer 1996. Available from 316½ E. Mitchell St., Petoskey, MI 49770.

Victoria Pope — "Trafficking in Women," *U.S. News & World Report*, April 7, 1997.

Robert Sarbag — "Hot Crime: Money Laundering," *Rolling Stone*, August 21, 1997.

Brian Sullivan — "International Organized Crime: A Growing National Security Threat," *Strategic Forum*, May 1996. Available from NDU Press, 300 Fifth Ave., Marshall Hall (Building 62), Fort Lesley J. McNair, Washington, DC 20319-5066.

Jeffrey Toobin — "Weak Chin: Why Vincent Gigante, Little Al, and Benny Squint Are History," *New Yorker*, August 4, 1997.

Ann Scott Tyson — "How the Nation's Largest Gang Runs Its Drug Enterprise," *Christian Science Monitor*, July 15, 1996.

Frank Viviano — "The New Mafia Order," *Mother Jones*, May/June 1995.

Gary Weiss — "The Mob on Wall Street," *Business Week*, December 16, 1996.

Phil Williams — "Transnational Criminal Organizations: Strategic Alliances," *Washington Quarterly*, Winter 1995.

Jeff Wise — "The Dragon's Teeth," *Far Eastern Economic Review*, June 13, 1996.

Gordon Witkin — "Stopping Cocaine South of the Border," *U.S. News & World Report*, January 29, 1996.

Tim Zimmerman and Alan Cooperman — "The Russian Connection," *U.S. News & World Report*, October 23, 1995.

INDEX